AF333697

FEMINISM AND WOMEN IN LEADERSHIP

FEMINISM AND WOMEN IN LEADERSHIP

VICENTE NARDI
EDITOR

Nova Science Publishers, Inc.
New York

For permission to use material from this book please contact us:
Telephone 631-231-7269; Fax 631-231-8175
Web Site: http://www.novapublishers.com

NOTICE TO THE READER

LIBRARY OF CONGRESS CATALOGING-IN-PUBLICATION DATA

Feminism and women in leadership / editor, Vicente Nardi.
   p. cm.
  Includes index.
  ISBN 978-1-60876-270-5 (hardcover)
  1. Feminism. 2. Feminism--Psychological aspects. 3. Leadership. I. Nardi, Vicente.
  HQ1155.F444 2009
  305.42--dc22
                2009049837

Published by Nova Science Publishers, Inc. ✛ *New York*

CONTENTS

Contents

PREFACE

Studies on both emotional intelligence and transformational leadership suggest that women are more transformational and emotionally intelligent in their leadership styles. In this book, several variables that may influence the relationship between emotional intelligence and transformational leadership are analyzed. A series of studies that examined gender-congenial variables and group variables and their impact on leadership emergence of women and men are summarized as well. In addition, the authors seek to understand the role of gender relations and gender identities in the context of doing qualitative research and their impacts in the ethics of conducting qualitative interviewing. Some of the problematic aspects to feminist engagement with adult male sexual victimisation is highlighted. In addition, the empirical research on the relationship of feminist attitudes and feminist identity to self-esteem and self-efficacy, weight concern, psychological well-being, relationship and sexuality, sexism and psychological distress, personality, and cognitions are reviewed.

Chapter 1 - Feminism has been theorized to have a number of benefits for women, including increased self-esteem and self-efficacy (Carter & Spitzack, 1990; McNamara & Rickhard, 1989; Morley, 1993), identity achievement (Stein & Weston, 1982), psychological well-being (Saunders & Kashubeck-West, 2006), and cognitive flexibility (Gerstmann & Kramer, 1997) as well as decreased weight concern (Guille & Chrisler, 1999), psychological distress (Landrine & Klonoff, 1997), and feelings of depression (Weitz, 1982). However measures of feminist attitudes and feminist identity have frequently been conflated in the research on this topic, such that most of the research on the relationship of feminism to mental health variables has assessed feminist attitudes rather than feminist identity. As a result, there is little research to support the possible benefits of adopting a feminist identity. In this chapter the empirical research on the relationship of feminist attitudes and feminist identity to self-esteem and self-efficacy, weight concern, psychological well-being, relationships and sexuality, sexism and psychological distress, personality, and cognitions will be reviewed. Due to the frequent conflation of feminist attitudes and feminist identity, the different relationships between mental health variables and feminist attitudes and feminist identity will be clearly delineated. Other critiques of the research on the relations between feminism and mental health variables will also be addressed.

Chapter 2 - The issue of adult male rape and sexual assault has been the subject of a significant increase in attention by scholars in the last two decades. This growth in the scholarly literature is similar to the large increase in research examining female sexual victimization from the 1970s onwards. Furthermore, over the last four decades many jurisdictions have adopted legal reforms that have included males as potential victims of rape. The research on adult male rape and sexual assault has examined this problem from a range of disciplinary perspectives and has developed in sophistication. Adult male rape is also an issue that has received increased attention from feminist scholars. Some of this literature has been, at best, ambivalent regarding the increasing societal and legal recognition of the problem of adult male sexual victimization. In other instances, male victimization has been treated in a dismissive manner. Up until now, this literature has received little in the way of serious sustained analysis. This chapter represents the beginning of an ongoing engagement by the authors with feminist theorizing on male rape.

In this particular work we highlight some of the problematic aspects of feminist engagement with adult male sexual victimization. First, this chapter will describe the incidence, prevalence, and impact of male rape. Second, it will examine how feminist theorizing can be problematic in providing robust explanations of rape which can accommodate the experiences of male victims. Finally, this chapter will engage in a critical evaluation of the claim that male rape victims are 'feminized' by rape, as well as claims regarding the treatment of male rape by the law and wider society.

Chapter 3 - Studies on both emotional intelligence and transformational leadership suggested that women are more transformational and emotionally intelligent in their leadership styles. However, few studies test this hypothesis experimentally. In this chapter, we analyze several variables that may influence the relationship between emotional intelligence and transformational leadership. Specifically, we summarize a series of studies that examined gender-congenial variables (e.g., whether participants study a gender-congenial major) and group variables (e.g., group cohesiveness) and their impact on leadership emergence of women and men. We interpret the results of our studies on the basis of Eagly and Karau's (2002) Role Congruity Theory and Eagly's Social Role theory (1987).

Chapter 4 - Our work points out that the prejudice against female leaders stems from gender stereotypes. That is, attributes that are perceived to be typical for men and women emerging from role-bound activities. Recent studies on the malleability of gender stereotypes show that they are flexible, dynamic structures that change with the passage of time. In this book chapter, we analyze people's stereotypic beliefs when evaluating men and women across time. In a study, we examined similarities and differences in beliefs about men and women of the past, present and future in Spain, and focus on the influence of an important demographic variable on these beliefs —the population size of people's location of residence. Results in the study showed that women of the present are estimated to be more masculine than are women of the past, and women of the future are expected to be more masculine than women of the present; whereas men are projected to increase in feminine attributes across years. Perceptions of men and women thus tend to converge with the passage of time. In less populated locations, however, men and women are more gender-stereotyped and, consequently, still shorter of equality than those in more populated areas. Participants who live in less populated, rural areas thus perceived less similarity between women and men's attributes than those who live in more populated, urban locations. We conclude that the study of dynamic gender stereotypes benefits from an extensive research in populations that vary in their demographic characteristics, and stress the importance of recent movements in rural areas supporting women's participation in the modernization process.

Chapter 5 - This chapter seeks to understand the role of gender relations and gender identities in the context of doing qualitative research and their impacts in the ethics of conducting qualitative interviewing. This discussion is informed by the research experience of two female researchers related with two different studies, with a particular focus on the process of conducting qualitative interviews with women and men in Portugal who had been medically diagnosed with infertility. Our aim is to focus on two main topics related to gender and ethics in the research relationships, in the context of studying infertility. First, the gender of the participant in the study: should we have interviewed women, men or couples? Should the interviewer be a woman or a man? Second, the construction of local ethics: is there a need for local ethical guidelines for researchers who use qualitative research in infertility? We will explore the emotions that we have experienced when doing qualitative research about infertility, illustrating that with empirical examples from our fieldwork. Those feelings were particularly acute due to two main factors: in the presence of social and gender inequalities (e.g., socioeconomic, professional and geographic inequalities in the access to fertility drugs for ovarian stimulation and women's physical and emotional discomfort within the fertility treatments); and by the fact that one of the researchers was confronted by some of the participants in the study with questions about her own fertility and her fulfillment of the role of being a mother. We call for a feminist research methods training program that takes into account the social, cultural, ethical and professional local contexts where the daily research relationship occurs.

Chapter 6 - In the United States, Japan, and many European countries, most research universities are placing increasing emphasis upon innovation, technology transfer and applied research. In all countries, across all sectors and in all fields, the percentage of women obtaining patents is not only less than their male counterparts but it is less than the percentage of women in science, technology, engineering, and mathematics (STEM) in the field in the country.

This raises several questions: First, what is the evidence that women aren't obtaining patents at the same rate as their male counterparts? Second, is this a feminist issue? Finally, what can we apply from feminist phase theories to close this gender gap in patenting?

What other problems and losses result from the boys' club that excludes women and results in a gender gap in patenting? First, women who are scientists lose. Second, science experiences a loss in attracting more individuals with creative ideas. Third, society loses because of fewer products.

Overall, both nationally and internationally, the gender gap in patents has shown some signs of closing over time. These studies provide some evidence for progression through the stages. Reaching the stage of inclusion seems distant, although some fields and sectors, such as the biotech start-ups, appear to be closer to inclusion.

Chapter 7 - Plant Biotechnology in Bulgaria has thirty five years of history. After the establishment of the first laboratory of *in vitro* cultures in the Institute of Genetics of the Bulgarian Academy of Sciences in the middle 1970's similar laboratories were organized in more than twenty other research institutes and universities. Major part of the personnel are women occupying different positions: head of units, project/group leaders, senior scientists, research and technical assistants. Many Bulgarian women working in this sphere have developed good scientific career contributing to development of many aspects of plant biotechnology. Leadership of women will be discussed in context of their participation in projects, outstanding research, tuition, expertise and motives to deal with plant biotechnology on the background of gender activities in biological sciences. The latter were compared with physical and mathematical sciences traditionally attracting more men. Survey was carried on three levels: (i) research organizations/institutes; (ii) research groups; (iii) researchers.

Chapter 8 - This chapter will look at feminist self-affirmation in mainstream popular music videos, and how the medium and its music has become the "most important cultural form for expressing third wave feminist perspectives" (Drake, 2002, p. 187). Recent work, in the late 2000s, by female popstar video musicians, Pink and Britney Spears suggest the conflation of celebrity, stardom and feminist practices of assertion to be prevalent. The concern with subjectivity is a dominant aspect of female music videos, in which the telling of a story with strong hints of autobiography abounds. The compelling nature of female music videos is attributable to the personal insights offered by the performers. As such a neo-romanticism associated with the cult of the artist and celebrity stature is conveyed. Social commentaries of success and survival address a female audience. Furthermore, there is an aggressive defiance in which the lyrics and the music video textually enact a challenge of the male domain, in which independence both financially as well as sexually and emotionally is paramount.

Chapter 9 - Women's satisfaction related to their marriage and work bring about interesting discussion in this study. Feminism has been opening work opportunities for women to be equal to men and to allow women to be more developed and independent in society. However, conflict of the double role—women's work and women's role in marriage as a wife and mother—to women seems continuously discussed. In general, conflicts occur as consequences between the two commitments, which are demanding that women perform excellently both in their marriage and at work. The conflicts include women's time management, priority need, energy division, decision making, love and attention, etc. Therefore, it is important to assess the level of women's satisfaction with regard to her work in order to identify how strongly a woman's work influences a woman's satisfaction in married life. In this study, we assess women's satisfaction in marriage with respect to several kinds of occupations from a quality perspective. The quality perspective offers a new way of assessing women's satisfaction by using a Quality Function Deployment (QFD) method. The QFD method, which is usually applied in industry, can be adopted in assessing women's satisfaction towards their marriage and work life. QFD produces a friendly interpretation of highly complex and intangible matters around married life; thus, it makes the assessment of women's satisfaction in marriage and work easier. By using QFD, we determine the variables and dimensions with respect to marital characteristics by integrating previous studies and considering expert opinions. Many activities carried out in married life are representative of a woman's role in marriage. In addition, QFD also compares the level of satisfaction with respect to a woman's occupation in a clearer and simpler way. The comparison leads to the identification of which dimension is the most satisfying and which one is less than the other, with respect to a different kind of occupation. In this study, we perform the QFD method on assessing women's satisfaction by utilizing data gathered from a questionnaire survey based on 587 respondents across West Malaysia, Malaysia. The effort to enhance women's satisfaction of their success in playing the double role in the marriage and at work is our main consideration. This study may contribute a new point of view regarding the progress of feminism in the social aspect and in women's quality of life.

Chapter 10 - In the United States, the number of women in Congress rarely rose above 2 per cent until the 1970s. Even then, remarked one commentator, they were "permanently excluded from the informal network of power relationships which is the key to the workings of that complex legislative machine:" (Gehlen, 1969: 36.). Pat Schroeder, who was elected to Congress in 1972 as one of 14 women, felt that she had "broken into and entered a private club", and describes the various indignities to which she and her female colleagues were exposed.(Schroeder, 1999: 19). A journalist who interviewed female congressmen found that women were totally excluded from a select circle run by the (male) Speaker of the House of Representatives, called the 'Board of Education' Some of her respondents had not even heard of it (Lynn, 1979: 413). Jeane Kirkpatrick, who served as a diplomat during the Nixon presidency and was a serious possibility for the Republican vice-presidential nomination in 1988. observed that men "do not bar women from taking part in politics, but only hamper their efforts to participate in power " (Kirkpatrick, 1974 : 20). During the Nixon presidency. women occupied no more than 13 of the 300 senior administrative positions.

Chapter 11 - In most bureaucracies, support for the assault victim comes at mid-level in the hierarchy. When, for example, a nurse is assaulted, she/he is most likely to seek assistance from another staff nurse or from the nurse manager. If a committee is formed about the high number of assaults, it usually begins at mid-range and is elevated as it becomes more formalized. In our case, violence concern started at the top of the hierarchal pyramid and led to the training of a team of counselors who intervene when an employee has been assaulted.

Chapter 12 - Often, women are considered victims of organized crime. A typical example is trafficking in women, where women are exploited in prostitution by criminal organizations. However, there are examples of women playing a quite different role in organized crime

In: Feminism and Women in Leadership
Editor: Vicente Nardi, pp. 1-27

ISBN: 978-1-60876-270-5
© 2010 Nova Science Publishers, Inc.

Chapter 1

LINKS BETWEEN FEMINISM AND MENTAL HEALTH: A REVIEW OF THE RESEARCH ON FEMINIST ATTITUDES, FEMINIST IDENTITY, AND MENTAL HEALTH VARIABLES

Heather Eisele and Jayne Stake*
University of Missouri, St. Louis, Missouri, USA

ABSTRACT

Feminism has been theorized to have a number of benefits for women, including increased self-esteem and self-efficacy (Carter & Spitzack, 1990; McNamara & Rickhard, 1989; Morley, 1993), identity achievement (Stein & Weston, 1982), psychological well-being (Saunders & Kashubeck-West, 2006), and cognitive flexibility (Gerstmann & Kramer, 1997) as well as decreased weight concern (Guille & Chrisler, 1999), psychological distress (Landrine & Klonoff, 1997), and feelings of depression (Weitz, 1982). However measures of feminist attitudes and feminist identity have frequently been conflated in the research on this topic, such that most of the research on the relationship of feminism to mental health variables has assessed feminist attitudes rather than feminist identity. As a result, there is little research to support the possible benefits of adopting a feminist identity. In this chapter the empirical research on the relationship of feminist attitudes and feminist identity to self-esteem and self-efficacy, weight concern, psychological well-being, relationships and sexuality, sexism and psychological distress, personality, and cognitions will be reviewed. Due to the frequent conflation of feminist attitudes and feminist identity, the different relationships between mental health variables and feminist attitudes and feminist identity will be clearly delineated. Other critiques of the research on the relations between feminism and mental health variables will also be addressed.

---

* Corresponding author: Department of Psychology, University of Missouri, St. Louis, MO 63121. E-mail: dr.heather.eisele@gmail.com

FEMINIST ATTITUDES AND FEMINIST IDENTITY

When examining the relationship between feminism and mental health variables, researchers have operationalized feminism either as feminist attitudes or as feminist identity. Further, feminist attitudes and feminist identity have frequently been used interchangeably, with measures of feminist attitudes presumed to measure feminist identity. However, feminist attitudes and feminist identity have distinct definitions. Feminist attitudes have been defined as a belief in the feminist goal of gender equality (Williams & Wittig, 1997; Zucker, 2004), whereas feminist identity involves both espousing feminist attitudes and explicitly identifying oneself as a feminist (Williams & Wittig, 1997; Zucker, 2004). Thus, explicit feminist self-identification is a primary requirement for a feminist identity (Ashmore, Deuz, & McLaughlin-Volpe, 2004).

Although feminist attitudes and feminist identity are highly correlated (Cowan, Mestlin, & Masek, 1992; Liss, Crawford, & Popp, 2004; Roy, Weibust, & Miller, 2007; Szymanski, 2004), they are not identical concepts. An analysis of six national public opinion polls conducted between 1972 and 1992 regarding feminist attitudes and feminist identification found that a two-factor model composed of feminist attitudes and feminist identity was a better fit than a one-factor model that combined these two concepts (Rhodebeck, 1996). Additionally, specific gender role attitudes regarding politics, work, and family did not predict feminist self-identification for women once demographic factors and general political attitudes were controlled (McCabe, 2005). Similarly, the predictors of feminist attitudes and feminist self-identification have been found to overlap, but not be identical (Williams & Wittig, 1997). Moreover, feminists engaged in significantly more activism, endorsed significantly less traditional gender role attitudes, and were less supportive of a sexual double standard than women who did not identify as feminists regardless of their espousal of feminist attitudes (Bay-Cheng & Zucker, 2007; Zucker, 2004). Thus, feminist attitudes and feminist identity appear to be two distinct concepts.

Measures of explicit feminist identity have rarely been included when assessing the relation of feminism to mental health variables—even in some of the measures that have been purported to measure feminist identity. For example, the three most commonly used measures of feminist identity, which are based on Downing and Roush's (1985) five stage model of feminist identity development, are the Feminist Identity Scale (FIS; Rickard, 1989), the Feminist Identity Development Scale (FIDS; Bargad & Hyde, 1991), and the Feminist Identity Composite (FIC; Fischer et al., 2000). Although these measures were designed to assess feminist identity development, no items pertain to explicit feminist identification. The term "feminist" is rarely used in the items of these measures. For example, only three items from the FIDS use the word "feminist," and only two of those items imply that an individual identifies with feminism (e.g., "Particularly now, I feel most comfortable with women who share my feminist point of view"). Therefore, it is conceivable that individuals could score highly on these measures without ever identifying themselves as feminists.

Indeed, the Synthesis subscale of feminist identity stage measures has not always significantly correlated with explicit feminist self-identification, despite being conceptualized as a higher stage of feminist identity. The Synthesis subscale of the FIC was not significantly correlated with explicit feminist self-identification (Saunders & Kashubeck-West, 2006; Szymanski 2004). Additionally, feminists, women who had high feminist attitudes but did not identify as feminists, and non-feminists did not differ on their Synthesis subscale scores on the FIS (Zucker, 2004). Thus, given that research has demonstrated that some of the subscales which purport to measure higher stages of feminist identity do not differentiate between feminists and non-feminists, these stage measures should be conceptualized as assessing different types of feminist attitudes, not feminist identity. Only measures that include assessment of explicit feminist self-identification should be considered measures of feminist identity. As a result, all research findings that utilized these measures will be discussed as measures of feminist attitudes rather than feminist identity.

FEMINISM AND MENTAL HEALTH VARIABLES

Feminism and Self-Esteem/Self-Efficacy

Feminist attitudes and self-esteem/self-efficacy. Positive relationships have been found between feminist attitudes and self-esteem/self-efficacy. Information on self-efficacy and self-esteem is combined in this section because self-efficacy has been conceptualized as a type of self-esteem (Maddux, 1991). Research on feminist attitudes and self-esteem/self-efficacy has typically supported a positive relationship for these variables. The Rosenberg Self-Esteem Scale (RSE; Rosenberg, 1965) was positively correlated with feminist attitudes for Euro American and non-Euro American adult women (Boisnier, 2003; De Man & Bentoit, 1982; Moradi & Subich, 2002). However Boisner found that race moderated the relationship between feminist attitudes and RSE scores, such that the relationship was positive for African American female college students, but negative for their Euro American peers. Moreover, RSE scores were negatively correlated with traditional gender role attitudes (Moradi & Subich, 2002). Thus, it appears that feminist attitudes are positively related to self-esteem and traditional gender role attitudes are negatively related to self-esteem, although there may be ethnoracial differences in this relationship.

The research on the relationship between self-acceptance and feminist attitudes in sexual minority women has been mixed. Self-acceptance of one's sexual identity can be conceptualized as a type of self-esteem for sexual minority women. This conceptualization is supported by studies that have demonstrated significant negative correlations between self-esteem and internalized homophobia for gay men and lesbians (Allen & Oleson, 1999; Haines et al., 2008; Nicholson & Long, 1990). Internalized homophobia in lesbians and bisexual women was negatively correlated with a range of feminist attitudes (range of -.17 to -.34) as well as positively correlated with traditional gender role attitudes (Szymanski, 2004). However, Leavy and Adams (1986) found that self-esteem and self-acceptance were not related to feminist attitudes in a sample of lesbian participants (-.14). However it is notable that the correlation from Leavy and Adam's study, while non-significant, is close to the lower end of the range of significant correlations from Szymanski's study. Thus the differences in the presence of significant results between these two studies may be due to power differences rather a contradiction in findings.

General personal self-efficacy is also positively related to feminist attitudes. Feminist attitudes predicted general personal self-efficacy among Women's and Gender Studies (WGS) students regardless of ethnicity or gender (Eisele & Stake, 2008) as well as for a sample of predominately Euro American female college students (Roy et al., 2007). Additionally, general feelings of empowerment were positively correlated with greater feminist attitudes for female college students, including feelings of control over one's decisions and optimism (Peterson, Grippo, & Tantleff-Dunn, 2008). Change in feminist attitudes over the course of WGS classes also predicted feelings of empowerment based on the class for male and female students of all ethnoracial backgrounds (Eisele & Stake, 2008). Increased feminist attitudes were also related to increased feelings of career self-efficacy for college women (Foss & Slaney, 1986).

Studies that assess engagement in activism also support the hypothesis that feminist attitudes are related to greater self-efficacy. Engagement in activism can be viewed as another way to assess self-efficacy, in that individuals who feel empowered regarding an issue must also feel that they have the ability to affect changes in their lives through engaging in activism related to that issue (Zimmerman, 1995). This conceptualization is supported by findings that individuals with high self-efficacy engaged in more activism than those with low self-efficacy (Markowitz, 1998; Zimmerman, Israel, Schulz, & Checkoway, 1992; Zimmerman & Rappaport, 1988). Specific to feminist activism, self-efficacy and pro-choice activism were related among members of pro-choice organizations for women from a range of ages (Kaysen & Stake, 2001). Therefore, empirical research supports the conceptualization of engagement in activism as a behavioral indicator of feelings of self-efficacy. Feminist attitudes have been found to be related to engagement in feminist activism, thereby supporting the hypothesis that feminist attitudes are positively related to self-efficacy. Feminist attitudes were positively correlated with belief in collective activism for female college students (Peterson et al., 2008). Additionally, feminist attitudes predicted intent to engage in feminist activism, while change in feminist attitudes over the course of a WGS class predicted change in intent to engage in activism for male and female college students from a variety of ethnoracial backgrounds (Eisele & Stake, 2008). Adult women with feminist attitudes reported that they engaged in more activism for women's rights than women who did not endorse feminist attitudes (Dauphinais, Barkan, & Cohn, 1992) and feminist attitudes were positively related to engagement in feminist activism for college aged and adult women (Liss et al., 2004; Szymanski, 2004). Thus, this research provides further evidence that feminist attitudes are linked to self-efficacy.

Feminist identity and self-esteem/self-efficacy. Only a few studies have addressed the relationship between explicit feminist identity and self-esteem or self-efficacy, but they provide support for the hypothesis that feminist identity is positively related to greater self-esteem and self-efficacy. Feminist identity predicted general personal self-efficacy, and change in feminist identity over the course of a WGS class predicted feelings of empowerment based on the class for male and female college students regardless of ethnoracial background (Eisele & Stake, 2008). Additionally, feminist identity predicted intent to engage in feminist activism and change in feminist identity over the course of a WGS class predicted change in intent to engage in activism for male and female college students regardless of ethnicity (Eisele & Stake, 2008). Moreover, feminist identity was positively correlated with engaging in feminist activism for adult women (Kelly & Breinlinger, 1995; Szymanski, 2004) and accounted for a unique amount of variance in predicting engagement in feminist activism among adult and college aged women (Nelson et al., 2008; Szymanski, 2004; Zucker, 2004). Indeed, feminist identity was the strongest predictor of feminist activism (Szymanski, 2004). Furthermore, women who identified themselves as feminists engaged in significantly more activism than non-feminist women and egalitarian women (Zucker, 2004), and feminist identity partially mediated the relationship between political attitudes and feminist activism for a sample of middle-aged female participants (Duncan, 1999).

Feminist identity has also been found to be indirectly related to self-efficacy and self-esteem. Feminist identity was negatively related to RSE scores through conformity to the feminine norms of focus on appearance, thinness, and involvement in romantic relationships as well as self-objectification for a sample of predominantly Euro American college and adult women (Hurt et al., 2007). In addition, internalized homophobia was negatively correlated with explicit feminist self-identification for a sample of predominantly Euro American adult sexual minority women (Syzmanski, 2004; Syzmanski & Chung, 2003), suggesting that women who identified as feminists had greater self-acceptance. Furthermore, the negative correlation between feminist identity and internalized homophobia was -.36, while the correlations between a range of feminist attitudes and internalized homophobia varied from -.34 to .09 (Szymanski, 2004).

Moreover, research suggests that feminist identity may be a better predictor of self-efficacy than feminist attitudes. Szymanski (2004) reported a positive correlation between feminist identity and engagement in activism of .76 while the positive correlations between a range of feminist attitudes and engagement in activism ranged from .03 to .62. Furthermore, feminist identity partially mediated the relationship between feminist attitudes and personal and collective self-efficacy at pretest and for change over time, such that feminist attitudes were only weakly related to self-efficacy once feminist identity was included in the analyses (Eisele & Stake, 2008). These findings were particularly strong for feminist activism. These findings support the importance of adopting feminist self-identification, particularly for engagement in feminist activism, and support the personal and social benefits of feminist identity.

Feminism and Psychological Well-Being

Recent research on the potential benefits of feminism has expanded to include assessment of general psychological well-being. This research has found that adult women with greater feminist attitudes (who were also likely to identify as feminists) and moderate feminist attitudes had a greater overall sense of psychological well-being than adult women with traditional gender role attitudes (Yakushko, 2007). Additionally, feminist attitudes and feminist identity together predicted overall psychological well-being for adult and undergraduate women, although feminist identity was not an independent predictor of well-being (Saunders & Kashubeck-West, 2006). Women with high and moderate feminist attitudes reported more personal growth than women with traditional role attitudes (Yakushko, 2007), while traditional gender role attitudes negatively predicted personal growth (Saunders & Kashubeck-West, 2006). Adult women with greater feminist attitudes reported more autonomy and purpose in life than women with moderate feminist or traditional gender role attitudes (Yakushko, 2007), although no differences were found among adult women of varying feminist attitudes in life satisfaction, self-acceptance, positive relationships, or environmental mastery (Yakushko, 2007). Furthermore, feminist identity was found to be indirectly negatively related to depressive symptoms through conformity to the feminine norms of focus on appearance, thinness, and involvement in romantic relationships as well as self-objectification for adult and undergraduate women (Hurt et al., 2007). Thus, it appears that feminist attitudes are related to psychological well-being, although the relationship of feminist identity to well-being less clear. However research does support that traditional gender role attitudes are negatively related to well-being and personal growth for women.

Feminism and Weight Concern

Feminist attitudes and weight concern. Research on the relationship between feminist attitudes and weight concern has yielded mixed results, with most studies finding no relationship between feminist attitudes and disordered eating behaviors, disordered eating attitudes, or body image (Cash, Ancis, & Strachan, 1997; Curtis & Comer, 2006; Dionne, Davis, Fox, & Gurevich, 1995; Fingeret & Gleaves, 2004; Grippo & Hill, 2008; Guille & Christler, 1999; Mahalik et al., 2005; Mintz & Betz, 1986; Ojerholm & Rothblum, 1999; Twamley & Davis, 1999; Xinaris & Boland, 1990). In addition, Eisele and Stake found that feminist attitudes did not predict disordered eating attitudes or body dissatisfaction among 435 male and female college students regardless of ethnic background (see Appendix for specific information on study aims, methods, results, limitations, and tables on this study). Furthermore, change in feminist attitudes did not predict change in disordered eating attitudes or body dissatisfaction among the same sample over the course of a WGS class. Moreover, change in the weight concern variables was unrelated to how relevant the students thought the class was to body image or their lives in general. These findings suggest that feminist attitudes are not related to weight concern and that extensive exposure to information on feminism did not impact students' weight concern, regardless of whether the class addresses this issue.

A few studies have found a relationship between feminist attitudes and weight concern. Snyder and Hasbrouck (1996) demonstrated that feminist attitudes were negatively correlated with bulimic behaviors, preoccupation with thinness, body dissatisfaction, and the disparity between participants' current and ideal physique in a sample of predominantly Euro American female college students. Conversely, traditional gender role attitudes were positively correlated with preoccupation with thinness, body dissatisfaction, and the disparity between participants' current and ideal physique (Snyder & Hasbrouck, 1996). Additionally, while feminist attitudes were unrelated to the Thinness subscale of the Conformity to Feminine Norms Inventory (CFNI), feminist attitudes were negatively correlated with the Investment in Appearance subscale in a sample of male and female college students (Mahalik et al., 2005). Furthermore, Peterson and colleagues (2006) found that, for female undergraduates exposed to information about feminism and feminist theory regarding body image for 15 minutes, increases in feminist attitudes were correlated with decreases in the importance of their physical appearance. Also, decreases in traditional gender role attitudes were correlated with decreases in anxiety about physical appearance (Peterson et al., 2006).

Feminist identity and weight concern. Similar to the research on feminist attitudes and weight concern, the research on feminist identity and weight concern is mixed. Additionally, little research is available regarding the relationship between feminist identity and weight concern, as explicit feminist self-identification has been assessed in only five studies regarding weight concern. Moreover, in one of those studies, feminist attitudes and feminist identity were combined into a single variable (Fingeret & Gleaves, 2004), so it is unclear how each of the two feminism variables were uniquely related to weight concern. Two of the remaining four studies found no relationship between explicit feminist identity and body image or negative eating attitudes for sexual minority or heterosexual undergraduate and adult women (Haines et al., 2008; Ojerholm & Rothblum, 1999). Furthermore, Eisele and Stake found that feminist identity did not predict disordered eating attitudes or body dissatisfaction among 435 male and female college students regardless of ethnic background. Moreover, change in feminist identity did not predict change in disordered eating attitudes or body dissatisfaction among the same sample over the course of a WGS class (see Appendix for specific information on study aims, methods, results, limitations, and tables). In addition, Swami, Salem, Furhan, and Tovee (2008) found that adult feminists and non-feminists both rated a body size that was underweight (based on the BMI) as the most attractive from a range of choices. However feminists perceived a wider range of body sizes as more attractive than nonfeminists (Swami et al., 2008). Furthermore, Kelson, Kearney-Cooke, & Lansk, (1990), found that Euro American female undergraduate feminists viewed their bodies as competent based on how healthy they felt and the internal sensations of their bodies rather than on their outward appearance. The authors found no relationship between satisfaction with their bodies or themselves in general and outward appearance for feminists (Kelson et al., 1990). Conversely, non-feminists used their outward appearance as a measure of how satisfied they feel with their bodies and themselves in general, as well as a measure of how well their bodies functioned (Kelson et al., 1990). Thus, there is some support for the supposition that feminist identity is related to decreased weight concern.

A review of the research suggests that there are several possible explanations for the mixed findings regarding the relationship of feminism to weight concern. One possible explanation for these contradictory findings is related to ethnoracial background. African American women have been hypothesized to have different cultural attitudes toward weight and be more accepting of larger body sizes (Crago et al., 1996; Gray, Ford, & Kelly, 1987; Parker et al., 1995; Patel & Gray, 2001; Powell & Kahn, 1995). Consistent with this hypothesis, African American participants in our study had significantly lower scores at pretest and across time on both weight concern variables than Euro American participants or participants from other ethnoracial groups. Thus, one possibility for the mixed findings is that the relationship between weight concern and feminist attitudes or feminist identity may exist for Euro American women, but not for African American women or women from other ethnoracial backgrounds. Alternatively, the weight concern of women of color may not be related to feminist attitudes or identity, but rather to another construct, such as womanist attitudes. The measures of feminist attitudes used in these studies may not be able to accurately represent women of color's gender role attitudes. Additionally, African American women have been less likely to identify as feminists than Euro American women (Boisnier, 2003; Eisele & Stake, 2008; Williams & Wittig, 1997), because of perceptions that the women's movement has not addressed topics that are of importance to them (Boisnier, 2003; Reid, 1984). Finally, it is also possible that because of differences in cultural attitudes toward women and body size (Crago, Shisslak, & Estes, 1996; Parker et al., 1995), feminist attitudes may not be an important factor in the attitudes of women of color, particularly African

American women, toward weight concern. Therefore, it is possible that weight concern among women of color may be related to another concept such as level of acculturation, rather than feminist identity. However a recent meta-analysis also demonstrated that there are few overall ethnic differences in body satisfaction between African American and Euro American women, although these differences are largest in college aged women (Grabe & Hyde, 2006). These findings suggest that the ethnoracial background explanation for the mixed findings may be more relevant for college students than older adults. Thus, it is unlikely that ethnoracial differences completely explain the mixed findings regarding feminism and weight concern.

Another possible explanation for the non-significant findings regarding feminism and weight concern is related to age. Most of the research on feminism and weight concern utilize samples that are composed exclusively of college students (Cash et al., 1997; Fingeret & Gleaves, 2004; Kelson et al., 1990; Mahalik et al., 2005; Mintz & Betz, 1986; Ojerholm & Rithblum, 1999; Peterson et al., 2006; Snyder & Hasbrouck, 1996; Twamley & Davis, 1999; Xinaris & Boland, 1990), yet Tiggeman and Stevens (1999) found that there was a negative correlation between these variables only for women aged 30 to 49. The authors suggested that these findings may be due to age differences in self-concept such that social messages about the importance of appearance are so entrenched in women under age 30 that they exist regardless of feminist identity or other aspects of their self-concept. Indeed, Kashubeck-West, Mintz, and Weigold (2005) found that 87% of a sample of college female undergraduates wanted to lose weight, even though only 4.3% met the criteria for being overweight, supporting the supposition that weight concern is pervasive for this age group. Tiggeman and Stevens proposed that women in their 30's and 40's place less importance on body image in their overall self-concept because the number of factors that are important to their self-concept increases. Thus, studies that utilize college students to assess for a relationship between feminism and weight concern may be less likely to find a relationship between these variables. However, it should also be noted that it is unclear whether the findings from Tiggemann and Steven's study are due to age or cohort effects. Furthermore, a recent study of Euro American women aged 40-89 found no relationship between feminist attitudes and weight concern or self-objectification (Grippo & Hill, 2008), suggesting that neither age nor cohort differences completely explain the mixed findings regarding feminism and weight concern.

Another possible explanation for the findings between feminism and weight concern is that the relationship between these variables may be indirect rather than direct. For example, Sabik and Tylka (2006) found that high feminist attitudes moderated the relationship between the frequency of recent and lifetime sexist events and disordered eating behaviors for female college undergraduates. Specifically, the frequency of lifetime and recent sexist events positively predicted disordered eating for women who were low (one standard deviation below the mean) in a type of feminist attitudes that included appreciation for engaging in feminist activism, but not for those high in that feminist attitude (Sabik & Tylka, 2006). Additionally, feminist attitudes have also been found to moderate the relationship between awareness of media images and internalizing a thin ideal among female undergraduates, such that women who had higher feminist attitudes had less thin-ideal internalization (Myers & Crowther, 2007). Moreover, feminist identity was indirectly related to disordered eating attitudes through a negative relationship to focusing on appearance, focusing on thinness, and involvement in romantic relationships, as well as self-objectification for female undergraduates and adult women (Hurt et al., 2007). Therefore, feminism may not be directly related to weight concern but rather influence the strength of the relationship between other variables, such as sexist events and weight concern. However, similarly to the research regarding direct relationships between feminism and weight concern, the research in this area is also mixed. Feminist attitudes did not moderate the relationship between awareness of appearance norms and internalization of those norms for undergraduate women (Twamley & Davis, 1999), nor did a combination of feminist attitudes and feminist identity (Fingeret & Gleaves, 2004). Neither did feminist attitudes moderate the relationship between social influence and internalization of a thin ideal for female college students (Myers & Crowther, 2007). Feminist attitudes also did not moderate the relationship between self-objectification and body dissatisfaction for adult Euro American women (Grippo & Hill, 2008). Thus it appears that the relationship between feminism and weight concern is complex and more research needs to be conducted to better understand how these variables may be related.

Finally, it is also possible that a strong relationship does not exist between feminism and weight concern, contrary to hypotheses on this topic (Guille & Chrisler, 1999; Rowland-Serdar & Schwartz-Shea, 1991). Rather other variables, which may be related to feminism, may have a stronger relationship to weight concern than either feminist attitudes or feminist identity. For example, while feminist attitudes predicted body image and eating disturbance, feelings of empowerment were a stronger predictor of these variables for undergraduate women (Peterson et al., 2008). Thus feminism could be indirectly related to weight concern, such as by increasing variables such as feelings of empowerment or self-esteem, rather than being directly related. However it is important to note that most of these studies have assessed feminist attitudes rather than feminist identity, so it is less clear how feminist identity is related to weight concern.

Feminism and Quality of Relationships/Sexuality

Despite pervasive stereotypes that feminism is not compatible with romantic relationships (Misciagno, 1997), research has demonstrated that feminist identity is positively related to romantic relationships and sexuality. Traditional gender role attitudes have been found to be related to decreased expectations for egalitarian relationships (Yoder, Perry, & Saal, 2007) and increased suppression of self-expression and needs within relationships (Witte & Sherman, 2002) in samples of predominantly Euro American college women. Increased feminist attitudes are also associated with engaging in a greater variety of traditionally masculine and feminine behaviors in dating situations in college undergraduates (Rickard, 1989). Furthermore, adult and college aged women who perceived their male partner to be a feminist reported healthier relationships, as measured by increased relationship quality, relationship stability, and equality (Rudman & Phelan, 2007). Moreover, men with feminist female partners also reported greater stability in their relationships, as well as increased sexual satisfaction, than men whose partners were not feminists (Rudman & Phelan, 2007). Additionally, undergraduate women with traditional gender role attitudes report decreased sexual assertiveness, including initiating sexual behaviors and engaging in safe sex (Yoder et al., 2007), whereas increased feminist attitudes are related to self-efficacy regarding condom usage and sexual satisfaction (Schick, Zucker, & Bay-Cheng, 2008). Feminist identity was related to greater positive affect and evaluation of sexual cues and less acceptance of a sexual double standard than nonfeminists, regardless of their endorsement of feminist attitudes for heterosexual undergraduate women (Bay-Cheng & Zucker, 2007).

Feminism and Coping with Sex Discrimination

Feminism has previously been demonstrated to increase awareness of sexism (Fischer & Good, 1994; Leaper & Brown, 2008), thus suggesting that feminist attitudes and identity could cause increased distress for some women. However feminist attitudes have been found to moderate the effects of sexist events on psychological distress, suggesting that while feminism increases awareness of sexism, it also provides a mechanism for coping with sexist events. Qualitative and quantitative studies have demonstrated that feminism helps women to cope with sexist events. Adult Euro American women with more feminist attitudes who were engaged in litigation over sexual harassment engaged in less self-blame than women with less feminist attitudes (Wright & Fitzgerald, 2007), and 78% of Euro American self-identified feminists in academia spontaneously reported that they believed feminism helped them to cope with experiences of sexism, especially related to occupational activities (Klonis, Endo, Crosby, & Worrell, 1997). Landrine and Klonoff (1997) found that the amount of variance accounted for by sexist events was greater for non-feminists than self-identified feminists on measures of somatic, obsessive-compulsive, interpersonal sensitivity, and depressive symptoms. Traditional role attitudes have been demonstrated to moderate the relationship between distress and sexual harassment such that adult and undergraduate women with greater traditional gender role attitudes experienced more psychological distress (Moradi & Subich, 2002). Additionally, Euro American female undergraduates with greater traditional gender role attitudes experienced more symptoms of Posttraumatic Stress Disorder in response to sexual harassment, while African American peers with greater traditional gender role attitudes experienced less satisfaction with life (Rederstorff, Buchanan, & Settles, 2007). Feminist attitudes also moderated the relationship between sexist events and disordered eating, such that, for female undergraduates who were low in feminist attitudes that endorsed engaging in feminist activism, sexist events positively predicted disordered eating (Sabik & Tylka, 2006). However it should be noted that feminist attitudes have not been found to be universally beneficial: African American female undergraduates who endorsed less traditional gender role attitudes had greater symptoms of PTSD when they experienced sexual harassment than their same-ethnic peers who endorsed greater traditional gender role attitudes (Rederstorff et al., 2007). The authors posited that African American women with a feminist awareness may also be more aware of social inequities and may experience a greater impact of those inequities (Rederstorff et al., 2007). Also, among undergraduate women, feminist attitudes associated with a newly developed feminist consciousness were directly and indirectly related to psychological distress through feelings of anger, whereas other types of feminist attitudes were not related to psychological distress or anger (Fischer & Good, 2004).

One qualitative study has partially supported the hypothesis that feminism moderates the effects of sexist events by assisting women in reframing sexism from a personal to a societal problem (Landrine & Klonoff, 1997). When asked directly about how feminism has helped them, 81% of participants indicated that feminism assisted them with framing the problems they faced, 61% reported that feminism assisted them to work with others to combat sexism, and 60% reported that feminism helped them feel courageous enough to combat sexism

(Klonis et al., 1997). These findings suggest that feminism can moderate the relationship between sexist events and distress several different ways, including helping women to reframe sexist events, encouraging women personally, and encouraging women to engage in collective activism.

Feminism and Personality Development

Feminism also appears to be related to personality variables. Female undergraduates who are higher in nontraditional, profeminist attitudes have been found to have higher scores on Erickson's (1950) identity achievement (Stein & Weston, 1982), suggesting that feminist attitudes are related to greater self-actualization in female college students. Fisher and colleagues (2000) also found support for a relationship between feminist identity and increased ego identity development among predominantly Euro American female undergraduates. Significant positive correlations were found between the Objective subscale of a measure of ego identity achievement and higher feminist attitudes, while significant negative correlations were found between feminist attitudes and the Foreclosed Identity subscale (Fisher et al., 2000). A significant positive correlation was found between the foreclosed identity subscale and traditional gender role attitudes (Fisher et al., 2000). These findings suggest that feminist attitudes are positively related to greater ego identity achievement. Increased feminist attitudes were also related to preferring group strategies to enhance self-concept rather than individual strategies among female undergraduates (Ng, Dunne, & Cataldo, 1995). Finally, the findings regarding instrumentality and expressiveness and feminism are mixed. Snyder and Hasbruck (1996) found no relationship between feminist attitudes and instrumentality or expressiveness among predominantly Euro American female undergraduates. Conversely, Saunders & Kashubeck-West (2006) found that feminist attitudes, but not feminist identity, were correlated with expressiveness and instrumentality in a more ethnically diverse sample of female adults and undergraduates. These findings suggest that feminist attitudes are related to positive aspects of personality development.

Feminism and Cognitive Development

Finally, it appears that feminist identity may be related to the way women think about issues (Gerstmann & Kramer, 1997). The subscales of the FIDS and FIS that assess traditional gender role attitudes were positively correlated with a measure of dualistic cognitive development among female undergraduates, suggesting that reductionist thinking is related to traditional gender role attitudes (Gerstmann & Kramer, 1997). Feminist attitudes associated with integrating feminism into one's identity from these two measures were positively correlated with measures of subjective and dialectical cognitive development, suggesting that feminist attitudes that endorse engaging in activism are related to more flexible cognitive development (Gerstmann & Kramer, 1997). Additionally, after the participants attended a women's studies class, the correlations increased between feminist attitudes associated with integrating feminism into one's identity and endorsement of activism and one or both of the measures of subjective and dialectical thinking (Gerstmann & Kramer, 1997). Also, after the women's studies class, the correlations between feminist attitudes assessed by the FIS and the measure of dualistic thinking changed from nonsignificant to significantly negative (Gerstmann & Kramer, 1997). While the authors did not test to see if the change in correlations was significant, these findings suggest that feminist attitudes are related to more flexible cognitive development among college women and that exposure to feminism may increase cognitive flexibility.

CRITIQUE OF THE CURRENT RESEARCH

Although the findings presented here suggest that feminist attitudes and feminist identity can be positive for women, three primary problems exist that limit the conclusions that can be drawn from the findings. These problems include an over-reliance on correlational statistics, utilization of samples primarily composed of Euro American college students, and problems with the measurement of feminist identity. Almost every study discussed in this section is limited by at least one of these problems, and many are limited by more than one of these issues.

Most studies conducted with the intention to analyze the effects of feminism cannot actually do so because they rely on correlational analyses. Correlations can only demonstrate that a relationship between two variables exist, but cannot determine causality or the direction of the relationship. For example, women who have feminist identities have been posited to have greater self-esteem (McNamara & Rickhard, 1989), and research has demonstrated that feminist attitudes and identity are related to higher self-esteem (De Man & Bentoit, 1982; Hurt et al., 2007; Moradi & Subich, 2002). However, because of the reliance on correlational analyses, the direction of this relationship cannot be determined. It is possible that feminist identity increases self-esteem in women; however it is also possible that women with higher self-esteem are more likely to identify as feminists. Alternatively, another variable, such as exposure to feminism, could increase both. Unfortunately, no studies have been conducted to provide evidence of causation, although some provide a stronger basis for inferring causality than others. Without studies to establish causation, neither the benefits nor the possible costs of feminist attitudes and/or feminist identity can be fully understood.

In addition, the samples that have been used to assess the correlates of feminist identity have also limited the generalizability of these studies. Most studies have relied primarily on participants who are Euro American college students. Few studies reported that their sample included non undergraduate participants and/or that more than 25% of the participants were from non-Euro American ethnoracial backgrounds. Because most samples of studies that assess feminist attitudes and identity utilize primarily Euro American college students, the generalizability of the findings from studies on feminism and mental health variables may be limited to this population. A comparison of the findings from several studies suggested that potential explanations for mixed findings are related to ethnic differences. For example, ethnic differences may account for, or partially account for, the mixed findings regarding feminism and weight concern. Moreover, the relationship between feminism and mental health variables may be different for women of different ethnoracial groups. For example, Rederstoff and colleagues (2007) found that feminist attitudes had a beneficial effect for Euro American women, but a negative effect for African American women. These findings demonstrate the importance of assessing the relationship of feminism to mental health variables for non-Euro American women to better understand how feminism may differentially affect them. Additionally, there is some research to suggest that age/cohort differences may also account for the mixed findings regarding feminism and weight concern. Most of the studies cited in this chapter did not indicate that they assessed whether there were differences in the study variables based on ethnoracial group, age, or other demographic variables. Furthermore, most studies have utilized samples composed of exclusively female participants, thereby ignoring the potential relationships between feminism and mental health variables for men and implying that men do not benefit from feminism. Thus, it is unclear whether the findings regarding the relationship of feminist attitudes and feminist identity to mental health variables are generalizable to women who are not Euro American college students or to men.

The final criticism of studies on the potential mental health benefits of feminism pertains to the measurement of feminist identity. As discussed previously, the three measures of feminist identity development are among the most commonly used assessment tools for feminist identity in this area of research. Because none of the three stages of feminist identity measures ask participants to identify themselves as feminists, we cannot be sure whether the studies that have used these measures are assessing feminist identity. As a result, no studies that utilized these measures were discussed as measures of feminist identity; rather they were conceptualized as measures of feminist attitudes. Few studies that assess mental health variables asked participants directly for feminist self-identification. Therefore, the amount of information available on the potential benefits of explicit feminist self-identification is limited. Given that some research has demonstrated not only that feminist attitudes and feminist identity are differentially related to mental health variables (Eisele & Stake, 2008; Szymanksi, 2004), but also that feminist identity mediates the relationship between feminist attitudes and mental health variables (Eisele & Stake, 2008), it is important that we better understand the relationship of explicit feminist identity to mental health variables.

CONCLUSION

Feminism has been posited to have mental health benefits for women, and the extant research in this area generally supports this hypothesis. Positive direct relationships have been demonstrated between feminism and mental health variables, including self-esteem, self-efficacy, psychological well-being, and relationship satisfaction. There has also been some more recent research to suggest that feminism's relationship to mental health variables may be complex and indirect, such as moderating the impact of distress from sexism. Unfortunately however, there are significant limitations to this research which limits its generalizability and our ability to better understand the nature of these relationships between feminism and mental health variables. Some of the mixed findings in the research may be due to these limitations, such as regarding the relationship between feminism and weight concern. More research needs to be conducted on the differential relationships of feminist attitudes and explicit feminist identification to mental health variables to better understand how feminism is related to positive outcomes for individuals. It is also important that future research utilize methodologies that provide for stronger inferences of causality and assess for complex, indirect relationships among feminist attitudes, feminist identity, and mental health variables.

In summation, although there is evidence to support the potential mental health benefits of feminism, the limitations of the available research have left us with many questions that still need to be answered.

REFERENCES

Allen, D. J., & Oleson, T. (1999). Shame and internalized homophobia in gay men. *Journal of Homosexuality, 37,* 33-43.

Ashmore, R. D., Deaux, K., & McLaughlin-Volpe, T. (2004). An organizing framework for collective identity: Articulation and significance of multidimensionality. *Psychological Bulletin, 130,* 80-114.

Bargad, A., & Hyde, J. S. (1991). Women's studies: A study of feminist identity development in women. *Psychology of Women Quarterly, 15,* 181-201.

Bay-Cheng, L. Y., & Zucker, A. N. (2007). Feminism between the sheets: Sexual attitudes among feminists, nonfeminists, and egalitarians. *Psychology of Women Quarterly, 31,* 157– 163.

Boisnier, A. D. (2003). Race and women's identity development: Distinguishing between feminism and womanism among Black and White women. *Sex Roles, 49,* 211-218.

Carter, K., & Spitzack, C. (1990). Transformation and empowerment in gender and communication courses. *Women's Studies in Communication, 13,* 92-111.

Cash, T. F., Ancis, J. R., & Strachan, M. D. (1997). Gender attitudes, feminist identity, and body images among college women. *Sex Roles, 36,* 433-447.

Cowan, G., Mestlin, M., & Masek, J. (1992). Predictors of feminist self-labeling. *Sex Roles, 27,* 321-330.

Crago, M., Shisslak, C. M., & Estes, L. S. (1996). Eating disturbances among American minority groups: A review. *International Journal of Eating Disorders, 19,* 239-248.

Curtis, M. J., & Comer, L. K. (2006). Vegetarianism, dietary restraint, and feminist identity. *Eating Behaviors, 7,* 91-104.

Dauphinais, P. D., Barkan, S. E., & Cohn, S. F. (1992). Predictors of rank-and-file feminist activism: Evidence from the 1983 general social survey. *Social Problems, 39,* 332-343.

De Man, A. F., & Benoit, R. (1982). Self-esteem in feminist and nonfeminist French-Canadian women and French-Canadian men. *Journal of Psychology, 111,* 3-7.

Dionne, M., Davis, C., Fox, J., & Gurevich, M. (1995). Feminist ideology as a predictor of body dissatisfaction in women. *Sex Roles, 33,* 277-287.

Downing, N. E., & Roush, K. L. (1985). From passive acceptance to active commitment: A model of feminist identity development for women. *Counseling Psychologist, 13,* 695-709.

Duncan, L. E. (1999). Motivation for collective action: Group consciousness as mediator of personality, life experiences, and women's rights activism. *Political Psychology, 20,* 611-635.

Eisele, H. E., & Stake, J. E. (2008). The differential relationship of feminist attitudes and feminist identity to self-efficacy. *Psychology of Women Quarterly, 32,* 233-244.

Enns, C. Z. (1997). *Feminist theories and feminist psychotherapies: Origins, themes, and variations.* New York: The Haworth Press.

Erickson, E. H. (1950). *Childhood and society.* New York: Norton.

Fingeret, M. C., & Gleaves, D. H. (2004). Sociocultural, feminist, and psychological influences on women's body satisfaction: A structural modeling analysis. *Psychology of Women Quarterly, 28,* 370-380.

Fischer, A. R., Tokar, D. M., Mergl, M. M., Good, G. E., Hill, M. S., & Blum, S. A. (2000). Assessing women's feminist identity development: Studies of convergent, discriminant, and structural validity. *Psychology of Women Quarterly, 24,* 15-29.

Fischer, A. R., & Good, G. E. (1994). Gender, self, and others: Perceptions of the campus environment. *Journal of Counseling Psychology, 41,* 343-355.

Fischer, A. R., & Good, G. E. (2004). Women's feminist consciousness, anger, and psychological distress. *Journal of Counseling Psychology, 51,* 437-446.

Foss, C. J., & Slaney, R. B. (1986). Increasing nontraditional career choices in women: Relation of attitudes toward women and responses to a career intervention. *Journal of Vocational Behavior, 28,* 191-202.

Garner, D. M., Olmstead, M. P., & Polivy, J. (1983). Development and validation of a multidimensional eating disorder inventory for anorexia and bulimia. *International Journal of Eating Disorders, 2,* 15-34.

Gerstmann, E. A., & Kramer, D. A. (1997). Feminist identity development: Psychometric analyses of two feminist identity scales. *Sex Roles, 36,* 327-348.

Grahe, S., & Hyde, J. S. (2006). Ethnicity and body satisfaction among women in the United States: A meta-analysis. *Psychological Bulletin, 132,* 622-640.

Gray, J. J., Ford, K. F., & Kelly, L. M. (1987). The prevalence of bulimia in a black college population. *International Journal of Eating Disorders, 6,* 733-740.

Grippo, K. P., & Hill, M. S. (2008). Self-objectification, habitual body monitoring, and body dissatisfaction in older Eurpoean American women: Exploring age and feminism as moderators. *Body Image, 5,* 173-182.

Guillc, C., & Chrisler, J. C. (1999). Does feminism serve a protective function against eating disorders? *Journal of Lesbian Studies, 3,* 141-148.

Haines, M. E., Erchull, M. J., Liss, M., Turner, D. L., Nelson, J. A., Ramsey, L. R., & Hurt, M. M. (2008). Predictors and effects of self-objectification in lesbians. *Psychology of Women Quarterly, 32,* 181-187.

Henley, N. M., Meng, K., O'Brien, D., McCarthy, W. J., & Sockloskie, R. J. (1998). Developing a scale to measure the diversity of feminist attitudes. *Psychology of Women Quarterly, 22,* 317-348.

Hurt, M. M., Nelson, J. A., Turner, D. L., Haines, M. E., Ramsey, L. R., Erchull, M. J., & Liss, M. (2007). Feminism: What is it good for? Feminine norms and objectification as the link between feminist identity and clinically relevant outcomes. *Sex Roles, 57,* 355-363.

Kashubeck-West, S., Mintz, L. B., & Weigold I. (2005). Separating the effects of gender and weight-loss desire on body dissatisfaction and disordered eating behavior. *Sex Roles, 53,* 505-518.

Kaysen, D., & Stake, J. E. (2001). From thought to deed: Understanding abortion activism. *Journal of Applied Social Psychology, 31,* 2378-2400.

Kelly, C., & Breinlinger, S. (1995). Identity and injustice: Exploring women's participation in collective action. *Journal of Community & Applied Social Psychology, 5,* 41-57.

Kelson, T. R., Kearney-Cooke, A., & Lansk, L. M. (1990). Body-image and body-beautification among female college students. *Perceptual and Motor Skills, 71,* 281-289.

Klonis, S., Endo, J., Crosby, F., & Worell, J. (1997). Feminism as life raft. *Psychology of Women Quarterly, 21,* 333-345.

Landrine, H., & Klonoff, E. A. (1997). *Discrimination against women: Prevalence, consequences, remedies.* Thousand Oaks, CA: SAGE Publications.

Leaper, C., & Brown, C. S. (2008). Experiences with sexism and feminist awareness among adolescent girls. *Child Development, 79,* 685-704.

Leavy, R. L., & Adams, E. M. (1986). Feminism as a correlate of self-esteem, self-acceptance, and social support among lesbians. *Psychology of Women Quarterly, 10,* 321-326.

Liss, M., Crawford, M., & Popp, D. (2004). Predictors and correlates of collective action. *Sex Roles, 50,* 771-779.

Liss, M., O'Connor, C., Morosky, E., & Crawford, M. (2001). What makes a feminist? Predictors and correlates of feminist social identity in college women. *Psychology of Women Quarterly, 25,* 124-133.

Maddux, J. E. (1991). Self-efficacy. In C. R. Snyder & D. R. Forsyth (Eds.), *Handbook of social and clinical psychology: The health perspective* (pp. 58-78). New York: Pergamon Press.

Mahalik, J. R., Morray, E. B., Coonerty-Femiano, A., Ludlow, L. H., Slattery, S. M., & Smiler, A. (2005). Development of the Conformity to Feminine Norms Inventory. *Sex Roles, 52,* 417-435.

Markowitz, L. (1998). After the organizing ends: Workers, self-efficacy, activism, and union frameworks. *Social Problems, 45,* 356-382.

McCabe, J. (2005). What's in a label? The relationship between feminist self-identification and "feminist" attitudes among U.S. women and men. *Gender & Society, 19,* 480-505.

McNamara, K., & Rickard, K. M. (1989). Feminist identity development: Implications for feminist therapy with women. *Journal of Counseling and Development, 68,* 184-189.

Mintz, L. B., & Betz, N. E. (1986). Sex differences in nature, realism, and correlates of body image. *Sex Roles, 15,* 185-195.

Misciagno, P. S. (1997). *Rethinking feminist identification: The case for de facto feminism.* Westport, CT: Praeger Publishers.

Moradi, B., & Subich, L. M. (2002). Feminist identity development measures: Comparing the psychometrics of three instruments. *Counseling Psychologist, 30,* 66-86.

Morgan, B. L. (1996). Putting the feminism into feminism scales: Introduction of a Liberal Feminist Attitude and Ideology Scale. *Sex Roles, 34,* 359-390.

Morley, L. (1993). Women's studies as empowerment of "non-traditional" learners in community and youth work training: A case study. In M. Kennedy, C. Lubelska, & V. Walsh (Eds.), *Making connections: Women's studies, women's movements, women's lives* (pp. 118-141). London: Taylor & Francis.

Myaskovsky, L., & Wittig, M. A. (1997). Predictors of feminist social identity among college women. *Sex Roles, 37,* 861-883.

Myers, T. A., & Crowther, J. H. (2007). Sociocultural pressures, thin-ideal internalization, self-objectification, and body dissatisfaction: Could feminist beliefs be a moderating factor? *Body Image, 4,* 296-308.

Nelson, J. A., Liss, M., Erchull, M. J., Hurt, M. M., Ramsey, L. R., Turner, D. L., & Haines, M. E. (2008). Identity in action: Predictors of feminist self-identification and collective action. *Sex Roles, 58,* 721-728.

Ng, S. K., Dunne, M., & Cataldo, M. (1995). Feminist identities and preferred strategies for advancing women's positive self-concept. *Journal of Social Psychology, 135,* 561-572.

Nicholson, W. D., & Long, B. C. (1990). Self-esteem, social support, internalized homophobia, and coping strategies of HIV+ gay men. *Journal of Consulting and Clinical Psychology, 58,* 873-876.

Ojerholm, A. J., & Rothblum, E. D. (1999). The relationships of body image, feminism, and sexual orientation in college women. *Feminism & Psychology, 9,* 431-448.

Parker, S., Nichter, M., Nichter, M., Vuckovic, N., Sims, C. & Ritenbaugh, C. (1995). Body image and weight concerns among African American and White adolescent females: Differences that make a difference. *Human Organization, 54,* 103-114.

Patel, K. A. & Gray, J. L. (2001). Judgment accuracy in body preferences among African Americans. *Sex Roles, 44,* 227-235.

Peterson, R. D., Grippo, K. P., & Tantleff-Dunn, S. (2008). Empowerment and powerlessness: A closer look at the relationship between feminism, body image, and eating disturbance. *Sex Roles, 5,* 639-68.

Peterson, R. D., Tantleff-Dunn, S., & Bedwell, J. S. (2006). The effects of exposure to feminist ideology on women's body image. *Body Image, 3,* 237-246.

Powell, A. D., & Kahn, A. S. (1995). Racial differences in women's desire to be thin. *International Journal of Eating Disorders, 17,* 1455-1460.

Rederstorff, J. C., Buchanan, N. T., & Settles, I. H. (2007). The moderating roles of race and gender-role attitudes in the relationship between sexual harassment and psychological well-being. *Psychology of Women Quarterly, 31,* 50-61.

Reid, P. T. (1984). Feminism vs. minority group identity: Not for Black women only. *Sex Roles, 10,* 247-255.

Rhodebeck, L. A. (1996). The structure of men's and women's feminist orientations: Feminist identity and feminist opinions. *Gender & Society, 10,* 386-403.

Rickard, K. (1989). The relationship of self-monitored dating behaviors to level of feminist identity on the FIS. *Sex Roles, 20,* 213-116.

Rosenberg, M. (1965). *Society and the adolescent self-image.* Princeton, NJ: Princeton University Press.

Rowland Serdar, B., & Schwartz-Shea, P. (1991). Empowering women: Self, autonomy, and responsibility. *The Western Political Quarterly, 44,* 605-624.

Roy, R. E., Weibust, K. S., & Miller, C. T. (2007). Effects of stereotypes about feminists on feminist self-identification. *Psychology of Women Quarterly, 31,* 146-156.

Rudman, L. A., & Phelan, J. E. (2007). The interpersonal power of feminism: Is feminism good for romantic relationships? *Sex Roles, 57,* 787-799.

Sabik, N. J., & Tylka, T. L. (2006). Do feminist identity styles moderate the relationship between perceived sexist events and disordered eating? *Psychology of Women Quarterly, 30,* 77-84.

Saunders, K. J., & Kashubeck-West, S. (2006). The relations among feminist identity development, gender role orientation, and psychological well-being in women. *Psychology of Women Quarterly, 30,* 199-211.

Schick, V. R., Zucker, A. N., & Bay-Cheng, L. Y. (2008). Safer, better sex through feminism: The role of feminist ideology in women's sexual well-being. *Psychology of Women Quarterly, 32,* 225-232.

Stake J. E., & Hoffmann, F. L. (2001). Changes in student social attitudes, activism, and personal confidence in higher education: The role of women's studies. *American Educational Research Journal, 38,* 411-436.

Stake, J. E., & Rose, S. (1994). The long term impact of women's studies on students' personal lives and political activism. *Psychology of Women Quarterly, 18,* 403-412.

Stein, S. L., & Weston, L. C. (1982). College women's attitudes toward women and identity achievement. *Adolescence, 17,* 895-899.

Snyder, R., & Hasbrouck, L. (1996). Feminist identity, gender traits, and symptoms of disturbed eating among college women. *Psychology of Women Quarterly, 20,* 593-598.

Swami, V., Salem, N., Furham, A., & Tovee, M. J. (2008). The influence of feminist ascription on judgments of women's physical attractiveness. *Body Image, 5,* 224-229.

Szymanski, D. (2004). Relations among dimensions of feminism and internalized homophobia in lesbians and bisexual women. *Sex Roles, 51,* 145-159.

Szymanski, D., & Chung, Y. B. (2003). Feminist attitudes and coping resources as correlates of lesbian internalized heterosexism. *Feminism & Psychology, 13,* 369-389.

Tiggemann, M., & Stevens, C. (1999). Weight concern across the lifespan: Relationship to self-esteem and feminist identity. *International Journal of Eating Disorders, 26,* 103-106.

Twamley, E. W., & Davis, M. C. (1999). The sociocultural model of eating disturbance in young women: The effects of personal attributes and family environment. *Journal of Social and Clinical Psychology, 18,* 467-489.

Weitz, R. (1982). Feminist consciousness raising, self-concept, and depression. *Sex Roles, 8,* 231-241.

Williams, R., & Wittig, M. A. (1997). "I'm not a feminist, but…": Factors contributing to the discrepancy between pro-feminist orientation and feminist social identity. *Sex Roles, 37,* 885-904.

Witte, T. H., & Sherman, M. P. (2002). Silencing the self and feminist identity development. *Psychological Reports, 90,* 1075-1083.

Wright, C. V., & Fitzgerald, L. F. (2007). Angry and afraid: Women's appraisal of sexual harassment during litigation. *Psychology of Women Quarterly, 31,* 73-84.

Xinaris, S., & Boland, F. J. (1990). Disordered eating in relations to tobacco use, alcohol consumption, self-control, and sex-role ideology. *International Journal of Eating Disorders, 9,* 425-433.

Yakushko, O. (2007). Do feminist women feel better about their lives? Examining patterns of feminist identity development and women's subjective well-being. *Sex Roles, 57,* 223-234.

Yoder, J. D., Perry, R. L., & Saal, E. I. (2007). What good is a feminist identity?: Women's feminist identification and role expectations for intimate and sexual relationships. *Sex Roles, 57,* 365-372.

Zimmerman, M. A. (1995). Psychological empowerment: Issues and illustrations. *American Journal of Community Psychology, 23,* 581-599.

Zimmerman, M. A., Israel, B. A., Schulz, A., & Checkoway, B. (1992). Further explorations in empowerment theory: An empirical analysis of psychological empowerment. *American Journal of Community Psychology, 20,* 707-727.

Zimmerman, M. A., & Rappaport, J. (1988). Citizen participation, perceived control, and psychological empowerment. *American Journal of Community Psychology, 16,* 725-750.

Zucker, A. Z. (2004). Disavowing social identities: What it means when women say, "I'm not a feminist but..." *Psychology of Women Quarterly, 28,* 423-435.

APPENDIX: STUDY AIMS, METHODS, RESULTS, AND TABLES FROM CURRENT STUDY

Method

Study Aims

Findings from extant research suggest that feminist attitudes and feminist identity may be related to self-weight concern. Based on this research, a study was developed to further assess relations between these variables while addressing limitations of previous research: the failure to distinguish between feminist attitudes and feminist identity and reliance on cross-sectional designs. The first objective of this study was to assess whether a relationship exists between feminist attitudes, feminist identity, and weight concern at a single point in time and for change over time. Measures of weight concern assessed body satisfaction and drive for thinness. It was expected that feminist attitudes and identity would be related to the weight concern variables at pretesting and that change in feminist attitudes and identity would be related to change in the weight concern variables over time. Given that no studies have assessed both feminist attitudes and feminist identity in such a way to test for their possibly differential relationships to weight concern, it was unclear whether feminist attitudes or feminist identity would be more closely related to weight concern. Additionally, given that previous research has demonstrated that exposure to feminist theories and information on feminism is related to decreased weight concern (Peterson et al., 2006), it was hypothesized that weight concern would decrease over the course of the WGS classes.

Participants

Participants were college students enrolled in WGS classes during the 2006 Spring semester. Twenty-nine WGS classes were surveyed for this study representing a broad range of topics including introduction to women's studies (6 classes), women and literature (6 classes), women and art (1 class), women's health issues (1 class), psychology of women (3 classes), women and history (2 classes), and other WGS topics in sociology and anthropology (7 classes) and the humanities (3 classes). Six hundred and sixty-nine students were present at the pretest survey, 604 of which provided usable data. Five hundred and seventy-three students were present at the posttest survey, 506 of which provided usable data. Twenty-three students declined to participate (3%) at the pretest and 33 students declined to participate (6%) at the posttest.

Pretest and posttest surveys were matched for 435 students (357 female and 78 male). The mean age for the final groups of participants was 22.11 years. The majority of students identified themselves as Euro American (74.7%) with the remaining students identifying themselves as African American (10.3%), Asian American (5.3%), Hispanic/Latino(a) (3.4%), Native American (.2%), Biracial/multiracial (1.8%), and "Other" (3.7%). The college level of the participants was as follows: first year (12.0%), sophomores (21.1%), juniors, (29.0%), seniors (36.6%), graduate students (.9%), and non-degree seeking (.2%).

Materials

Feminist identity. The amount of feminist identity endorsed by participants was measured by two scales. The 4-item Self-Identification as a Feminist scale (SIF) was developed to assess explicit feminist self-identification and support of feminist values (Szymanski, 2004). Two items assessed participants' willingness to identify privately and publicly as a feminist (e.g., "I consider myself a feminist") and two items assessed the extent to which participants support feminist values and goals (e.g., "I support the goals of the feminist movement"). Each item is rated on a 5-point Likert scale, ranging from 0 (*strongly disagree*) to 4 (*strongly agree*). Internal consistency of the SIF was .93 in Szymanski (2004); in the current study it was .90 for the pretest and .92 for the posttest. Additionally, the SIF was correlated -.44 with traditional gender role attitudes (Szymanski, 2004).

The second scale of feminist identity was a single test item developed by Myaskovsky and Wittig (1997). The item asks participants to indicate on a 7-point Likert scale the statement that best applies to them. The statements ranged from, "I do not consider myself a feminist at all, and I believe feminists are harmful to family life and undermine relations between men and women," (0) to "I call myself a feminist around others and am currently active in the women's movement" (6). This test item was correlated .48 to .59 with the following variables: positive opinion of the women's movement, positive evaluations of feminists, exposure to feminism, recognition of sexism, and belief in collective social activism (Myaskovsky & Wittig, 1997).

The relation between the two feminist identity scales was reviewed to determine whether they could be combined into a single measure of feminist identity. The single feminist identity statement correlated .67 to .80 with the items from the 4-item measure in the pretest and .70 to .82 for the posttest. Furthermore, when the two scales were combined, the alpha coefficient for the current study was .93 for the pretest and .94 for the posttest. Given the relationship between these two scales, they were combined into a single 5-item measure of feminist identity for the purposes of this study.

Feminist attitudes. Feminist attitudes were measured with a 12-item scale that asked participants to rate how approving their attitudes are toward nontraditional gender roles. Ten of the 12 items were original items from the Global Goals subscale of the Liberal Feminist Attitude and Ideology Scale (LFAIS; Morgan, 1996). The remaining 2 questions were items from the Gender Roles subscale of the LFAIS (Morgan, 1996). A positively worded item is "A woman should have the same job opportunities as a man;" a negatively worded item is "Although women can be good leaders, men make better leaders." Participants were asked to rate each statement using a 7-point Likert scale, ranging from 0 (*strongly disagree*) to 6 (*strongly agree*). The total LFAIS score significantly correlated .61 with feminist identity, .68 with support of feminism, and .39 with Liberalism (Morgan, 1996). Additionally, it was not significantly correlated with a measure of social desirability (Morgan, 1996). The alpha coefficient for the Global Goals subscale was .80 and the Gender Roles subscale was .77 (Morgan, 1996). The alpha coefficient for the current study for all 12 items was .79 for the pretest and .83 for the posttest.

Weight concern. Participants' weight concern was assessed with a measure of body image and a measure of disordered eating attitudes. Participants' body image was assessed with the 9-item Body Dissatisfaction subscale and their preoccupation with being thin was assessed with the 7-item Drive for Thinness subscale of the Eating Disorder Inventory (EDI; Garner, Olmstead, & Polivy, 1983). The Body Disatisfaction subscale assessed participants' belief that parts of their bodies are too large, specifically their stomachs, thighs, buttocks, and hips while the Drive for Thinness subscale assessed participants' concern with dieting, preoccupation with weight, and pursuit of thinness. Participants were asked to rate the extent of their agreement with the subscale statements on a 0 (*Never*) to 5 (*Always*) Likert scale. Negative statements from the Body Dissatisfaction subscale were slightly reworded so that they will begin with the phrase "I worry that" rather than the phrase "I think that." The reason for this change was that the original stem "I think that" may have elicited responses that focused on factual information about participants' bodies. The items were reworded to help elicit responses that focused on participants' concern about their bodies. An example of a negatively worded item is "I worry that my buttocks are too large." Items that were positively worded were reverse scored, so that higher scores on the items indicated greater body dissatisfaction or drive for thinness. The alpha coefficient for the Body Dissatisfaction subscale for a sample of women who had been diagnosed with anorexia was .90; the alpha coefficient was .85 for the Drive for Thinness subscale (Garner et al., 1983). In a sample of female college students the alpha coefficient for the Body Dissatisfaction subscale was .91 and for the Drive for Thinness subscale was .85 (Garner et al., 1983). The alpha coefficient for the current study for the Body Dissatisfaction subscale was .90 for the pretest and the posttest; for the Drive for Thinness subscale the alpha coefficient was .91 for the pretest and .92 for the posttest.

Class relevance. To assess class relevance, participants were asked to answer four items in the posttest regarding how much they believed that the WGS class they attended was relevant to them personally. The first three items ask participants to rate how relevant the class was to their life, their life choices, and their interactions with others with a 7-point Likert scale, ranging from 0 (*Not at all*) to 6 (*Extremely*). The fourth item asks participants to identify on the same 7-point Likert scale to how relevant the class materials were to body image. The alpha coefficient for the current study for was .92 for the all the first three items and .83 for all four relevance items. Because the item that assessed the relevance of the class to weight concern correlated .29 to .34 with the remaining three items, and given the lower alpha coefficient for all 4 items, it was decided to assess general class relevance with the mean of the first three items. The fourth item was tested separately.

Procedure

Data collection occurred during the Spring semester of 2006 on six university and junior college campuses in two Midwestern states. The Spring 2006 course catalogues for those institutions were first reviewed to identify semester-long classes that were listed as WGS classes and were potentially suitable for the study. The researchers contacted professors of the identified classes to introduce the general purpose of the study and asked if they were willing to allow their class to participate. The researchers also asked professors to identify the extent that their class was relevant to the role of women in present day society on a 1 (*not at all*) to 5 (*a great deal*) Likert scale. If professors answered this question with a 4 (*quite a bit*) or 5 (*a great deal*), the researchers asked the professors if they would agree to allow data collection during class time at the beginning and end of the semester. Professors from 29 of the classes agreed to this request, and their classes were surveyed.

Participants completed the pretest surveys during their normal class time within the first 2 weeks of the semester and the posttest surveys within the last 2 weeks of the semester. The researcher or one of the four research assistants attended the class and explained to students that the goal of the study was to better understand students' experiences and attitudes and that their participation in the project was voluntary. The researcher stressed that participants' responses would be held strictly confidential, that only the researchers would see their responses, and that participants should not put their names on their answer sheets. A code was used to match participants' responses at the beginning of class with their responses at the end of class. Participants were given consent forms before completing the survey and were encouraged to ask any questions they might have as they completed the questionnaire. Additionally, students were informed that the survey was confidential and that the professor of the class would not have access to the survey forms. The professor either left the room or was seated away from the students during administration of the questionnaire so that students would not be influenced by the possibility that their professor might observe their responses. No incentives or penalties were given for participation or nonparticipation in the study.

Results

Preliminary Analyses

Transformation and missing data. The dataset was assessed for missing data. If a scale was missing 3 items or less, the remaining corresponding items were averaged and that score was entered for the missing item(s). Items that were negatively worded were reverse scored before the mean scores were calculated. The mean scores for all scales were assessed for skewness. Feminist attitudes scores were negatively skewed; it was reverse scored and a log transformation was applied to normalize the distribution.

Completers vs. non-completers. Participants who completed the pretest only and those who completed the pretest and posttest were compared to assess for possible group differences. A series of univariate analyses of variance (ANOVA) indicated that there were no differences between these two groups regarding demographic or study variables.

Time by gender effects. Preliminary analyses were conducted first to assess for the presence of a main effect of time for the study variables and for the presence of gender effects. A 2 x 2 (time by gender) multivariate analysis of variance (MANOVA) yielded a significant main effect for time, $F(6, 422) = 12.98$, $p < .001$, $\eta^2 = .16$. Paired samples t-tests indicated that the feminism variables increased over the course of the semester, but the weight concern variables did not (see Table A1).

The 2 x 2 MANOVA also yielded a significant main effect for gender, $F(6, 421) = 13.34$, $p < .001$, $\eta^2 = .15$. Repeated measures ANOVAs revealed that women reported higher scores than men at both time periods for all study variables (see Table A2). Based on these analyses, gender was controlled in the main analyses. No interaction effects were found for gender.

Table A1

Comparison of Pretest and Posttest Variable Scores ($N = 435$)			
Variable	Pretest	Posttest	Paired Samples T-test
LFAIS	5.20 (.57)	5.29 (.59)	$t\,(427) = 4.86$***
FEMID	3.54 (1.47)	3.71 (1.56)	$t\,(434) = 3.80$***
EDI- BD	2.32 (1.17)	2.30 (1.17)	$t\,(434) = -.51$
EDI-DT	2.04 (1.28)	2.09 (1.34)	$t\,(434) = .94$

Note. LFAIS and FEMID have a 0-6 scale. EDI-BD and EDI-DT have a 0-5 scale.
*** p < .001.

Time by ethnicity effects. Preliminary analyses were conducted to assess for differences between ethnoracial groups in the study variables at pretesting and over time to determine whether ethnoracial group needed to be controlled in the main analyses. Participants had the option of choosing one of seven different categories of ethnoracial identification. Given the small sample sizes for some of the ethnoracial groups, a 6 x 4 MANOVA (ethnoracial group by study variables) was conducted to determine if the groups could be combined into larger categories based on similarities in pretest and change scores (Native Americans were not included in the analyses because only one participant reported this ethnic identity). A main effect was found for ethnicity, F (6, 419) = 8.96, p < .001, η^2 = .11. Univariate analyses revealed that, overall, African American participants reported significantly different scores than individuals from other ethnoracial groups on some of the study variables. African American participants had significantly lower feminist identity, body dissatisfaction, and drive for thinness scores than Asian Americans and other non-Euro American participants at pretesting and Asian American, Latino/a/Hispanic, and biracial participants across time. Given that individuals from non-Euro American ethnoracial groups reported similar scores on the study variables at pretesting and across time, with the exception of African Americans, participants' ethnoracial identification was recoded into a new ethnicity variable. This new ethnicity variable included the categories: Euro American, African American, and Other Non Euro American.

A 2 x 3 MANOVA (time by ethnoracial group) with the four measures of student change yielded a significant main effect for ethnicity, F (8, 417) = 6.49, p < .001, η^2 = .11. Additional repeated measures ANOVAs revealed that African American participants had significantly lower feminist identity, drive for thinness, and body dissatisfaction scores at pretesting and across time than the other two ethnoracial groups (see Table A3). No interaction effects were observed. Because ethnoracial differences were found in the pretest variable scores and across time, ethnicity was controlled in the main analyses.

Table A2

Gender Differences ($N = 430$)			
Pretest Variable	Males	Females	F score
LFAIS	4.86 (.66)	5.26 (.53)	F (1, 428) = 28.64, d = .67***
FEMID	2.68 (1.63)	3.69 (1.39)	F (1, 433) = 31.95, d = .67***
EDI- BD	1.59 (1.06)	2.46 (1.14)	F (1, 433) = 37.80, d = .79***
EDI-DT	1.49 (1.26)	2.13 (1.25)	F (1, 433) = 22.19, d = .51***
Posttest Variables			

Table A2 (Continued)

LFAIS	4.90 (.70)	5.37 (.53)	$F(1, 426) = 41.38, d = .76***$
FEMID	2.92 (1.71)	3.87 (1.50)	$F(1, 426) = 27.20, d = .59***$
EDI- BD	1.63 (.99)	2.44 (1.16)	$F(1, 426) = 34.76, d = .75***$
EDI-DT	1.52 (1.24)	2.21 (1.33)	$F(1, 426) = 16.51, d = .54***$

*** p < .001.

Table A3

Ethnic Differences (N = 433)			
Pretest Variable	Euro American	African American	Other Non Euro American	F score
American				
LFAIS	5.20 (.58)	5.14 (.59)	5.25 (.54)	$F(2, 425) = .473, \eta^2 = .00$
FEMID	3.60 (1.48)[a]	2.87 (1.20)[b]	3.71 (1.48)[a]	$F(2, 430) = 5.06, \eta^2 = .02**$
EDI- BD	2.42 (1.17)[a]	1.64 (.98)[b]	2.26 (1.17)[a]	$F(2, 430) = 8.94, \eta^2 = .04***$
EDI-DT	2.15 (1.27)[a]	1.22 (.94)[b]	2.07 (1.36)[a]	$F(2, 430) = 11.66, \eta^2 = .05***$
Posttest Variables				
LFAIS	5.30 (.59)	5.20 (.61)	5.32 (.61)	$F(2, 423) = .64, \eta^2 = .00$
FEMID	3.80 (1.58)[a]	2.78 (1.26)[b]	3.95 (1.56)[a]	$F(2, 430) = 7.35, \eta^2 = .03*$
EDI- BD	2.38 (1.17)[a]	1.58 (.89)[b]	2.42 (1.20)[a]	$F(2, 430) = 9.87, \eta^2 = .05**$
EDI-DT	2.17 (1.33)[a]	1.27 (.99)[b]	2.29 (1.40)[a]	$F(2, 430) = 11.56, \eta^2 = .05**$

Note. Variables with different superscripts are significantly different.
*** p < .001. ** p < .01. * p < .05.

Age/year in college effects. Regression analyses were undertaken to assess the relation of age and year in college to each of the study variables to determine whether these variables needed to be controlled in the main analyses. Age was only a significant predictor for drive for thinness at pretest, $\beta = -.15, p < .01$. Therefore, age was controlled for in the main pretest regression analyses for drive for thinness.

Relation between Pretest Feminist Attitudes, Feminist Identity, and Weight Concern

A primary goal of this study was to assess the relation between feminist attitudes, feminist identity, and weight concern at pretesting. To do so, a series of three regression analyses were conducted using the pretest scores. The demographic variables of gender and ethnoracial group (as well as age for drive for thinness) were controlled by entering them in the first step of all regression equations. In the first regression analysis, the relation between pretest feminist attitudes and pretest feminist identity was assessed. In the second set of regression analyses, the relation between pretest feminist attitudes and pretest drive for thinness and body dissatisfaction were tested in separate analyses. In the third set of regression analyses, the relation between pretest feminist identity and pretest drive for thinness and body dissatisfaction were tested in separate analyses.

In the first set of pretest regression analyses, feminist attitudes significantly predicted feminist identity, $\beta = .49$, $p < .001$, $\Delta R^2 = .23$. In the second set of pretest regression analyses, feminist attitudes did not significantly predict drive for thinness or body dissatisfaction. In the third set of pretest regression analyses, feminist identity did not significantly predict drive for thinness or body dissatisfaction.

Relation between Change in Feminist Attitudes, Feminist Identity, and Self-Efficacy

A second goal of this study was to assess the relation between change in feminist attitudes, feminist identity, and weight concern. A series of three regression analyses were conducted that were congruent with the analyses conducted with the pretest variables. However, in this set of analyses, the relation between change over time in the variables was assessed rather than the relation between the variables at a single point in time. Relevant demographic variables were entered in the first step of the analyses. To assess change in the outcome variables, pretest scores corresponding to the outcome measure being tested were entered into the regression equation in the second step of the regression analysis. By controlling for pretest scores, the results from the analyses represented the relation between the predictor variables and the residual (change) scores. In the case of the predictor variables, however, change scores were utilized rather than pretest and posttest scores because of multicollinearity problems.

In the first set of change analyses, change in feminist attitudes significantly predicted change in feminist identity, $\beta = .09$, $p < .001$, $\Delta R^2 = .01$. In the second set of change analyses, change in feminist attitudes did not significantly predict change in drive for thinness or body dissatisfaction. In the third set of change analyses, change in feminist identity did not significantly predicted change in drive for thinness or body dissatisfaction.

Class Relevance

In the final set of analyses, general class relevance was assessed using regression analyses to determine if it was related to change in the study variables. In these analyses, demographic variable scores, pretest study variable scores, and general class relevance scores were entered as predictor variables. Posttest study variable scores were entered as the outcome variables. Each dependent variable was assessed in a separate regression analysis. Additional regression analyses were conducted similarly to the general class relevance analyses, except the score of the item assessing class relevance to weight concern was entered instead of general class relevance scores. Neither general class relevance nor the relevance of the class to weight concern predicted change in body dissatisfaction or drive for thinness.

Study Limitations

It should be noted that there some limitations were present in this study. First, a measure of liberal feminist ideology was utilized to assess feminist attitudes, yet feminism is not a monolithic construct. Many forms of feminism exist, and liberal feminist ideology is only one type of feminist ideology (Enns, 1997). Although all feminist ideologies have the same underlying principles of valuing women's perspectives, gender equality, and awareness of sexist social structures and practices, each has a different focus and identifies a different location for the source of sexism (Enns, 1997). However, intercorrelations between different ideologies of feminist attitudes generally demonstrate significant positive relationships between liberal feminism and other feminist ideologies, except cultural feminism (Henley, Meng, O'Brien, McCarthy, & Sockloskie, 1998; Liss, O'Connor, Morosky, & Crawford, 2001; Szymanski, 2004), suggesting that the findings from studies that utilize liberal feminist attitude measures will generalize to most other feminist ideologies. Even so, little data on this topic is available, and it is possible that findings from studies that utilize measures of liberal feminist ideology may not fully generalize to individuals who endorse other feminist ideologies.

The second limitation of this study was that the length of time between the pretest and posttest was limited to approximately 4 months. It is possible that more change in the study variables would have been found if a longer longitudinal design had been utilized. However, previous research has found that changes in attitudes and engagement in feminist activism among WGS students have stayed relatively constant in the 9 months after the class ended (Stake & Rose, 1994). It does not appear, therefore, that a follow-up survey after the classes ended would have found additional change in the feminism study variables. Longer exposure to feminism in WGS classes, however, has been found to result in more student change (Stake & Hoffman, 2001), suggesting that more change in the variables may be found if participants attend subsequent WGS classes.

A third limitation of this study is that, given the setting of a WGS class, some students may have felt compelled to provide more socially desirable responses regarding feminist attitudes and feminist identity. This pressure may have increased over the course of the semester as students spent more time in the class. Thus, students' scores in feminist attitudes and feminist identity could have been artificially inflated, especially at posttesting. However, research has previously demonstrated that the measures of feminist attitudes and feminist identity utilized in this study are not significantly related to social desirability (Morgan, 1996; Szymanski, 2004). Additionally, no relation has previously been found between social desirability and feminist attitudes at posttesting for WGS classes (Bargad & Hyde, 1991). Thus, given previous research on this topic and the steps taken to ensure confidentiality listed in the methods section, it is unlikely that students' responses were influenced by social desirability.

Conclusion

While few of the hypotheses of this study were supported, our findings are consistent with most of the extant research on this topic. Weight concern did not change over the course of the WGS classes, nor was it related to feminist attitudes or feminist identity at pretest or over time. However, this finding is consistent with most of the previous research in the area, as few studies have demonstrated a direct relationship between feminism and weight concern. Most of this research has assessed the relationship of feminist attitudes to weight concern, rather than feminist identity. Some studies have found that feminist attitudes moderate the relationship of another variable, such as sexist events, to weight concern. However the findings in this area are mixed as well. Future research should assess the potentially unique role of feminist identity to weight concern, given the lack of research regarding explicit feminist self-identification. Previous research has demonstrated that feminist identity plays an important and unique role in mental health variables over and above feminist attitudes (Eisele & Stake, 2008), and further research needs to be conducted to ascertain whether this finding extends to weight concern. Future research should particularly assess the potential role of feminist identity to weight concern, particularly as a moderating variable, and address whether feminist attitudes and identity are related to weight concern through other variables, such as empowerment. In conclusion, while most of our hypotheses regarding feminism and weight concern were not supported, there is much research that still needs to be conducted on this topic.

In: Feminism and Women in Leadership
Editor: Vicente Nardi, pp. 29-48

ISBN: 978-1-60876-270-5
© 2010 Nova Science Publishers, Inc.

Chapter 2

MALE VICTIMS OF RAPE: FEMINISM, LAW AND SCHOLARSHIP

Joanna Jamel and Philip N.S. Rumney

Department of Criminology, Kingston University, London, England.
Bristol Law School, University of the West of England, Bristol, England

ABSTRACT

The issue of adult male rape and sexual assault has been the subject of a significant increase in attention by scholars in the last two decades. This growth in the scholarly literature is similar to the large increase in research examining female sexual victimization from the 1970s onwards. Furthermore, over the last four decades many jurisdictions have adopted legal reforms that have included males as potential victims of rape. The research on adult male rape and sexual assault has examined this problem from a range of disciplinary perspectives and has developed in sophistication. Adult male rape is also an issue that has received increased attention from feminist scholars. Some of this literature has been, at best, ambivalent regarding the increasing societal and legal recognition of the problem of adult male sexual victimization. In other instances, male victimization has been treated in a dismissive manner. Up until now, this literature has received little in the way of serious sustained analysis. This chapter represents the beginning of an ongoing engagement by the authors with feminist theorizing on male rape.

In this particular work we highlight some of the problematic aspects of feminist engagement with adult male sexual victimization. First, this chapter will describe the incidence, prevalence, and impact of male rape. Second, it will examine how feminist theorizing can be problematic in providing robust explanations of rape which can accommodate the experiences of male victims. Finally, this chapter will engage in a critical evaluation of the claim that male rape victims are 'feminized' by rape, as well as claims regarding the treatment of male rape by the law and wider society.

INTRODUCTION

The issue of adult male rape and sexual assault has been the subject of a significant increase in attention by scholars in the last two decades. This growth in the scholarly literature is similar to the large increase in research examining female sexual victimization from the 1970s onwards (Kelly, 1988). Furthermore, over the last four decades many jurisdictions have adopted legal reforms that have recognized males as potential victims of rape (Rumney, 2008; Raitt and Ferguson, 2006). The research on adult male rape and sexual assault has examined this problem from a range of disciplinary perspectives and has developed in sophistication. Adult male rape is also an issue that has received increased attention from feminist scholars. Some of this literature has been, at best, ambivalent regarding the increasing societal and legal recognition of the problem of adult male sexual victimization. In other instances, male victimization has been treated in a dismissive manner. Up until now, this literature has received little in the way of serious sustained analysis. This chapter represents the beginning of an ongoing engagement by the authors with feminist theorizing on male rape.

In this particular work we highlight some of the problematic aspects of feminist engagement with adult male sexual victimization. First, this chapter will describe the incidence, prevalence, and impact of male rape. Second, it will examine how feminist theorizing can be problematic in providing robust explanations of rape which can accommodate the experiences of male victims. Finally, this chapter will engage in a critical evaluation of the claim that male rape victims are 'feminized' by rape, as well as claims regarding the treatment of male rape by the law and wider society.

THE INCIDENCE, PREVALENCE AND IMPACT OF MALE RAPE

While it has been recently claimed that there is only 'a small amount of research literature on male victimization' and that it would be 'foolhardy to attempt to put a figure on the extent of the problem' as the 'precise figure remains elusive' (Graham, 2006: 188, 189), the reality is that male rape has been the subject of a growing body of work from a range of disciplines. In epidemiological research from the United States, Sorenson et al. found that 7.2% of adult males (over the age of 16) reported being a victim of unwanted 'sexual contact' (Sorenson et al., 1987). A more recent British study of 2,474 men found that 2.89% of men disclosed being a victim of sexual assault as adults (that is, over the age of 16) and 5.35% had been victims of child sexual abuse. This research also found that homosexuality was a significant risk factor associated with sexual victimization. Males with a history of consensual sex with other males were six times more likely to report victimization than males with no such history (Coxell et al., 1999). In an earlier British study of 930 gay men, F.C.I. Hickson et al. identified a significant number as victims of non-consensual sex. Of those surveyed it was found that 257 (27.6 per cent) men reported that they had been 'subjected to non-consensual sex at some point in their lives.' Of these, it was found that 45.2 per cent (99) had been anally penetrated, and in another 11 cases (5 per cent) there had been an unsuccessful attempt at anal penetration (Hickson et al., 1994). In a survey of 287 gay men in Vancouver, one third were found to have 'been forced to have sex against their will at least once in their lives' (Janoff, 2005).

As a result of what appears to be a significant difference in victimization rates between men and women, it is worth considering some of the implications this has for feminist theorizing. For example, it might be suggested that according to feminist conceptualizations of female rape, the prevalence of which signifies the eligibility of its survivors for political and symbolic 'victim' status (see: Kelly, Burton and Regan, 1996). Consequently, it may be suggested that due to the reported lower incidence of male rape that its victims are ineligible for the same 'victim' status as their female counterparts. Indeed, might the recognition of male rape victims undermine radical feminists' gender inequality argument based on the homogeneity of gender where all males are 'oppressors' and all females are 'victims' within the patriarchal power structures of Western society. This approach echoes feminist rejection of gender neutral rape legislation such as the Criminal Justice and Public Order Act 1994, on the basis that having a rape law that applies equally to males and females devalues the notion of rape as a 'gendered' crime perpetrated by men against women (Gillespie, 1996: 151) Radical feminists such as Catherine MacKinnon provide conflicting perspectives arguing against gender-neutral laws on the basis that they obscure the sex-based harms done to women (MacKinnon, 1990), while favoring a gender-neutral anti-pornography ordinance (Rumney, 2007) and in later work arguing for the extension of laws to protect males, as well as females, who are victims of sexual harassment (MacKinnon, 1997).

Another source of information concerning sexual victimization is official crime statistics. In England and Wales, the most recent officially recorded rates of rape victimization are for the 2008-2009 period in which 12,165 female rapes and 968 male rapes were recorded by the police (Walker, Flatley, Kershaw, and Moon, 2009).Therefore, male rape victims account for about eight per cent of all recorded rapes in England and Wales. In the United States, due to variations across states with regard to their respective laws, it is difficult to gauge the prevalence of adult male sexual victimization. In 2007, according to the FBI Uniform Crime Reports the number of forcible rapes of women was 90,427 while male rape victimization is encompassed under the categories of aggravated sexual assault and sex offences depending on the situational characteristics and injuries sustained (FBI, 2008). In addition, there is also the problem of under-reporting which affects not only male, but also female rape figures (Kelly, Lovett and Regan, 2005). As a result, crime statistics are not a reliable way of judging the rate of victimization (Coxell, Mezey, and Kell, 2000). Research by the charity organization Survivors UK suggests that males may not report to the police for many different reasons, including: 'not knowing that it is a crime'; 'fear of not being believed'; and 'concerns that sexuality may become an issue' (HMCPSI/HMIC, 2002; Abdullah Kahn, 2008; Rumney, 2008). Other factors may include the male's conceptualization of the incident (Allen, 2002) and the availability of social support networks as well as the prevalence of myths and misconceptions constructed about male rape victims which may affect their sense of self. For example, (i) men cannot be raped (Stermac et al., 2004); (ii) males should be able to defend their sexual zones (Groth and Burgess, 1980); (iii) only gay men get raped (Stermac et al , 2004); (iv) men cannot sexually perform unless sexually aroused (Smith, Pine, and Hawley, 1988); (v) men are sexually available at all times to take advantage of opportunities for sex (Clements-Screiber and Rempel, 1995), (vi) the impact of rape on men is less severe than on female rape victims (Stermac et al., 2004). Due to male rape being perceived as a homosexually motivated offence (McMullen, 1990) and the antagonistic undertones of heterosexist society's treatment of members of the gay community (despite its acceptance on some levels); it is not surprising that many heterosexual and homosexual victims alike are silent regarding their victimization. The perception that the police service will be particularly unsympathetic to gay victims may also help to explain research findings which suggest that fewer homosexual victims of male rape report to the police than heterosexual victims (Hodge and Canter, 1998; Abdullah-Kahn, 2008).

The impact of male sexual victimization is often very serious (Sarrel and Masters, 1982; Myers, 1989; Isely, 1991; Huckle, 1995; Mezey and King, 2000, Walker et al, 2005; Walker et al., 2005a). Researchers suggest that males who have been subject to sexual victimization experience similar types of psychological *sequelae* as female victims, although there are also differences (Mezey and King, 1989; Schack, 2004; Tolin and Foa 2008: 977). Reactions to male rape can include depression, anger, desire for revenge, sexual problems, concerns regarding sexuality and masculinity, difficulty with trusting others and self-harm (Mezey and King, 1989; Coxell and King, 1996; Allen, 2002; Elliott, Mok, and Briere, 2004; Walker et al., 2005; Willis, 2009). Recent control group research by Elliott et al. (2004) and Walker et al. (2005a) found that sexually assaulted males were significantly more likely to report traumatic reactions than males in control groups who had not been victims of sexual assault. It is evident that not all male victims suffer similar levels of psychological trauma as there are a number of factors which are influential in this regard. For example, reactions may be influenced, firstly, by the coping strategies of the victim (Olff, Langeland, Draijer, and Gersons, 2007) and, secondly, their social support network (Ozer, Best, Lipsey and Weiss, 2008). Tolin and Foa (2008: 63) found that women and girls were more likely than boys to exhibit PTSD symptoms, suggesting: 'Thus, one possible interpretation of the higher frequency of PTSD among women and girls is that they are more likely than their male counterparts to experience sexual assault and abuse.' However, on closer analysis they concluded that the difference in PTSD rates could not be explained solely be sexual victimization rates. Another aspect of reported differential rates of PTSD derives in part, from research reviewed by Tolin and Foa which examines the possible influence of socially ascribed gender behavior on self-reports that may result in males being less willing to admit to fear. The research in this regard, however, is regarded as 'mixed' (Tolin and Foa, 2008: 66).

Male rape victims also experience difficulties when accessing their social support network in times of crisis. These may originate in the socialization process through which males learn that the expression of emotions and discussion of emotive topics do not conform to gender ascribed normative masculine behavior (Parsons and Bales, 1956). Therefore, there is likely to be a dissipation of their peer social network when sensitive topics such as sexual victimization are raised. Indeed, male victims report a range of negative reactions by others when reporting to friends and relatives including disbelief, threats and laughter (Johnston, 1996, Scarce, 1997; Walker et al, 2005). Negative responses to disclosure are also found in the historical literature. In his examination of legal and social responses to male rape in late imperial China, Anthony Sommer found evidence that the stigma of being penetrated was also shared by family members and that sometimes 'such shame provoked family members to violent acts against the penetrated male himself' (Sommer, 2000: 150). Further, the unwillingness of some males to seek assistance may hinder their access to medical services. Research has also found that female rape victims do not perceive themselves as 'patients' and therefore treatment is not part of their internal discourse (Foa, Rothbaum, Riggs and Murdock, 1991). Similarly reasoning may well apply to male victims.

FEMINIST APPROACHES TO RAPE

Before progressing further, it is important to highlight the variety of feminist approaches which attempt to explain the perpetuation of male violence against women. Furthermore, it is beneficial to clarify the diversity within feminism which is often inadvertently homogenized by referring to 'feminists' in a general sense. This chapter will outline the ideologies of liberal feminists, radical feminists (who are our main focus), Marxist and social feminists in their explanation of the prevalence of rape and consider the conceptual problems posed to these perspectives by male rape.

Firstly, 'Liberal feminists focus on social justice, consisting largely of legalized access and equal opportunity for success rather than specific protections from violence against women' (Martin, Vieraitis, and Britto, 2006: 324). Liberal and radical feminists (to a lesser extent) suggest that gender equality regarding education, politics and the law should result in a decrease in female victimization, and lower rape rates. This is known as the 'amelioration hypothesis' (Whaley and Messner, 2002). Enns (1992) considers oppression as a result of gender inequality across educational, legal and socio-political contexts to be the product of rigid gender role socialization processes. The application of this theorization to male rape suggests that gender inequality also negatively affects male victims as their gender constructs them as members of the dominant and powerful in-group. Thus, their victimization is hidden or unrecognized and they are inhibited from seeking social and legal recourse for their victimization. Alternatively, some radical feminist theorists suggest that gender equality may increase rape victimization rates as a consequence of a temporary male backlash (Russell, 1975). This sexually violent attack against females is perceived as serving a cathartic role for men to reclaim the perceived loss of power as a result of gender equality. In relating this conceptualization to male rape victims the cathartic role would also be to reclaim power but not as a result of gender inequality. Rather, as a result of the pressure of aspiring to hegemonic status and the rigidity of this form of masculinity.

Secondly, Marxist feminism considers that male violence against women is the result of the power differential based on gendered class positions within society. This imbalance of power between men and women is further exacerbated by sexual difference (Martin et al., 2006). However, the rape of male victims cannot be explained by this approach as they are treated as occupying a dominant class position. It may be suggested that their rape victimization may remove their socially ascribed access to the dominant class and relegate them to the subordinate class on a par with female rape victims.

Thirdly, Socialist feminists combine the ideologies of Marxist and radical feminists whereby females' 'absolute' economic and gender equality will influence rape rates as women occupy a singular role as a class within the fiscal system. (Martin et al., 2006). In the labor market where the current positions of males (the bourgeoisie) and women (the proletariat) become more balanced, in order to obtain a cathartic release from this perceived reduction in socio-economic power, males will seek to re-affirm their power through violence against the encroaching proletariat according to socialist feminists. Again, the existence of male rape victims provides considerable problems for its application to male rape. It is suggested that the dominant class raping members of their own social group may be to reinforce their dominant position and progress their aspiration to hegemonic male status (Connell, 1995).

Fourthly, according to Martin et al. (2006) the primary concern of radical feminists relates to rape and violence against women (see Brownmiller, 1975; MacKinnon, 1989; Russell, 1975), the origins of which are seen to be the result of the social stratification system based on patriarchal norms that reinforces gender-based inequalities regarding access to resources and women's dependence on males for physical and economic protection. Thus, gender role norms which sexually objectify women and advocate their ownership condone a culture where sexual aggression and violence are in adherence with the dominance ascribed by the male sex role. Radical feminists consistently overlook men's lack of 'agency' when sexually victimized and weakens their theoretical perspective as it implies that all men are potential aggressors and all women are potential victims. This conceptualization is particularly problematic regarding male rape where both the aggressor and victim are male. Helliwell (2000) suggests there is a 'heterosexual matrix' where there are two distinct types of person (male and female) between whom there is an imbalance of power within society. In accordance with this theory, the pervasiveness of this heterosexual matrix is further highlighted by the feminization of the male as a consequence of their sexual victimization.

Marcus (1992: 391) has argued rape is 'a scripted interaction in which one person auditions for the role of rapist and strives to manoeuvre another person into the role of victim ... a process of gendering which we can attempt to disrupt' (Butler, Scott and Marcus, 1992: 391, as cited in Mardorossian (2002: 752), but the script pre-exists the act of violence and only 'momentarily' creates the identities of rapist and victim when enacted. By contrast, other scholars see rape as more structured form of victimization, beyond temporary interactions. McGlynn (2008: 77-78) has argued that '[t]he term rape ... is widely accepted as describing harms against women by men. While it does, and should encompass the rape of men, it must also not be forgotten that this is primarily a crime by men against women'. This view of rape is linked to a radical feminist critique of heterosexual relations, the aim of which is to reinforce heterosexist social structures within patriarchal society: 'Heterosexism is an ideological system that rejects and stigmatizes non-heterosexual forms of behavior, identity, relationships and communities' (Schneider, 2001: 459). Rape is therefore seen as a form of social control of women:

> While men are capable of being raped, they are not subjected to the pervasive threat of rape which faces women in the present culture. Nor are they raped at the horrifyingly (if controversial) numbers that women are. The fact that men can be, but are not often raped emphasizes the extent to which rape enforces a systematic (i.e., consistent, although not necessarily conscious) sexualized control of women (Cahill, 2000: 45).

Radical feminist perspectives suggest the gendered crime of rape is condoned by society's patriarchal structures and reinforced through socialization practices which debilitate both males and females. Bourdieu (1998/2001: 53) suggests a core motivation for male rape '[m]anliness, it can be seen, is an eminently relational notion, constructed in front of and for other men and against femininity, in a kind of fear of the female, firstly in oneself'. The social control which the 'fear of rape' instills in females results in self-monitoring of behavior. But, what radical feminists historically failed to acknowledge was that females do not have sole ownership of rape victimhood, and that their theoretical perspectives tend to be uncompromisingly gendered. Radical feminists' contributions to political and legislative decision-making may, to some degree, have negatively affected male rape victims resulting in a lack of acknowledgment of their needs. Yet, it can be argued that there are links between male rape and radical feminist theorizing on female rape. Cahill (2000) highlights the gender specific stigma attached to male rape victimization whereby they are demoted from a dominant to a subordinate status due to the passivity and submissiveness (feminine characteristics) of victimhood and are therefore defined as a 'social woman'.

In Western societies, sexuality and personal identity are intrinsically linked according to Helliwell (2000), who highlighted the Foucauldian perception that sex is the covert element that underpins our sense of self. Therefore, the act of rape is a penetration of the self and violation of the person's core corporeal boundaries (Sanday, 1990). Thus, in this sense the violation of the corporeal self can be debilitating irrespective of gender. According to Cahill (2000: 44) 'Foucault viewed the desexualization of rape as a liberating blow against the disciplining discourse which constructed sexuality as a means of social and political power'. Nevertheless, while a Foucauldian perspective may be considered useful in facilitating the recognition of male rape victims by removing the sexual element and focusing instead on the issue of power, the fact that rape is a violent act and the mode sexual, is challenging. In addition, the impact of the rape on male victim's sexual identity (Garnets, Herek, and Levy, 1990; Myers, 1989) would also be negated according to this view.

VICTIMOLOGY, FEMINISM AND MALE RAPE

Radical feminists have been victimology's harshest critics due to its alleged victim-blaming perspectives particularly regarding rape and neglect of women and feminist perspectives (Naffine, 1997). Victimology is a sub-discipline of criminology, the pioneers of which are von Hentig (1948) and Mendelsohn (1947), who developed the concepts of 'victim proneness' and 'victim culpability' respectively. But it is to Wolfgang (1958), and his pivotal concept of 'victim precipitation' developed from his research on identified patterns found in criminal homicides, that is the focus here. An example of this precipitation by victims within an encounter is as follows: the victim instigates the conflict between himself/herself and the offender which ultimately leads to their demise. 'Victim precipitation' was then controversially applied by Amir (1971) to the crime of female rape in his so-called 'Philadelphia Study'. The concept of 'victim precipitation' is often mistakenly perceived as a being victim-blaming or holding the victim accountable for their behavior (for example, by inviting the offender for coffee and frequenting risky venues such as clubs and bars late at night) (Weis and Borges, 1973). Similar reasoning is sometimes applied to male rape victims (Rumney and Hanley, 2009).

A critical radical victimology emphasized a crisis in criminological victim research and a number of objections were proposed, one of which was the claim that victims were being held responsible for their own criminal victimization. These perceptions of 'victim precipitation' are strongly rebuked by Fattah (1994) who argued that victimologists should not be held responsible for how their concepts are misinterpreted and furthermore, that the victim's behavior is not assessed so there are no moral judgments made in this regard. Thus, the focus is on the situational rather than the behavioral context of the rape incident for purposes of the current discourse. Schneider (2001) also stated that victim precipitation is the issue, not 'coresponsibility' and there is no intention to 'degrade' victims or to 'scapegoat' them. Instead, it is suggested that the aim is to develop victim-oriented programs of crime prevention. However, by this focus on crime prevention, one can argue that there is the implication that the victim needs to change their behavior in order to prevent their criminal victimization. Schneider (2001) also emphasized that the underlying theory of victim precipitation is that of symbolic interaction which does not excuse the offender from sole responsibility for the act of rape. Another point Schneider made is that by denying a victim-offender relationship, the victim will exhibit a reaction of 'learned helpless' as they will always consider themselves at risk of sexual attack by a male predator. Nonetheless, a question arises about male rape victims who are not generally socialized to consider that they are at risk of sexual attack. When males are subjected to rape, it is often beyond the boundaries of their experience and can result in a crisis of masculine identity and sexual orientation, as well as a fear of other males. Thus, the act of rape is a form of social control of women and men (Chapleau, Oswald and Russell, 2008). Fewer men than women may fear rape, or structure their behavior in order to avoid it (Abdullah-Kahn, 2008: 163-167), but focus group research involving student participants strongly suggests that participants judge the credibility of male rape complainants on the basis that males should perceive certain forms of behavior to be risky or dangerous and act accordingly to avoid it. In these discussions direct comparison with cases of female rape are made on the basis that if a woman would view a situation as dangerous (for example, going back to a man's apartment alone), a male should do so as well (Rumney and Hanley, 2009).

Furthermore, considering radical feminists' significant contribution to defining rape within legal and social contexts (Rozee and Koss, 2001) should they not be assisting all victims of male violence? Otherwise, the radical feminist approach is undermined suggesting that their aims are more about progressing their political aims than actively reducing the problem of male violence at a societal level (Dutton and Nicholls, 2005). However, radical feminists would argue that because females account for the majority of rape victims then it is appropriate for their limited resources to be directed to this gender group (Jones and Cook, 2008). However, by this token these feminists may be criticized as reinforcing the gender dichotomy within society by re-affirming homogenous gender groups. Thus, the underlying gendered basis of social power structures are reaffirmed and serve to negate the male rape victim's experience as they are still considered to belong to the dominant group.

In order to circumvent this flawed response to the crime of rape by the criminal justice system, some feminist legal scholars advocate redress through the channels of civil justice in the United States. The advantage of this being that the female rape victim will have more control over her legal representation and agency of the case. However, such tort procedures also have inherent '... anti-victim biases, such as comparative fault unique to civil proceedings' (Rozee and Koss, 2001: 304). This would also apply to male rape victims and indeed, victim blaming attitudes are in evidence within the focus group research on male rape (Rumney and Hanley, 2009). Comparative fault is where the victim is held partially accountable for her/his behavior thus there are echoes of victimological perspectives such as Mendelsohn's 'victim culpability' in their victimization. Furthermore, in order for females to change their behavior to prevent possible rape victimization this would contravene '...rights guaranteed by the Constitution such as the "freedom to travel"' (304). Also, in order to comply with the 'reasonable woman standard' how might that compare to a 'reasonable man standard'? If females can be deemed eligible for a duty of care by a third party regarding sexual victimization should this not also apply to male rape victims? The answers to such questions are not forthcoming and are proving to be thorny issues which theorists are not keen to address.

FEMINIST ENGAGEMENT WITH MALE RAPE: TWO CASE STUDIES

The last four decades of feminist research has provided a unique and pivotal insight into the nature, impact and prevalence of male sexual aggression against women and children. There can be little doubt that for many feminist scholars, particularly those from a radical perspective, the problem of male sexual aggression figures centrally in the lives of women and girls (Walby, 1990; Caringella, 2009), and indeed, it is seen as a 'key element in male power over and control of women' (Hester et al, 1996: 3). In addition to the scholarly attention given to female victims, feminist engagement with the issue of rape has taken the form of political organizing, lobbying and creating support services for female victims (Spohn and Horney: 1992; Jones and Cook, 2008). By contrast, constructive feminist engagement with victims of rape who happen to be male has, until recently, been largely absent. Historically, feminist engagement with the issue of male rape showed a reluctance to recognize the harm when a male was sexually violated. For example, Joanna Bourke has found evidence of nineteenth-century feminists devaluing the trauma suffered by young males coerced into prostitution, by suggesting that the harm suffered by young women was greater than that suffered by their male counterparts (Bourke, 2007: 240-241). Echoing her nineteenth century predecessors, Shere Hite has devalued the trauma suffered by male victims of sexual assault by claiming, wrongly, that certain forms of sexual assault could not be humiliating to a male victim (Hite, 1981: 749). In more recent times, there is evidence of a tendency to dismiss the importance of male rape as an issue worthy of analysis by criticizing any attention it receives. This has included describing a large-scale study of male rape as a 'matter for concern' because a similar study was not being conducted of female victims. (Gillespie, 1996: 161). More recently, Patricia Novotny has argued that media coverage of the sexual abuse of boys by Roman Catholic clergy was 'hardly newsworthy' (Novotny, 2003: 745). Ruth Graham has argued that in discussions leading up to the legal recognition of male rape by the UK Parliament in 1994 male victims of anal rape were 'privileged' and little attention was given to female victims of anal rape (Graham, 2006). Graham's claims in this regard are factually incorrect and based on a serious misreading of sources (Rumney, 2008; Rumney and Jamel, 2009b). It is worth pointing out that in the lead up to this legal change, it was one of the very few occasions when male rape received some degree of, albeit limited, attention. Prior to this time, in virtually every other Parliamentary debate, as well as in the media and scholarly literature the overwhelming focus had been on the rape of women. This of course, is understandable to the extent that most victims of rape are female. It is unfortunate, however, that on the one occasion when males did receive some specific attention it is immediately interpreted as 'privileging,' rather than addressing an issue that previously had been largely ignored within Parliamentary debates and many areas of legal reform.

Interestingly, some radical feminists have applied their theories regarding the social construction of rape to male victims, as have a number of writers sympathetic to feminist principles (Pelka, 1992; Scarce, 1997; Kendall, 2004; Funk, 2006). Catherine MacKinnon, for example, has argued:

> Implicit is an insistence that men cannot be sexually dominated in their social status or roles as men. The denial that interactions among men can have a sexual component, and that sexual abuse of men is gendered, are twin features of the social ideology of male dominance with which amici are familiar as experts. In this ideology, men are seen as sexually invulnerable. This image protects men from much male sexual violence and naturalizes the sexual abuse of women, making it seem that women, biologically, are sexual victims. Denying that men can be sexually abused as men thus supports the gender hierarchy of men over women in society. The illusion is preserved that men are sexually inviolable, hence naturally superior, as the sexual abuse of men by men is kept invisible. (MacKinnon, 1997: 20-21)

Some other feminist scholars have actually engaged in empirical research that has examined the experience of male victims. Lees, for example, has examined criminal justice responses to male rape (Lees, 1997; Gregory and Lees, 1999). These scholars see the existence of male rape as supporting feminist arguments concerning the nature and prevalence of male power. Jeanne Gregory and Sue Lees have noted that male and female rape 'can both be seen as forms of promoting dominant hegemonic heterosexuality.' (Gregory and Lees, 1999: 131) In earlier work, Lees argued that 'to embrace non-consensual buggery of men under the same legislation [as women] is not, in my view, to deny the relation between rape whether of men or women and male domination, and in particular, domination of the particular hegemonic form of macho masculinity characteristic of western cultures' (Lees, 1997: 91). Like Lees, other feminist scholars have argued that rape laws should recognize male victimization (see for example, Scutt, 1976; Tong, 1984; Hall, 1989).

(i) The 'Gendering' of Male Victims

This section will analyze a particular example of feminist theorizing as it pertains to male rape. It is a long established claim by some feminist theorists that men who are raped are also gendered female by the experience (see for example, Rush, 1990; Gillespie, 1996; Mooney, 2006). For example, Catherine MacKinnon has argued that:

> 'Men who are sexually assaulted are thereby stripped of their social status as men. They are feminized: made to serve the function and play the role customarily assigned to women as men's social inferiors.' (MacKinnon, 1997: 19)

MacKinnon, and most other writers in this area, appear to view the process of feminization as resulting from rape or sexual assault. Others appear to endorse a subtle shift in emphasis by arguing that men are raped 'as women': 'Further, even men who are homosexually assaulted are actually assaulted as women, because they are feminized and stripped of their social status [as] men' (internal quotation marks omitted) (MacGrady and Van Doren, 2002: 404). It is often the case that the notion of gendering is used to treat male rape as a 'dismissive footnote' (Bourke, 2007: 240). To some feminists, the notion of gendering justifies shifting attention away from male victims by re-characterizing their victimization as something involving females. For example, in a report published by the *Research Centre for Law, Gender and Sexuality*, the authors state the following:

> Rape law sets the boundaries within which it is acceptable for men to have sex. It is about *men's* not women's sexuality: men act, women are acted upon; men force, women succumb; men are the subjects, women are the objects. This is the case even where both the parties involved are men; as has frequently been observed, the raped man is culturally feminised [sic] by the act of rape. (RCLGS, 2006: 4-5)

For the rest of the report male victims are simply ignored. Thus, the recasting of male rape victims as 'culturally feminized' serves the purpose of obscuring the recognition of male victimization. Other feminists appear to use the notion of gendering to justify the exclusion of male victims from the definition of rape (Rush, 1990). The use of gendering to shift the focus of attention away from male victims has been questioned by Sivakumaran, (2005:1283) who has argued that the feminization of raped males and the 'equation of femininity and weakness' falls 'within the scope of the objectives of the women's movement'.

Recently, Elsje Bonthuys has stated that: 'Instances of male rape proceed from and reinforce the very sexist structures and discourses which are found in the rape of women' (Bonthuys, 2008: 254). However, unlike some other feminist scholars, Bonthuys does not deny or diminish the problem of adult male rape. On the contrary, she explores similarities between male and female sexual victimization, as well as aspects that are specifically gendered, in a way that does not undermine the recognition of male rape as a social problem. In so doing, she draws on the research literature that examines the meaning of impact of male rape (Bonthuys, 2008). By contrast, most feminist scholars who obscure male rape by placing it under the umbrella of female victimization rarely draw on the growing literature on male sexual victimization (Rumney and Jamel, 2009b).

The notion that men are 'culturally feminized' by rape has some support in prison rape research. Several studies have found that inmates who rape other men refer to their victims in gendered terms. Some men are told that they are 'women,' 'wives,' 'bitches' or 'tramps' (Human Rights Watch, 2001; Talvi, 2002; Gear, 2007). Furthermore, some male victims feel that their sense of masculinity is undermined by victimization (Allen, 2002). It could also be argued that by being penetrated, a man is placed in the female role in heterosexual sex, that is, of the person who is penetrated. Consequently, by being placed in a female role he is 'feminized' and less of a man. Historically, this view of the penetrated male has influenced legal responses to male rape victims. Sommer notes that in late imperial China the penetrated male suffered great social stigma. Whilst legal codes recognized that young males could be victims of rape perpetrated by older males, outside of this situation '[m]ales were not expected to be weak … They were not supposed to be penetrable at all, but rather penetrators, subjects rather than objects of action. Even so, Qing law acknowledged that males could be raped, and that they might consent to sodomy. But for this penetrability to make sense, the male had to be somehow less than male' (Sommer, 2000: 132). Furthermore, he observes that in 'late imperial China, common sense held that to be penetrated would profoundly compromise a male's masculinity; for this reason, powerful stigma attached to a penetrated male' (Sommer, 2000: 117-118). More recent research that has examined the attitudes of gay males who engage in anal intercourse supports these early findings. As a result of socially ascribed gender roles, some gay males see the penetrator as male and the penetrated as female (Kippax and Smith, 2001: 418, 420).

Some feminist scholars who argue male victims are gendered female also argue that laws that recognize that men can be victims of rape 'disguise' or 'cover up' gendered violence against women and that they 'extinguish difference[s]' between men and women (Mooney, 2006: 62; Mooney 2008) There are several ways of responding to this argument. First, the legal recognition of male rape is an acknowledgement of reality: men are sometimes victims of non-consensual penetrative sex. Far from obscuring the reality of rape, it recognizes its breadth. Secondly, gender-neutral rape laws do not prevent the identification of harms that are inflicted on women as victims of rape. For example, despite the fact that rape is defined in English law as involving either a male or female victim, this has not prevented the courts from identifying pregnancy, resulting from rape, as an aggravating factor in sentencing guidelines (*Millberry*, 2003: para 10). If gender–neutral rape laws did indeed 'extinguish differences' between the sexes such a sex-based consequence of rape could not be recognized. It might also be added that those who argue that gender-neutral laws 'disguise' the gendered nature of rape do not identify any mechanism by which this is achieved. Thirdly, those scholars who argue that men are gendered female by rape are themselves obscuring the gendered reality of male rape and the specific needs and beliefs that surround male sexual victimization. One could also argue that such feminist theory actually obscures the specific victimization of women (as well as men) by conflating the rape of men and women. This appears to undermine the specific recognition of women's experiences that feminist scholars argue is important (Mooney, 2006; MacKinnon, 1990).

It is appropriate to consider whether this gendering theory is a fully accurate account of the male experience. There are at least two issues here. Firstly, while it is undoubtedly the case that some male rapists use female epithets to humiliate their victims, this is not the totality of the experience of male victims. In many cases of male rape female epithets are not reported either by victims or the perpetrators of male rape (Groth, 1979). Second, there is actually a danger that by describing raped males as feminized this is actually contributing to the misunderstandings and negative social attributions that surround this crime. Raped men are still male and referring to them as female is unlikely to promote understanding or assist their recovery, particularly for those who *do* struggle with their sense of sexual identify and masculinity following rape. A wounded sense of masculinity does not turn a man into a woman. This suggests a one-dimensional view of men who are defined primarily by their sense of masculinity and little else. Furthermore, social attitudes that ascribe to male rape victims a lack of masculinity or who are 'feminized' fail to fully recognize, as Bourke has done, that 'each and every body is permeable and appropriable' (Bourke, 2007: 247), including the masculine body.

Another problem with the gendered female theory is that those who use it have given little thought to the limits of this concept or indeed, how it could be applied in other contexts. To illustrate the problem, we can apply the notion of gendering to a rape case that recently attracted international media attention. In 2008, there was extensive media coverage of the case of a 42 year old woman who had been locked in a cellar in Austria for 24 years, repeatedly raped by her father and had given birth to seven of his children. Media reports suggested that, as a result of her abuse and incarceration she was 'psychologically extremely disturbed' (Connolly, 2008). Applying the feminist gendering theory to this case, one could argue that given this woman's incarceration and systematic abuse at the hands of her father, her experience might be viewed as similar to the experience of incarcerated males who are repeatedly raped by other prisoners and unable to escape (Human Rights Watch, 2001; Banbury, 2004). As a result, could it not be argued that this woman was 'gendered male' by her experience of rape and incarceration? However, outside of possibly giving us an understanding of the psychological impact of sexual victimization in the context of imprisonment, such analysis would appear to be of limited utility and, we would argue, describing her as having being gendered male adds little to the analysis. However, precisely the same can be said when males are said to have been gendered female. This is not to totally reject the gendering theory. Rather it is to raise questions regarding its uses and limits.

(ii) Catherine A. MacKinnon, Andrea Dworkin and Male Rape

Catherine MacKinnon and Andrea Dworkin have made a huge contribution to feminist theorizing and activism in the fields of legal and social equality. Little attention, however, has been paid to their more limited writings on male sexual victimization. This section will focus on one common issue that arises in both their writings on rape, that is, the relative treatment of male and female rape victims. This issue has been the subject of recent claims that male rape victims, or at least some groups of them, receive preferential treatment by society and the legal process, compared with female victims (Rumney, 2008). However, this is not a new phenomenon. One of the earliest examples of this claim is from Andrea Dworkin, who, when writing in 1989 , stated:

> 'Society's general willingness to do anything necessary to protect boys and men from male sexual aggression is testimony to the value of a male life. Society's general refusal to do anything meaningful to protect women and girls from male sexual aggression is testimony to the worthlessness of a female life' (Dworkin, 1989: 56).

Similarly, Catherine MacKinnon has recently suggested that: 'When [men] are sexually violated, especially if they are straight and white and adult, it is not generally disbelieved or simply tolerated or found entertaining or defended ...' (MacKinnon, 2006: 74) This statement appears to suggest that all males are not 'generally disbelieved' as a matter of normative treatment by society, but that men who are straight and white are in a particularly privileged position. In suggesting a distinction between differing groups of males, MacKinnon acknowledges that some males may be unequal compared to other males in a similar way to the ways in which women are unequal to men: 'on the basis of their race, ethnicity, religion, and sexuality, plus class ...' (MacKinnon, 2006: 107) To a degree, this may well be an accurate acknowledgement of the social forces that can impact on men's relative social position. For example, gay men face physical and sexual assault as part of homophobic attacks and are also targeted for rape within prisons where they often appear to receive little protection from authorities (Human Rights Watch, 2001; Janoff, 2005; Banbury, 2004; Pattavina, 2007). They also face potentially unsympathetic and victim-blaming attitudes in response to their sexual victimization, which may, in part result from homophobic attitudes (Eigenberg, 1989; Pelka, 1995; Scarce, 1997; Mitchell and Hirschman 1999; White and Kurpius, 2002; Wakelin and Long, 2003; Doherty and Anderson, 2004; Davies and Rogers,

2006; Anderson, 2007; Rumney, 2009a). Further, it may be the case that homosexual males face particular problems being believed. For example, because some people may assume that their sexuality or sexual history makes consent more likely when a rape is alleged.

However, it should not be assumed that by comparison to gay male, a heterosexual male is in a privileged position. Evidence suggests that heterosexual males do not experience unquestioning acceptance of their reports of sexual victimization (Rumney, 2008). One of the reasons for this can be found in social attitudes towards male rape. In focus group research in which participants discussed vignettes depicting an allegation of male rape, Anderson and Doherty found that 'the projection of a gay identity onto an alleged victim (and this may happen to any victim, regardless of his sexual identity) results in reframing the depicted rape as a consensual sexual encounter' (Anderson and Doherty, 2008). Recent focus group research by Rumney and Hanley has found that when participants were asked to consider whether a rape has taken place in a series of vignettes, decision-making was influenced by a range of myths and misunderstandings. For example, many participants expected a genuine male victim to resist his attacker and be physically injured. For others, there was a fixed expectation that a genuine male rape victim would report immediately to the police. When complainants did not respond as expected many participants viewed the complainant as less credible (Rumney and Hanley, 2009). In reality, however, many males 'freeze' when being raped as a result of fear and do not resist their attacker(s), while some delay reporting as a result of concerns regarding the police response to their complaint (King and Woollett, 1997; Rumney, 2001; Abdullah-Kahn, 2008). While for some participants, homosexuality was seen as an important factor in undermining complainant credibility, the focus group research does not suggest that any particular group of male victims are 'not generally disbelieved' or that there exists a 'general willingness to do anything necessary' to protect men from sexual violence. Indeed, this research suggests that male victims who engage in particular forms of behavior (e.g. walking down an alleyway, or going to the home of a man they have known for a short time) are viewed in a similar way to female victims and described as 'stupid' or wanting to be raped. Furthermore, some participants have difficulty believing men can be physically raped at all and others are readily prepared to claim, on spurious grounds, that a male rape complainant is making a false allegation (Anderson and Doherty, 2008; Rumney and Hanley, 2009).

Further still, male victims who do report to the police recount some positives responses, but others are met with insensitivity, disbelief, dismissive treatment and encouragement to drop their allegations (Lees, 1997; Gregory and Lees, 1999; Rumney, 2008; Abdullah-Kahn 2008). Research involving police officers indicates that many hold victim-blaming attitudes and have little understanding of the reality of men's experiences of sexual victimization. Some officers also exhibit homophobic attitudes towards male victims (Abdullah-Kahn 2008).Recommendations have also been made based on the findings of evaluative research on the specialist police response to rape victims. It has been suggested that specialist police training programmes on rape victim care could be improved by highlighting the complexities of male rape in relation to its impact on victims' masculinity and the influence of gender-based negative responses on their recovery process (see Jamel, Bull, and Sheridan, 2008). Thus, increasing the breadth of police training regarding their response to male rape victims. The aim of such research is to improve the police service response to male rape survivors so that the attention given to this subject within training programmes approaches that given to female rape victims.

Examination of rape and sexual assault trials involving male complainants provides further evidence that male rape complainants are not given preferential treatment, as Dworkin and MacKinnon suggest, compared with female complainants (Rumney 2001, Rumney, 2008b).

CONCLUSION

This chapter has begun a process of evaluation of feminist theory as it pertains to adult male rape and sexual assault. It has not been possible to provide a detailed analysis of all feminist theorizing in this area. Rather, this chapter has sought to sketch the ways in which various strands of feminism deal with male victims and to examine in detail certain ways in which particular issues are approached. In some respects, feminist engagement with male rape is troubling. For example, the claim that male victims, or certain groups of male victims, receive privileged treatment has been repeated with increasing frequency. The problem with this claim, however, is that it is often on no reliable research evidence (Rumney, 2008; Rumney and Jamel, 2009b). A related point is by what process do scholars make such questionable claims? Outside of a misreading of evidence or making claims unsupported by evidence, many feminist writings concerning male victimization do not draw on our growing knowledge of this subject. For some leading theorists their best analysis docs draw on the research literature (MacKinnon, 1997), while at other times they provide no evidential support for their claims which are in fact, contradicted by the evidence that does exist. Even work that purports to be a detailed analysis of scholarship concerning male rape (Graham, 2006), on closer inspection is fundamentally flawed as a result of the author's unfamiliarity with the existing contemporary research literature (Rumney and Jamel, 2009b).

Furthermore, if feminist scholars continue to emphasize that male victim are feminized - that they are socially positioned in the same way as female victims, then it becomes harder for feminists to emphasize the distinctive nature of female victimization. In terms of theoretical engagements with male rape, emphasizing the notion of the feminized male also makes it harder for significant numbers of feminists to justify the otherwise complete exclusion of men from their analysis. Indeed, it could also be argued that the logical result of emphasizing the feminization of males is for feminists to reconceptualise their political goals and those of service providers in order to facilitate the inclusivity of males who wish to deliver such services which encompass '... prevention and programm[es] by men for men, and about male violence against women (and men and boys)' (Maier, 2008, p. 98). If feminists were prepared to engage in such a venture this would not require them to ignore the uniquely gendered aspects of rape such as the fact that women make up most of its victims or that feminist writings or services for victims should reflect such realities. But it would involve a recognition that if the problem of rape and sexual assault is to be properly addressed it will require attention being given to all the victims and perpetrators of rape. Challenging rape and the culture that supports it will not be successful if it is left unchallenged in any part of our society.

REFERENCES

Abdullah-Khan, N. (2008). *Male Rape: The Emergence of a Social and Legal Issue* (Houndmills: Palgrave MacMillan).

Allen, S. (2002). 'Male Victims of Rape: Responses to a Perceived Threat to Masculinity', in C. Hoyle & R. Young (Eds.) *New Visions of Crime Victims* (Oxford: Hart).

Amir, M. (1971). *Patterns of Forcible Rape* (Chicago: University of Chicago Press).

Anderson, I. (2007). 'What is a Typical Rape? Effects of Victim and Participant Gender in Female and Male Rape Perception', *British Journal of Social Psychology*, Vol.46, 225.

Anderson, I. & Doherty, K. (2008). *Accounting for Rape Psychology: Feminism and Discourse Analysis in the Study of Sexual Violence* (London: Routledge).

Banbury, S. (2004). 'Coercive Sexual Behaviour in British Prisons as Reported by Adult Ex-Prisoners', *Howard Journal*, Vol.43, 113.

Bonthuys, E. (2008). 'Putting Gender into the Definition of Rape or Taking it Out?' *Feminist Legal Studies Vol.16*, 249.

Bourdieu, P. (1998/2001). *Masculine domination* (R. Nice, Trans.) Cambridge: Polity.

Bourke, J. (2007). *Rape: A History from 1860 to the Present* London: Virago.

Brownmiller, S. (1975). *Against Our Will: Men, Women and Rape.* Harmondsworth: Penguin.

Cahill, A. J. (2000). 'Foucault, Rape, and the Construction of the Feminine Body,' *Hypatia, Vol.15*, 43.

Caringella, S. (2009). *Addressing Rape Reform in Law and* Practice New York: Columbia University Press.

Chapleau, K. M. Oswald, D. L. & Russell, B. L. (2008). 'Male Rape Myths: The Role of Gender, Violence, and Sexism,' *Journal of Interpersonal Violence, Vol. 23*, 600.

Clements-Schreiber, M. E. & Rempel, J. K. (1995). 'Women's Acceptance of Stereotypes about Male Sexuality: Correlations with Strategies to Influence Reluctant Partners,' *The Canadian Journal of Human Sexuality, Vol.4*, 223.

Connell, R. W. (1995). *Masculinities.* Cambridge: Polity Press.

Connolly, K. (2008). 'Horror in a Cellar: Woman Tells of 24 years of Imprisonment and Rape by her Father,' guardian.co.uk 28 April 2008 http://www.guardian.co.uk/world/2008/apr/28/austria.internationalcrime.

Coxell, A. King, M. B. Mezey, G. C. & Gordon, D. (1999). 'Lifetime Prevalence, Characteristics, and Associated Problems of Non-Consensual Sex in Men: Cross Sectional Survey,' *British Medical Journal, Vol. 318*, 846.

Coxell, A. W. Mezey, G. C. & Kell, P. (2000). 'Sexual Molestation of Men: Interviews with 224 Men Attending a Genitourinary Medicine Service,' *International Journal of STD and AIDS, Vol.11*, 574.

Davies, M. & Rogers, P. (2006). 'Perceptions of Male Victims in Depicted Sexual Assaults: A Review of the Literature,' *Aggression and Violent Behaviour, Vol.11*, 367.

Doherty, K. & Anderson, I. (2004). 'Making Sense of Male Rape: Constructions of Gender, Sexuality and Experience of Rape Victims', *Journal of Community and Applied Social Psychology*, Vol.14, 85.

Dutton, D. G. & Nicholls, T. L. (2005). 'The Gender Paradigm in Domestic Violence Research and Theory: Part 1 - The Conflict of Theory and Data,' *Aggression and Violent Behavior*, Vol.10, 680.

Dworkin, A. (1989). *Pornography: Men Possessing Women* New York: JP Dutton

Elliott, D. M. Mok, D. S. & Briere, J. (2004). 'Adult Sexual Assault: Prevalence, Symptomatology, and Sex Differences in the General Population,' *Journal of Traumatic Stress, Vol. 17*, 2004, 203.

Eigenberg, H. (1989). 'Male Rape: An Empirical Examination of Correctional Officers' Attitudes toward Rape in Prison,' *Prison Journal, Vol.69*, 39.

Enns, C. Z. (1992). 'Towards Integrating Feminist Psychotherapy and Feminist Philosophy,' *Professional Psychology: Research and Practice, Vol.23*, 453.

Fattah, E. A. (1994). 'Some Problematic Concepts, Unjustified Criticism and Popular Misconceptions,' in G. F. Kirchoff & E. Kosovoski & H. J. Schneider (Eds.) *International Debates of Victimology* (82-103), Moenchengladbach: World Society of Victimology.

FBI (2008). http://www.fbi.gov/ucr/cius2007/offenses/violent_crime/forcible_rape.html.

Foa, E. B. Rothbaum, B. O. Riggs, D. S. & Murdock, T. B. (1991). 'Treatment of Postraumatic Stress Disorder in Rape Victims: A Comparison Between Cognitive-Behavioural Procedures and Counselling,' *Journal of Consulting and Clinical Psychology Vol.59*, 715.

Funk, R. E. (2006). 'Queer Men and Sexual Assault: What Being Raped Says about Being a Man', in C. Kendall & W. Martino (Eds.) *Gendered Outcasts and Sexual Outlaws: Sexual Oppression and Gender Hierarchies in Queer Men's Lives* New York: Routledge.

Garnets, L. Herek, G. & Levy, B. (1990). 'Violence and Victimization of Lesbians and Gay Men,' *Journal of Interpersonal Violence, Vol.5*, 366-383.

Gear, S. (2007). 'Behind the Bars of Masculinity: Male Rape and Homophobia in and about South African Men's Prisons' *Sexualities* Vol. 10, No. 2, 209-227.

Hester, L. Kelly, L. & Radford, J. (Eds.) *Women, Violence and Male Power: Feminist Activism, Research and Practice* Buckingham: Open University Press.

Graham, R. (2006). 'Male Rape and the Careful Construction of the Male Victim', *Social & Legal Studies, Vol.15*, 187.

Gregory, J. & Lees, S. (1999). *Policing Sexual Assault.* London: Routledge.

Groth, A. N. & Burgess, A. W. (1980). 'Male rape: offenders and victims,' *American Journal of Psychiatry, Vol.137*, 806.

Hall, C. (1988). 'Rape: The Politics of Definition,' *S. AFR. L. J. Vol. 105*, 67.

Helliwell, C. (2000). 'It's Only a Penis: Rape, Feminism, and Difference,' *Signs, Vol.25*, 789.

HMCPSI/HMIC (2002). [Her Majesty's Crown Prosecution Service Inspectorate/Her Majesty's Inspectorate of Constabulary], *A Report on the Joint Inspection into the Investigation and Prosecution of Cases Involving Allegations of Rape* (London. HMCPSI/HMIC).

Hickson, F. C. I. Davies, P. M. Hunt, A. J. Weatherburn, P. McManus, T. J. & Coxon, A. P. M. (1994). 'Gay Men as Victims of Nonconsensual Sex', *Archives of Sexual Behavior, Vol.23*, 281.

Hite, S. (1981). *The Hite Report on Male Sexuality.* London: Optima.

Hodge, S. & Canter, D. (1998). 'Victims and Perpetrators of Male Sexual Assault', *Journal of Interpersonal Violence Vol.13*, 222.

Huckle, P. L. (1995). 'Male Rape Victims Referred to a Forensic Psychiatric Service', *Med Sci Law, Vol.35*, 187.

Human Rights Watch (2001). *No Escape: Male Rape in U.S. Prisons*. New York: Human Rights Watch.

Jamel, J., Bull, R., & Sheridan, S. (2008) 'An investigation of the specialist police service provided to male rape survivors'. *International Journal of Police Science & Management, Vol. 10,* 486.

Janoff, D. V. (2005). *Pink Blood: Homophobic Violence in Canada* Toronto: University of Toronto Press.

Jones, H. & Cook, K. (2008), *Rape Crisis: Responding to Sexual Violence* Russell House Publishing Ltd.

Johnston, L. (1995). 'Homeless Sex Scandal', *The Big Issue*, 11–17th September, 11.

Kelly, L. Burton, S. & Regan, L. (1996). 'Beyond Victim or Survivor: Sexual Violence, Identity and Feminist Theory and Practice,' in L. Adkins & V. Merchant (Eds.) *Sexualizing the Social: Power and the Organization of Sexuality* (77-101) Basingstoke: Macmillan.

Kendall, C. N. (2004). 'Gay Male Pornography and Sexual Violence: A Sex Equality Perspective on Gay Male Rape and Partner Abuse', *McGill Law Journal, Vol.49,* 877.

King, M. & Woollett, E. (1997). 'Sexually Assaulted Males: 115 Men Consulting a Counselling Service', *Archives of Sexual Behavior, Vol.26,* 579.

Kippax, S. & Smith, G. (2001). 'Anal Intercourse and Power in Sex Between Men', *Sexualities Vol.4,* 413.

Lees, S. (1997). *Ruling Passions: Sexual Violence, Reputation and the Law*. Buckingham: Open University Press.

MacKinnon, C. A. (1989). *Toward a Feminist Theory of the State* Cambridge. MA: Harvard University Press.

MacKinnon C. A. (1990). 'Liberalism and the Death of Feminism,' in Dorchen Leidholdt & Janice G. Raymond (Eds.) *The Sexual Liberals and the Attack on Feminism.*

MacKinnon C. A. (1997). 'Oncale v. Sundown Offshoreservices, Inc., 96-568 Amici Brief in Support of Petititoner,' *UCLA Women's L. J. Vol.8,* 9.

Mackinnon, C. (2006). *Are Women Human? And Other International Dialogues*. Cambridge: Harvard University Press.

MacGrady, K. A. & Van Doren, J. W. (2002). 'AALS Constitutional Law Panel on Brown, Another Council of NICAEA?' *Akron L. Rev. Vol 35,* 371.

Maier, S. L. (2008). 'Are rape crisis centers feminist organizations?' *Feminist Criminology 82.*

Mardorossian, C. M. (2002). 'Toward a new feminist theory of rape,' *Signs Vol.27,* 743-775.

Martin, K., Vieraitis, L. M & Britto, S. (2006). Gender Equality and Women's Absolute Status: A Test of the Feminist Models of Rape. *Violence Against Women, Vol.12,* 321.

McMullen, R. (1990). *Male Rape: Breaking the Silence on the Last Taboo*. London: Gay Men's Press.

Mendelsohn, C.M. (1947). 'New Bio-Psychosocial Horizons: Victimology,' *American Law Review, Vol.13,* 649.

Mezey, G. & King M. (1989). 'The Effects of Sexual Assault on Men: A Survey of 22 Victims', *Psychological Medicine, Vol.19,* 205-209.

Mezey, G. C. & King, M. B. (Eds.) (2000). *Male Victims of Sexual Assault* second ed. Oxford: Oxford University Press *Millberry* [2003] 1 WLR 546.

Millberry [2003] 2 Cr.App.R.(S) 31

Mitchell, D. & Hirschman, R. (1999). 'Attributions of Victim Responsibility, Pleasure and Trauma in Male Rape' *Journal of Sex Research, Vol.36,* 369.

Mooney, A. (2006). 'When a Woman Needs to be Seen, Heard and Written as a Woman: Rape, Law and an Argument Against Gender Neutral Language,' Int'l J. Semiotics L. 39.

Myers, M. F. (1989). 'Men Sexually Assaulted as Adults and Sexually Abused as Boys,' Archives of Sexual Behavior, *Vol.18,* 203.

Naffine, N. (1997). *Feminism & Criminology,* Cambridge: Polity Press.

Novotny, P. (2003). 'Rape Victims in the (Gender) Neutral Zone: The Assimilation of Resistance?', *Seattle Journal for Social Justice, Vol.1,* 743.

Olff, M. Langel &, W. Draijer, N. & Gersons, B. P. R. (2007). 'Gender differences in postraumatic stress disorder,' *Psychological Bulletin, Vol.133,* 183.

Ozer, E. J. Best, S. R. Lipsey, T. L. & Weiss, W. S. (2008). 'Predictors of Posttraumatic Stress Disorder and Symptoms in Adults: A Meta-Analysis,' *Psychological Trauma, Theory, Research, Practice in Policy, 3.*

Pattavina, A. Hirschel, D. Buzawa, E. Faggiani, D. & Bentley, H. (2007). 'A Comparison of the Police Response to Heterosexual Versus Same-Sex Intimate Partner Violence', *Violence Against Women, Vol.13,* 374.

Pelka, F. (1995). 'Raped: A Male Survivor Breaks His Silence', in P. Searles & R. J. Berger (Eds.) *Rape and Society: Readings on the Problem of Sexual Assault* Boulder, CO: Westview Press.

Raitt, F. & Ferguson, P. (2006). 'Re-defining Rape,' *Edinburgh Law Review, Vol.10,* 185.

RCLGS (2006). *Response to the Office for Criminal Justice Reform's Consultation Paper: 'Convicting Rapists and Protecting Victims of Rape – Justice for Victims of Rape'.*

Rozee, P. D. & Koss, M. P. (2001). 'Rape: A century of resistance,' *Psychology of Women Quarterly, Vol.25,* 295.

Rumney, P. (2007). 'In Defence of Gender Neutrality within Rape,' *Seattle Journal for Social Justice, Vol.6,* 481.

Rumney, P (2008). 'Policing Male Rape and Sexual Assault', *Journal of Criminal Law, Vol.71,* 67.

Rumney, P. (2008b). 'Gender Neutrality, Rape and Trial Talk,' *International Journal for the Semiotics of Law, Vol.21,* 139.

Rumney, P. & Hanley, N. (2009). 'The Mythology of Male Rape: Social Attitudes and Law Enforcement,' in C. McGlynn & V. Munro (Eds.) *Rethinking Rape Law: National, International and European perspectives* Routledge-Cavendish (forthcoming).

Rumney, P. (2009a). "Gay Victims of Male Rape: Law Enforcement, Social Attitudes and Barriers to Recognition,' *International Journal of Human Rights, Vol.13,* (forthcoming).

Rumney, P. & Jamel, J. (2009b). *'The Not So Carefully Constructed Male Victim: A Response to Ruth Graham'.* This Working Paper can be accessed via the Social Science Research Network: http://www.ssrn.com/.

Rush, F (1990). 'The Many Faces of Backlash,' in Dorchen Leidholdt & Janice G. Raymond (Eds). *The Sexual Liberals and the Attack on Feminism.*

Russell, D. E. H. (1975). *The Politics of Rape.* New York: Stein and Day.

Russell, D. E. H. & Bolen, R. M. (2000). *The Epidemic of Rape and Child Sexual Abuse in the United States.* London: Sage Publications Ltd.

Sanday, P. R. (1990). *Fraternity gang rape: Sex, brotherhood and privilege on campus.* New York: New York University Press.

Sarrel, P. M. & Masters W. H. (1982). 'Sexual Molestation of Men by Women', *Archives of Sexual Behavior, Vol.11*, 117.

Scarce, M. (1997). *Male on male rape: The hidden toll of stigma and shame.* Cambridge: Perseus Publishing.

Schack, A. V. (2004). 'Prior History of Physical and Sexual Abuse Among the Psychiatric Inpatient Population: A Comparison of Males and Females,' *Psychiatric Quarterly Vol.75*, 343.

Schneider, H. J. (2001). Victimological developments in the world during the past three decades: A study of comparative victimology - Part 2. *International Journal of Offender Therapy and Comparative Criminology, 45*, 539-555.

Scutt, J. A. (1976). 'Reforming the Law of Rape: The Michigan Example,' *Austl. L. J. Vol. 50*, 615.

Sivakumaran, S. (2007). 'Sexual Violence Against Men in Armed Conflict', *European Journal of International Law, Vol.18*, 253.

Smith, R. E., Pine, C. J. & Hawley, M. E. (1988). 'Social cognitions about male victims of female sexual assault,' *The Journal of Sex Research, Vol.24*, 101.

Sommer, M. H. (2000). *Law, Sex, and Society in Late Imperial China* Stanford: Stanford University Press.

Sorenson, S. B. Stein, J. A. Siegel, J. A. Golding, J. M. & Burnam, M. A. (1987). 'The prevalence of adult sexual assault: The Los Angeles Epidemiologic Catchment Area Project,' *American Journal of Epidemiology, Vol.126*, 1154.

Spohn, C. & Horney, J. (1992). *Rape Law Reform: A Grassroots Revolution and its Impact.*

Stermac, L. del Bove, G. & Addison, M. (2004). 'Stranger and acquaintance sexual assault of adult males,' *Journal of Interpersonal Violence, Vol.19*, 901.

Talvi, S. J. A. (2002). 'Prison's Shameful Secret,' *The Nation* September 9th http://www.thenation.com/doc/20020923/talvi20020909.

Tolin, D. F. & Foa, E. B. (2008). 'Sex Differences in Trauma and Post-Traumatic Stress Disorder: A Quantitative Review of 25 Years of Research,' *Psychological Trauma, Theory, Research, Practice and Policy, Vol. S*, 37.

Tong, R. (1984). *Women, Sex and the Law.* Rowman and Allanheld.

U. S. Department of Justice (2008). http://www.ojp.usdoj.gov/ bjs/pub/ascii/cv07.text.

Von Hentig, H. (1948). *The Criminal and his Victim: Studies in the sociobiology of crime* New Haven: Yale University Press.

Wakelin, A. & Long, K. M. (2003). 'Effects of Victim Gender and Sexuality on Attributions of Blame to Rape Victims', *Sex Roles Vol.49*, 477.

Walby, S. (1990). *Theorizing Patriarchy.* Oxford: Blackwell.

Walker, J. Archer, J. & Davies, M. (2005). 'Effects of Rape on Men: A Descriptive Analysis,' *Archives of Sexual Behaviour, Vol. 34*, 69.

Walker, J. Archer, J. & Davies, M. (2005a). 'Effects of Male Rape on Psychological Functioning', *British Journal of Clinical Psychology, Vol.44*, 225.

Walker, A., Flatley, J., Kershaw, C., and Moon, D. (2009) Crime in England and Wales 2008-2009: Volume 1: Findings from the British Crime Survey and police recorded crime. London: Home Office.

Weis, K. & Borges, S. S. (1973). 'Victimology and Rape: The Case of the Legitimate Victim,' *Issues in Criminology, Vol.8*, 71.

Whaley, R. B. & Messner, S. F. (2002). 'Gender Equality and Gender Homicides,' *Homicide Studies Vol. 6*, 188.

White, B. H. & Kurpius, S. E. R. (2002). 'Effects of Victim Sex and Sexual Orientation in Perceptions of Rape', *Sex Roles, Vol.46*, 191.

Willis, D. G. (2009). 'Male-on-Male Rape of an Adult Man: A Case Review and Implications for Interventions,' *Am Psychiatr Nurses Assoc, Vol.14*, 454.

Wolfgang, M. E. (1958). *Patterns of criminal homicide* Philadelphia: Pennsylvania Press.

In: Feminism and Women in Leadership
Editor: Vicente Nardi, pp. 51-73

ISBN: 978-1-60876-270-5
© 2010 Nova Science Publishers, Inc.

Chapter 3

ARE WOMEN MORE EMOTIONALLY INTELLIGENT IN THEIR LEADERSHIP STYLE THAN MEN? THE ROLE OF GENDER-CONGENIAL AND GROUP VARIABLES

Esther López-Zafra[1] and Rocio Garcia-Retamero[2,3]
[1]University of Jaén (Spain)
[2] University of Granada (Spain),
[3]Max Planck Institute for Human Development (Berlin, Germany),

ABSTRACT

Studies on both emotional intelligence and transformational leadership suggested that women are more transformational and emotionally intelligent in their leadership styles. However, few studies test this hypothesis experimentally. In this chapter, we analyze several variables that may influence the relationship between emotional intelligence and transformational leadership. Specifically, we summarize a series of studies that examined gender-congenial variables (e.g., whether participants study a gender-congenial major) and group variables (e.g., group cohesiveness) and their impact on leadership emergence of women and men. We interpret the results of our studies on the basis of Eagly and Karau's (2002) Role Congruity Theory and Eagly's Social Role theory (1987).

INTRODUCTION

Through history a great debate about leadership has taken place. Mainly, discussions have focused on two aspects: the first is whether a leader was born or made, and the second relates to whether leaders had exceptional intelligence. Typical examples about leaders (e.g. Alexander Magnus or Caesar Augustus) take us back us to the idea that these people were truly exceptional in their character and their intelligence. Thus, it has long believed that leadership should be based on the individual and his or her characteristics rather than on

---

* Corresponding author: E-mail: elopez@ujaen.es. Tel: +34 953 211990. Fax: +34 953 211881.

social situations or the group leader and followers (although research showed that group processes are central for understanding leadership). On the other hand, the study of emotional intelligence is relatively recent but went through a fast development both in research and applications in contexts such as education, organizations, and health. In this chapter we review several studies focused on the relationship between emotional intelligence and transformational leadership that show that gender and group variables are also important to explain this relation.

LEADERSHIP

There are several characteristics that are perceived to be relevant for leadership emergence, such as certain mental abilities (Atwater, Dionne, Avolio, Camobreco, & Lau, 1999; Atwater & Yammarino, 1993; House & Aditya, 1997), personality traits as extraversion or emotional stability (Hoogh, Hartog, & Koopman, 2005; Houghton, Bonham, Neck, & Singh, 2004), leadership behaviors (Mackenzie, Podsakoff, & Rich, 2001), and the degree of a person's physical attractiveness (Weierter, 1997), among others. Recent studies suggest that emotions also play a crucial role in the perception and emergence of leaders in groups (Pescosolido, 2002) as leaders' cues influence implication and performance of the workers (D'Intino, Goldsby, Houghton, & Neck, 2007). For instance, the passion they bring to what they do (Marques, 2007), and also the individual's charisma and empathy, influence whether they are perceived as true leaders (Conger, 1999; Conger & Kanungo, 1998; Kellet, Humphrey, & Sleeth, 2002, 2006) or as having effective leadership skills (Cooper & Sawaf, 1997; Grossman, 2000). These perceptions, in turn, make leadership emergence more plausible.

Transformational Leadership Style

There are many typologies of leadership that Bass (1990) reviewed in the Stodgill's Handbook of Leadership and Leadership Styles. As this author pointed out, leadership styles are "alternative ways in which leaders structure interactive behaviors to carry out their roles as leader" (Bass, 1990, p. 27). According to this definition, a leadership style involves both the structure and behavior of the interaction with members of the group and playing the leading roles. Based on these three aspects, we see that the style is much larger concept that emphasizes both the task and relationships as well as the status of the leader (López-Zafra & Morales, 2007).

Although there are different typologies about leadership, there are two that have attracted more attention and research: Lewin's leadership styles and Bass' transformational leadership style (see López-Zafra & Morales, 2007, for a review). The most effective leadership style in contemporary's organizations is the transformational leadership.

Transformational Leadership is a concept proposed by Burns (1978) and further developed by Bass and colleagues (Avolio, 1999; Avolio & Bass, 2002; Avolio, Bass, & Jung, 1995). This leadership style involves establishing oneself as a role model by gaining the trust and confidence of the followers (Bass, 1985, 1998). This style is in clear contrast with other styles such as transactional leadership, which involves management in the more conventional sense of clarifying subordinates' responsibilities, rewarding them for meeting objectives, and correcting them for failing to meet objectives. M.L.Q. (Multifactorial Leadership Questionnaire) is the instrument usually used to measure leadership style. It is integrated by the following factors: (a) *Charisma or idealized influence* is shown by leaders who act as role models, create a sense of identification with a shared vision, and instill pride and respect from association with them; (b) *inspirational motivation* is shown by leaders who use emotional support and exhibit excitement about goals and future states; (c) *intellectual stimulation* is shown by leaders who encourage their followers to rethink their conventional practices and ideas and increase problem solving; (d) *individualized consideration* is shown by leaders whose behavior communicates personal respect to followers and who attend to their individual needs. *Transactional leadership* is assessed by two subscales: (a) *Management by exception* is shown by leaders who monitor performance and take corrective action as necessary and (b) *contingent reward* is shown by leaders who provide tangible or intangible support and resources to followers in exchange for their efforts and performance; finally, *Laissez faire* is the avoidance or absence of leadership. As we will analyze below, these components include an important emotional component.

An impressively wide corpus of research has addressed this topic because transformational leaders are generally very efficient (Bass, 1996, 1998, 1999; Conger & Hunt, 1999; Eagly & Johannsen-Schmidt, 2001; Hunt, 1999; Kirkpatrick & Locke, 1996; López-Zafra, 2001; López-Zafra & Morales, 1999, 2007; Lowe, Kroeck, & Sivasubramaniam, 1996), motivate their followers to improve their performance (Conger & Kanungo, 1998; House, 1977) and are more satisfied (Lowe et al., 1996; Srivastava & Bharamanaikar, 2004). In a similar vein, the relationship between transformational leaders and their followers is very emotional. For instance, transformational leaders generally use emotional support, and are able to spread their emotions about what they expect from their followers (Avolio & Bass, 2002; Bass, 1996; López-Zafra, 2001). These leaders are also able to benefit from their followers' emotional commitment (Dionne, Yammarino, Atwater, & Spangler, 2004). Moreover, positive emotions as enthusiasm or happiness may be passed through empathy and inspirational motivation (Lewis, 2000). An emotional intelligent leaders also manage conflict avoiding negative emotions, looking for constructive conflict resolution strategies and establish cooperation and trust among group members, contributing to a collective emotion (George, 2000). Furthermore, these leaders present several non-verbal emotional cues that make them more effective and charismatic leaders (Weierter, 1997). This pattern of behavior makes transformational leaders superior leaders for many contemporary organizations.

Transformational Leadership and Gender

Transformational leadership style emerges as an important variable to explain gender differences on leadership. Specifically, Eagly and Johannsen-Schmidt (2001) show in their meta-analysis that there is a relationship between democratic and transformational leadership, although the results are mixed due to context and type of study (see López-Zafra & Morales, 2007 and Molero, Cuadrado, Navas, & Morales, 2007; for similar results). Specifically, women show higher transformational leadership style than men. They also showed higher person orientation as well as a leadership style more democratic and communal than that of men. This makes women show more transformational leadership characteristics (Eagly& Johannsen-Schmidt, 2001). In fact, in a meta-analysis, these authors found that women are more transformational leaders than men (Eagly, Johannensen-Schmidt, & van Engen, 2003; see also Eagly & Carli, 2007; Eagly and Johannensen-Schmidt, 2001; Garcia-Retamero & López-Zafra, 2002, 2006a, 2006b).

Due to the supportive and considerate behaviors, transformational leadership may be advantage for women (Porterfield & Kleiner, 2005), and may very well allow women to excel as leaders (Eagly, 2003, 2004, 2007). In line with this, the interesting question would be whether emotional intelligence is related to these emotional characteristics of transformational leadership? If so, women may find a way to avoid prejudice against them as leaders.

EMOTIONAL INTELLIGENCE

The concept of emotional intelligence was introduced by Salovey and Mayer (1990), but it was Goleman who promoted the topic in a book entitled Emotional Intelligence (see Goleman, 1995). Since this early publication, a wide range of authors have addressed the concept in different theoretical models (e.g., Bar-On & Parker, 2000; Ciarrochi, Forgas, & Mayer, 2001; Mayer & Salovey, 1997; Parker, Taylor, & Bagby, 2001). For instance, the model of Mayer and Salovey (1997) focused on emotional constructs such as the ability to perceive, glean information from, and manage one's own and others' emotions (Mayer & Salovey, 1997; Salovey & Mayer, 1990).

Emotional Intelligence and Gender

The analyses of gender differences on emotional intelligence have often yield a clear advantage for women (Ciarrochi, Chang, & Caputi, 2000; Dawda & Hart 2000; Mayer, Caruso, & Salovey, 1999; see also Extremera, Fernández-Berrocal, & Salovey, 2006 and Van Rooy, Alonso, & Viswesvaran, 2005). Women are socialized in feelings and are more expressive than men, their gender characteristics include being supportive and affective and take care of children, and these feminine characteristics involve emotions.

However, this higher score on emotional intelligence may be related to a component of emotional intelligence more than to other components or even to the measurement instrument used. In fact, Ciarrochi et al (2000) showed that women scored significantly high in General emotional intelligence, Attention, Clarity and Regulation of emotions measured by TMMS whereas Dawda and Hart (2000), did not find any difference between total scores on EQ-i and Bar-On, Brown, Kirkcaldy, and Thomé (2000) find some results with no significant differences between men and women on general emotional intelligence, but find differences on emotional intelligence components. We may deduce that women have higher interpersonal abilities than men whereas they are good in tolerance to stress and impulse control (Candela, Barberá, Ramos, & Sarrió, 2002) and this is what some results show, specifically women score higher than men in EQ-i "social skills" factor, but when it gets a global score are the men scoring higher than women (Petrides & Furnham, 2000). Also here it seems that gender stereotypes affect perceptions of emotional intelligence. Emotional intelligence is seen as an attribute of women, so that individuals would rate women higher in emotional intelligence (e.g. children assessing emotional intelligence of their mothers), again it seems that the gender stereotypes affect perceptions but referring to global punctuation while when making estimates on specific aspects of emotional intelligence, the stereotyped perception of emotional intelligence as an attribute of women decreases (Petrides, Furnham, & Martín, 2004).

Some studies also found an interaction between emotional intelligence and age. Thus, it is observed that women among 20 and 40 years old scored higher than men (Sutarso, 1999) and the differences in EQ-i factors between men and women vary by age (Ugarriza, 2001), so that a pattern is shown suggesting that emotional intelligence increases with age (Van Rooy et al., 2005). Also, the study by Bar-On et al. (2000) found no significant differences between men and women on general emotional intelligence but on the specific aspects of emotional intelligence. Therefore, women exceed men on interpersonal relationships whereas men exceed women on copying with stress and impulse control. This is coherent with the result that women have more social interactions and better well-being than men (Rose, 1995).

In sum, there are differences on specific aspects of the emotional intelligence between men and women (Candela et al., 2002), but further research is needed.

EMOTIONAL INTELLIGENCE AND TRANSFORMATIONAL LEADERSHIP

Several studies were influenced by the theoretical models of Salovey et al.(1997) and Goleman (1996, 1999) and focused on the relationship between emotional intelligence and other constructs such as mental health and physical well-being (Donaldson & Bond, 2004), or life satisfaction (Augusto, López-Zafra, Martínez, & Pulido, 2006b, Livingstone & Day, 2005; Wolfradt, Felfe, & Koster, 2002), among others. Other studies addressed the relationship between emotional intelligence and work-related variables such as emotional work (Wong & Lang, 2002), stress perceptions in the workplace (e.g. Augusto, López-Zafra, Berrios, & Aguilar-Luzón, 2008; Moïra, Luminet, & Menil, 2006; Bar-On et al., 2000), satisfaction (Augusto et al., 2006a, 2006b) performance (Boyatzis, 2006; Cote & Miners, 2006) or attitudes toward work (Lopes, Grewal, Kadis, Gall, & Salovey, 2006). But, even given the importance of leadership as a main group process in organizations, the relationship among both constructs has been exposed theoretically but scarcely empirically studied (Barbuto & Burbach, 2006).

Researchers also focused on leaders' ability to recognize others' emotional expressions, how leaders use emotions to supervise their followers in work groups, and how emotions are used to develop leadership skills (e.g., Caruso, Mayer, & Salovey, 2002). Emotional intelligence is related both to emotions and intelligence but it is different from them (Mayer, Roberts, & Barsade, 2007). Both types of intelligences predict leaders' performance, but the most important competencies are the ones related to emotional intelligence (Boyatzis, 2006) and even could compensate a lower intelligence in other areas. Thus, Cote and Miners (2006) show that emotional intelligence, measured by MSCEIT, predicted task performance of managers in a higher extent for those with lower cognitive intelligence. Also, some empirical works have presented evidence of a positive relation between emotional intelligence and leadership effectiveness (Kerr, Garvin, Heaton, & Boyle, 2006; Leban & Zulauf, 2004; Rosete & Ciarrochi, 2005; Wong & Law, 2002), leadership self-efficacy (Villanueva & Sánchez, 2007), and of the potential use of emotional intelligence in organizational studies (Law, Wong, & Song, 2004).

Moreover, changes from a rational to a dynamic system in the organizations, has yield to the need of more flexible and horizontal structures to obtain an advantage in the competition. Thus, along with individual characteristics, evidence suggests that social abilities are crucial in leader's performance and efficacy. Moreover, emotional intelligence emerges as a construct of remarkable efficiency; therefore, it should be an important element in the effectiveness of leadership (Prati, Douglas, Ferris, Ammeter, & Buckley, 2003). These considerations on the best execution of people with high emotional intelligence as well as its predictive ability on people who may have a high potential for leadership (Dries & Pepermans, 2007), along with a higher efficacy and performance of transformational leaders, has led many professionals in different fields (academic, applied or educational communities) to request the development of training programs in Emotional Intelligence for leaders and managers (Groves, McEnrue, & Shen, 2008). But it is also necessary, not only to take into account competencies for an excellent leadership but other factors that may enhance the efficacy of the increase of emotional intelligence among managers and potential managers in organizations. Among these factors are individual characteristics (e.g., openness to experience), labor (e.g. emotional work) or organizational (e.g., degree of change; McEnrue, Groves, & Shen, 2008).

These abilities and capacities are crucial in leadership emergence because they are perceived positively by leaders' followers. Furthermore, as we mentioned above, several authors have pointed out that the relationship between transformational leaders and their followers is very emotional. Yet most of the work that has focused on transformational leadership and emotions is theoretical (e.g., Bass, 2002; Brown & Moshavi, 2005; Sosik & Mergerian, 1999). The relationship between these concepts has been considered in only a few empirical studies to date (e.g., Barbuto & Burbach, 2006; Barling, Slater, & Kelloway, 2003). In general, evidence of the relationship between emotional intelligence and TL has been reported (Downey, Papageorgiou, & Stough, 2006; Palmer, Walls, Burgess, & Stough, 2001; Sivanathan & Fekken, 2002) although in other reports, these results were not replicated (Brown, Bryant, & Reilly, 2006).

Transformational Leadership, Emotional Intelligence, and Gender

As we have seen above, there is a fairly well developed literature about gender differences in both emotional intelligence and transformational leadership separately.

Bearing these results in mind, it could be assumed that female leaders, especially those who score high in emotional intelligence, might be more transformational than male leaders. Previous research, however, did not support this hypothesis. Specifically, Mandell and Pherwani (2003) showed that emotional intelligence predicts transformational leadership regardless of gender. An explanation of this result is that gender per se might not influence emotional intelligence when predicting transformational leadership, but rather the key factor would be gender identity. In line with this alternative hypothesis, previous research has shown that individuals' feminine stereotypic characteristics predict transformational leadership (Cuadrado, 2004; Hackman, Furniss, Hills, & Paterson, 1992; Kent & Moss, 1994; López-Zafra & Morales, 1998, 2007), regardless of their gender (López-Zafra & Olmo, 1999).

The results of works that empirically address this relation are of great significance. Specifically, Sosik, and Megerian (1999) propose that four of the leadership characteristics are clearly overlapped with high levels of emotional intelligence. The first one refers to the adherence to the professional interaction norm that they consider a demonstration of charisma or idealized influence. The second one is motivation and the third is related to intellectual stimulation, that is, the leader has to motivate and stimulate the intellectual development and this is achieved with support among the members of the group and conflict management, making the group progress in efficacy. The forth element refers to the individualized consideration as the transformational leaders focus on each member of the group to make him/her feel important and necessary for the group. Also, Barling et al. (2003) found out that the emotional intelligence is related to idealized influence, individualized consideration and inspirational motivation, three components of transformational leadership. Furthermore, DeCremer & van Knippenberg (2002) report that charisma, the main attribute of transformational leadership, is central to create a cooperation feeling among group members. Moreover, the leader charisma is more important than the subordinate's perception of justice in a cooperative context.

In sum, results show that these concepts are related, thus, accumulated research on emotional intelligence shows that can predict outcomes related to leadership and performance, so that, it is worth further research on this relationship.

Our works go one step further and analyze other variables that may influence this relationship. Specifically, we think that there might be some group variables that might influence the relationship between emotional intelligence and transformational leadership. For example, cohesive groups improve the relationships between their members (Levine & Moreland, 1998), showing a strong positive relationship between cohesion and team success (Carron, Bray, & Eys, 2002). When analyzing leadership and cohesion, results show that a significant relationship exists between leader behaviors, such as training, giving feedback, and team cohesion (Murray, 2006). This pattern of relationships and behaviors in groups that are highly cohesive, are well established to be related with the leadership process. However, there is no study that relates these two concepts with Emotional Intelligence.

Other variables that may be related are gender-congenial variables (e.g., the social categories that individuals belong to). For example, there is a fairly well develop literature about congruency and women leadership, that is, women are less prejudiced when working in a feminine industry that is congruent with her gender role (Eagly, 2007; Eagly & Carli, 2007; Eagly & Karau, 2002; Garcia-Retamero & López-Zafra, 2006a, 2006b, 2009). But other contexts may also have gender-congenial characteristics. For example, the academic discipline that a person selects might be important because the extent to which a leader is perceived to be transformational is mediated by their environment (i.e., whether it is male- or female-congenial; Garcia-Retamero & López-Zafra, 2006b). Male students often choose some disciplines (e.g. engineering) to a larger extent than female students do, and vice versa. As a consequence, these disciplines are perceived as male-congenial and female-congenial, respectively.

STUDIES ABOUT EMOTIONAL INTELLIGENCE AND TRANSFORMATIONAL LEADERSHIP

To shed some light in the aspects commented above we carried out two research focusing on a) some group variables that affect leadership emergence; b) gender-congenial variables that may affect the relationship between transformational leadership and emotional intelligence.

Study 1. The Role of Group Variables (Cohesiveness) on the Relation between Transformational Leadership and Emotional Intelligence and Their Impact on Leadership Emergence

If we may establish a relationship between transformational leadership and emotional intelligence and also gender plays a role in this relation, then we may predict that an individual that has these characteristics may emerge more frequently as a leader. Furthermore, individuals who have high emotional intelligence would emerge more frequently as leaders than low emotional intelligence individuals because they are more transformational in their leadership style (see Figure 1), and also this could be easily the case in high cohesive groups more than in low cohesive groups.

To test this model we carried out a study (López-Zafra, Garcia-Retamero, & Augusto, 2008) in which two hundred and ten undergraduates (45 men and 165 women) from Health Sciences studies (median age= 19 years, range 17-47) completed a 30-minute set of questionnaires that measured their socio-demographic status and the perceived degree of cohesiveness of their class group, and their emotional intelligence and leadership style. Afterwards, they selected from their group those who they thought would be good and bad leaders, respectively. Individuals were assigned to a high- (n = 85) or a low-cohesion (n = 125) group, depending on their estimations of the degree of cohesiveness of their own group.

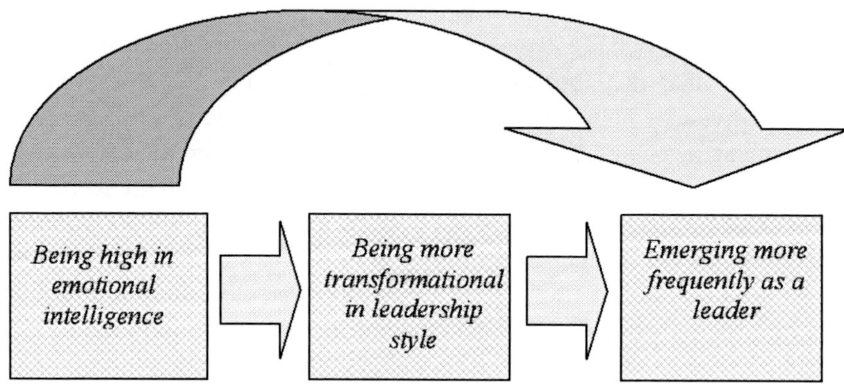

Figure 1. Model of relationships among dimensions.

Emotional Intelligence was measured by the Spanish version of the Trait Meta Mood Scale (TMMS-24; Salovey, Mayer, Goldman, Turvey, & Palfai, 1995; Spanish version by

Fernández-Berrocal, Extremera, and Ramos, 2004), which is a 24-item questionnaire that identifies three interpersonal factors: emotional clarity (an individual's tendency to distinguish their own emotions and moods), emotional regulation (an individual's tendency to regulate their own feelings), and emotional attention (conveys the degree to which an individual tends to observe and think about their own feelings and moods). And leadership was measured by a reduced Spanish version of the *Multifactorial Leadership Questionnaire* (MLQ) by López-Zafra (1998). This instrument is made up of 22 items and has convergent validity with the MLQ (Bass, 1985).

Participants' estimations showed that female participants thought that they would be evaluated more positively than male participants ($M = 1.62$, SD = .75, vs. $M = 1.2$, SD =.43), $F(1, 208) = 23.84$, $p < .001$. And also female participants had a higher degree of affinity than male participants ($M = 2.12$, SD = 0.99 vs. $M = 2.54$, SD = 1.04) and perceived the class group as more cohesive than male participants ($M = 2.78$, SD = .72, vs. $M = 3.20$, SD = .86) $F(1, 208) = 23.85$, $p < .001$ and $F(1, 208) = 6.07$, $p = .01$, respectively.

To test the influence of participants' emotional intelligence on their leadership style, they were classified as high or low in emotional clarity, emotional regulation, and emotional attention, depending on whether their scores were above or below the median of the group (see Extremera & Fernández-Berrocal, 2005).

In sum, when analyzing each of the emotional intelligence components interaction with leadership styles, we found that participants who had high emotional clarity evaluated themselves as more transformational in their leadership style than those who had low emotional clarity. This pattern of results emerged in both the high- and low-cohesion group ($p < .001$, and $p < .001$, respectively). However, the difference between participants high and low in emotional clarity was greater in the high-cohesion group than in the low-cohesion group ($p < .001$). The simple Cohesiveness × Emotional clarity interaction in transactional and laissez-faire leadership did not yield any significant results.

On the other hand, participants who were high in emotional regulation evaluated themselves as more transformational in their leadership style than those who were low in emotional regulation. This difference was higher in the high-cohesion group than in the low-cohesion group ($p = .037$). Finally, participants who were high in emotional attention did not evaluate themselves as more transformational in their leadership style than those individuals who were low in emotional attention (see table 1).

To measure leadership emergence, we computed the number of positive choices minus the number of negative choices that each participant received. Both positive and negative choices were weighted (with weights of 3, 2, and 1), according to the order in which that participant was selected (i.e., first, second, or third). The higher the order was, the larger the weight. Those individuals who received only one positive or negative choice were not considered in our analyses.

To test whether individuals who were high in emotional intelligence emerged more frequently as leaders as a result of being more transformational in their leadership style, we analyzed the correlation between participants' scores in the components of emotional intelligence and in transformational leadership, the correlation between participants' scores in transformational leadership and the weighted measure of leadership emergence, and the correlation between participants' scores in the components of emotional intelligence and the weighted measure of leadership emergence. Our results show that the correlation between emotional intelligence and transformational leadership and the correlation between transformational leadership and leadership emergence were high. However, the correlation between emotional intelligence and leadership emergence did not differ from zero. Furthermore, this pattern of results emerged more clearly in the high-cohesion group than in the low-cohesion group (see table 2).

**Table 1. Influence of Emotional intelligence factors
and group cohesiveness on leadership style**

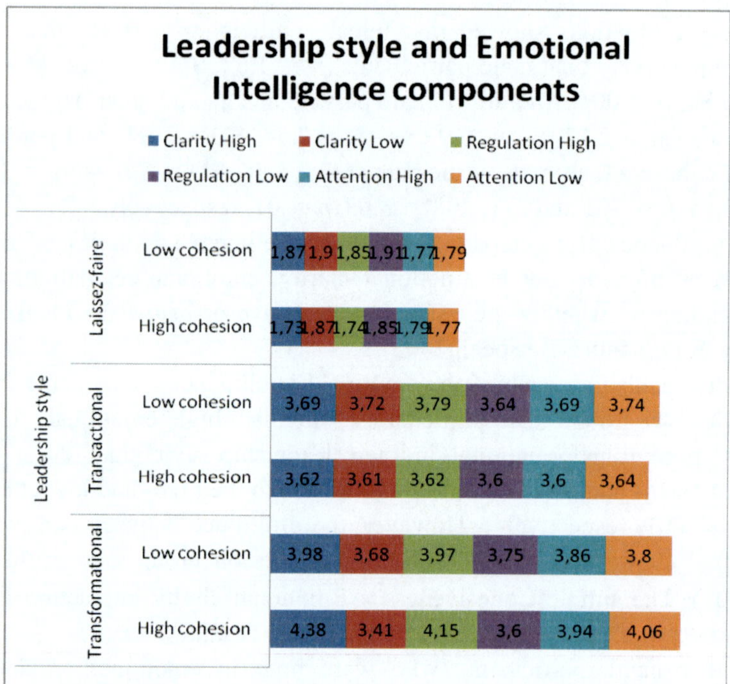

**Table 2. Influence of Emotional Intelligence and Group
Cohesiveness on Leadership Emergence**

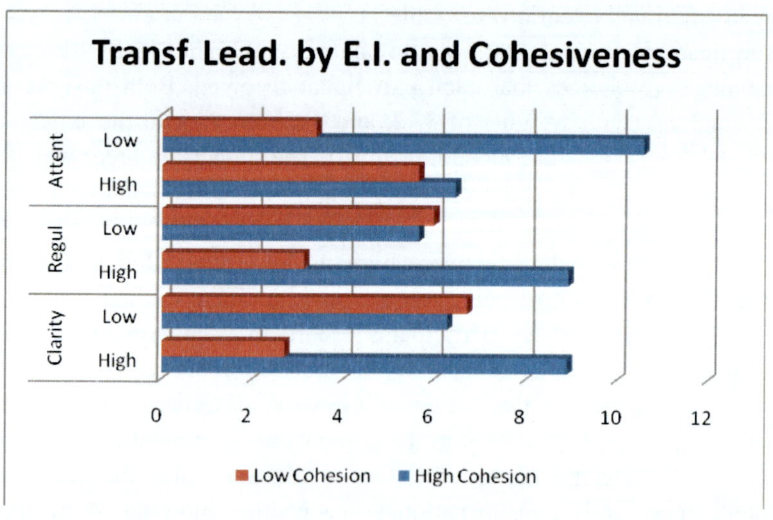

To analyze the influence of the components of emotional intelligence and the leadership style on leadership emergence we conducted a stepwise regression analysis. Our results show that both transformational leadership and transactional leadership styles were the best predictors for leadership emergence. Specifically, transformational leadership had a greater impact on the emergence of leadership ($\beta = 5.58$; $p < .001$) whereas transactional leadership was a negative predictor ($\beta = -1.73$; $p < .05$). That is, the more transformational and the less transactional a person is, the more likely it is that they will emerge as a leader. The results of these analyses support the hypothesis that individuals high in emotional intelligence emerge more frequently as leaders because they are more transformational in their leadership style.

Summing up, this research evaluated the extent to which emotional intelligence and transformational leadership are related concepts. The results in our study showed that individuals high in both emotional clarity and emotional regulation (two key components of emotional intelligence) evaluated themselves as more transformational in their leadership style than those individuals low in both components. On the contrary, there were no differences between high and low in emotional attention individuals and their transformational leadership style.

From these results we may assert that understanding and regulating followers' emotions seem to be more important to transformational leadership than feeling others' emotions. Our results are in line with findings by Salovey, Woolery, Stroud, and Epel (2002). These authors showed that individuals that score high in emotional attention often report more anxiety than individuals with low scores in this variable. A possible explanation is that the latter are not as aware of and worried about their affects and use more effective strategies in their relationships (Gohm, 2003). In sum, all these results show that emotional clarity and emotional regulation are good predictors of positive outcomes whereas emotional attention is not.

Furthermore, individuals who were high in transformational leadership and low in laissez-faire leadership emerged very frequently as leaders in an informal context. These individuals were selected very often as good leaders and less often as bad leaders by their classmates. As predicted, this was especially the case in high-cohesion groups. Our results highlight the importance of cohesiveness as a predictor of how much influence the relationship between emotional intelligence and transformational leadership will have on the emergence of leadership. Note that to lead; a leader needs a unified group of followers and cohesiveness is a key concept in the analysis of group behavior because it differentiates mere social categories from real groups (see Carron & Bradley, 2000).

Supporting our model, the correlation between participants' scores in emotional intelligence and those in transformational leadership was very high. Also, the correlation between participants' scores in transformational leadership and scores in leadership emergence was very high. But, the correlation between emotional intelligence and leadership emergence was not substantial and did not differ from zero. This result supports the idea that transformational leadership can be thought of as a construct that modulates the relationship between emotional intelligence and leadership emergence, influencing the constructive group dynamic and the emergence of a leader. So that, to emerge as leaders in a class context, individuals high in emotional intelligence needed to be transformational in their leadership style. Simply being high in emotional intelligence did not seem to be enough. As in the previous results, this was especially the case in the high-cohesion group.

In sum, our study contributes to knowledge about emotional intelligence and transformational leadership in several ways. First, our results support the recent attempts to investigate affective processes in leadership (e.g., Dasborough & Ashkanasy, 2002; George, 2000). Second, we show that the relationship between transformational leadership style and emotional intelligence plays a crucial role in the emergence of leaders, but the impact is mediated by group cohesiveness. Finally, we also show that possessing the emotional intelligence components of emotional clarity and regulation promoted the perception of an individual as a leader, but only if these individuals were transformational in their leadership style. In line with other research (e.g., Eagly et al, 2003), our study also revealed that being laissez-faire correlates negatively with the emergence of leadership. It seems to be easier for an individual who has spent time in a group and feels connected to their group members to emerge as a leader if they are transformational in leadership style and high in emotional intelligence. Therefore, emotions and affect are key aspects in the perception of individuals as transformational leaders (Brown & Keeping, 2005).

In our study, participants selected from among their classmates those they thought would be good and bad leaders. Therefore, leadership emergence was based on group members' judgments. However, participants evaluated themselves on the leadership styles and emotional intelligence scales. Consequently, their scores could be inflated (López-Zafra, 1998). In future research it would be interesting to have external ratings of the emergent leaders. Another question requiring future research is whether our results also hold in a formal leadership context (i.e., managers in a workplace).

In summary, the findings of this study are a promising starting point for future research in formal contexts and also have a direct implication for training leaders and coaches. It is important to train leaders not only about effective behaviors but also about understanding and managing emotions, as they both influence cohesion and, consequently, results from the group.

Study 2. The Impact of Gender-Congenial Variables on the Relationship between Transformational Leadership and Emotional Intelligence

As seen in study 1, there are some group variables that may influence the relationship between emotional intelligence and transformational leadership. Also as referred in the literature women may be more transformational and less transactional in their leadership style, more emotionally intelligent and more feminine than men.

In a study (López-Zafra, Garcia-Retamero, & Berrios, in revision) we wanted to analyze these aspects considering gender-congenial variables (discipline of studies) and also test whether Transformational leadership is predicted by Emotional intelligence and femininity. As far as the predictions about the impact of gender-congenial disciplines are concerned, we hypothesized that students from feminine gender-congenial disciplines are more transformational, emotionally intelligent, and feminine, than students from masculine gender-congenial disciplines that are the way around (more transactional, less emotionally intelligent and masculine).

Four-hundred and eighty Spanish undergraduates (190 men and 290 women) completed a 30-minute set of questionnaires that measured their socio-demographic status; their emotional intelligence (TMMS), leadership style (MLQ), and gender identity (short version of Bem's

Sex Role Inventory (BSRI, Bem, 1974). The participants had a median age of 20.31 years (SD = 1.8; range 17-47). They were all students from three different disciplines (Psychology, n = 237, 170 females and 67 males; Engineering sciences, n = 88; 11 females and 77 males; and Economics, n = 155; 109 females and 46 males).

To select which students were going to participate in our study, we took into account the gender-congeniality of the major they were studying following several criteria. Specifically, we considered 1) the percentage of male-female students in each discipline in Spain, 2) a pretest about the perceptions undergraduates have about the different disciplines, and 3) the mathematical content of the discipline. Taking into account these three criteria, we considered three levels of gender-congeniality of the disciplines: masculine-congenial, feminine congenial and neutral. In particular, Psychology was considered as a female- congenial discipline whereas Engineering sciences were considered a male-congenial discipline. Economics was considered as a gender neutral discipline; as the proportion of women in this discipline is high and the mathematical content is higher than in Psychology but much lower than in engineering sciences.

As a first step in analysis of the data, the correlations between all scales and subscales were computed. Masculinity and femininity were negatively correlated. Masculinity was also significantly related to individual consideration (i.e., one of the factors of the transformational leadership scales) and management by exception (i.e., one of the factors of the transactional leadership scale). In contrast, femininity was positively correlated to all transformational leadership subscales and the contingent reward transactional leadership subscale. In addition, when considering the global transformational leadership scale, results showed that transformational leadership is positively correlated to femininity and the three components of emotional intelligence. In contrast, transactional leadership is negatively correlated to masculinity and positively correlated to femininity, emotional clarity and emotional regulation from the emotional intelligence subscales.

Regarding to the hypothesis that women are more transformational in their leadership style, more emotionally intelligent, and more feminine than men. Results showed significant main effects of sex of participant and discipline. However, the interaction between these factors was not significant. In line with this hypothesis, women's scores in femininity were higher than those of men $F(1, 467) = 6.29$, p=.002. However, there is a main effect of gender on transactional leadership, whereby women are more transactional in their leadership style than men $F(1, 474) = 5.10$, p = .000. An explanation of this result is that women score higher on contingent reward than men ($M = 3.94$, $SD = .08$ vs. $M = 3.71$, $SD = .05$; $F(1, 471) = 4.38$, $p = .037$. Furthermore, women's scores in emotional regulation were lower than those of men $F(1, 475) = 9.57$, $p = .002$. In contrast, women did not have higher scores than men on the emotional clarity and emotional attention (see table 3).

Similarly, when considering high and low scores on the dependent variables, we hypothesize that individuals who are high in emotional intelligence or transformational leadership are more feminine and less transactional and masculine than individuals who are low in both emotional intelligence and transformational leadership. We created a new variable based on the classification of participants as high or low in these factors depending on whether their scores were above or below percentile 33 and 67, respectively (see Extremera & Fernández-Berrocal, 2002, and López-Zafra & del Olmo, 1999 for a similar procedure).

Table 3. Scores for the dimensions by Sex

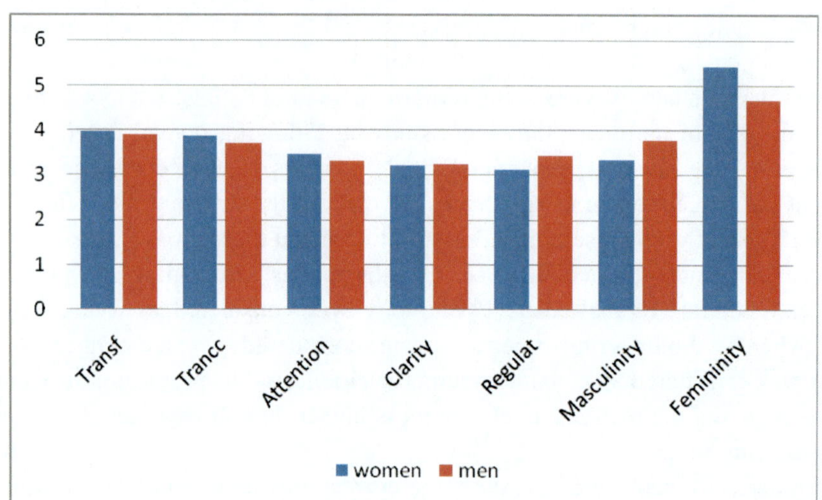

We conducted t-test to analyze differences between individuals who score high and low in the dimensions mentioned above. Results showed that individuals who scored high in transformational leadership also scored higher in femininity, global transactional leadership; contingent reward (a transactional leadership subscale, and the subscales of emotional intelligence for emotional attention; for emotional clarity and for emotional regulation) than individuals who score low in transformational leadership. However, individuals with low scores in transformational leadership, scored higher in management by exception (a transactional leadership subscale than individuals who scored high in transformational leadership (see Figure 2).

Figure 2. Means for the dimensions of the study by Low or High scores in Transformational Leadership.

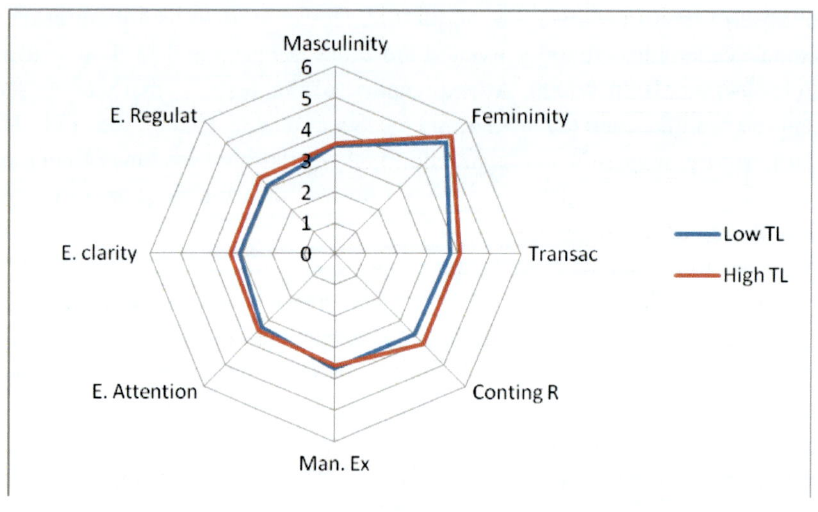

In sum, our research evaluated the extent to which transformational leadership, emotional intelligence and gender are related concepts. And results in our study showed that women are more feminine than men. However, in contrast with our hypothesis, women scored higher than men in transactional leadership. This result is due to a high score in contingent reward and it has been shown that women generally are higher than men in this variable (Eagly et al., 2003). Therefore, this result is in line with previous research.

In line with our hypothesis, individuals high in transformational leadership scored also higher in femininity, the three subscales of emotional intelligence and contingent reward (a transactional leadership subscale) than individuals who scored low in transformational leadership, whereas these individuals scored higher in management by exception (a transactional leadership subscale). These results are very interesting as the important theme is being high or low in transformational leadership, regardless of gender. Several studies have shown that gender differences in transformational leadership are not so important and that men who are more transformational are also more feminine (Hackman et al, 1992; Kent & Moss, 1994; López-Zafra & Del Olmo, 1999; López-Zafra & Morales, 1998, 2007). We also found that high scores in emotional clarity and regulation are fairly well related to transformational leadership subscales. Once again, these results are related to those that show that emotional clarity and emotional regulation are good predictors of positive outcomes, whereas emotional attention is not (Extremera et al., 2006; Salovey et al., 2002)

Furthermore, our results about the potential predictability of Emotional intelligence and gender identity on transformational leadership show that femininity, emotional clarity and emotional regulation are predictors for transformational leadership. As Mandell and Pherwani (2003) showed, emotional intelligence predicts transformational leadership regardless of sex. Consequently, with our research we go one step further by showing that gender identity is the key variable instead of sex.

Finally, individuals who study a female congenial discipline scored higher in femininity and emotional attention than individuals studying a male congenial discipline, whereas students from a gender neutral discipline are higher in emotional regulation than students from a feminine or masculine discipline (see table 4). This result is consistent with studies that show that women score higher than men in emotional attention (Extremera et al. 2006).

In the same vein, a relationship between femininity and emotional attention may be established. Interestingly, participants who study Economics are higher in emotional intelligence than participants who study other disciplines as they have a high emotional regulation, medium emotional clarity, and low emotional attention. Results by Salovey et al. (2002) show that those individuals that score high in emotional attention often report more anxiety than individuals with low scores in this variable. A possible explanation is that the latter are not so aware and worried about their affect and use more effective strategies in their relations (Gohm, 2003). High scores in emotional clarity and emotional regulation are also related to high satisfaction and low anxiety (Extremera et al., 2006; Fernández-Berrocal, Extremera, & Ramos, 2003). In a similar vein, emotional regulation correlates positively with physical and mental health (Extremera & Fernández-Berrocal, 2002). In summary, all these results show that emotional clarity and emotional regulation are reliable predictors of positive outcomes whereas emotional attention is not.

Table 4. Scores in the Dimensions by gender-congenial discipline

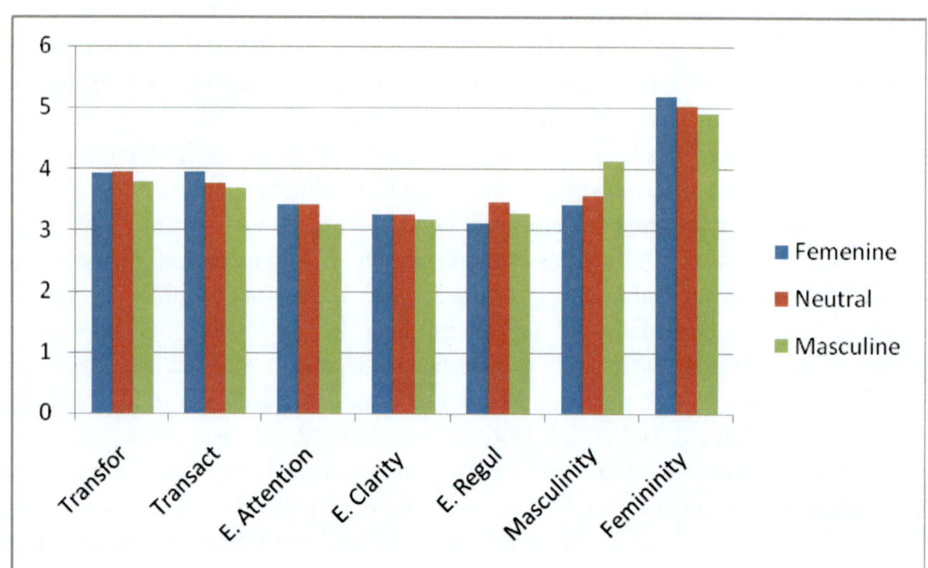

In summary, our study contributes to knowledge about transformational leadership, emotional intelligence, and gender identity in several ways. First, it supports the relationship between these three dimensions. Second, we show that gender-congenial variables (e.g. discipline) are related to these concepts. We show that emotional clarity and emotional regulation are the emotional intelligence subscales best related to transformational leadership. Finally, we also show that having feminine characteristics and having the emotional intelligence components of emotional clarity and regulation are predictors of transformational leadership style.

REFERENCES

Atwater, L. E., Dionne, S. D., Avolio, B., Camobreco, J. F. & Lau, A. W. (1999). A longitudinal study of the leadership development process: Individual differences predicting leader effectiveness. *Human Relations, 52*, 1543–1562.

Atwater, L. E. & Yammarino, F. J. (1993). Personal attributes as predictors of superiors' and subordinates' perceptions of military academy leadership. *Human Relations, 46*, 645–668.

Augusto, J. M., López-Zafra, E., Martínez, R. & Pulido, M. (2006). Perceived emotional intelligence and life satisfaction among university teachers. *Psicothema, 18*, 152–157.

Augusto-Landa, J. M., López-Zafra, E., Berrios-Martos, M. P. & Aguilar-Luzón, M. C. (2008). The relationship between emocional intelligence, occupational stress and health in nurses. A questionnaire survey. *International Journal of Nursing Studies, 45 (6)*, 888-901.

Avolio, B. J. (1999). *Full leadership development: Building the vital forces in organizations.* London: Sage.

Avolio, B. J. & Bass, B. M. (2002). *Developing potential across a full range of leadership: Cases on transactional and transformational leadership.* Mahwah, NJ: Lawrence Erlbaum Associates.

Avolio, B. J., Bass, B. M. & Jung, D. I. (1995). *MLQ multifactor leadership questionnaire: Technical report.* Palo Alto, CA: Mind Garden.

Barbuto, J. E. & Burbach, M. E. (2006). The emotional intelligence of transformational leaders: A field study of elected officials. *The Journal of Social Psychology, 146,* 51–64

Barling, J., Slater, F. & Kelloway, E. K. (2003). Transformational leadership and emotional intelligence: An exploratory study. *Leadership and Organization Development Journal, 21,* 157–161.

Bar-On, R. & Parker, D. A. (2000). *The handbook of emotional intelligence.* San Francisco: Jossey-Bass.

Bar-On, R., Brown, J. M., Kirkcaldy, B. D. & Thomé, E. P. (2000). Emotional expression and implications for occupational stress: An application of the Emotional Quotient Inventory (EQ-i). *Personality and Individual Differences, 28,* 1107–1118.

Bass, B. M. (1985). *Leadership and performance beyond expectations.* New York: Free Press.

Bass, B. M. (1990). *Bass and Stodgill's handbook of leadership.* (3º ed.). Nueva York: The Free Press.

Bass, B. M. (1996). *A new paradigm of leadership: An inquiry into transformational leadership.* Alexandria, VA, US: U.S. Army Research Institute for the Behavioral and Social Sciences.

Bass, B. M. (1998). *Transformational leadership: Industry, military and educational impact.* Mahwah, NJ: Lawrence Erlbaum Associates.

Bass, B. M. (1999). Two decades of research and development in transformational leadership. *European Journal of Work and Organizational Psychology, 8,* 9–32.

Bass, B. M. (2002). Cognitive, social, and emotional intelligence of transformational leaders. In R. E. Riggio, S. E. Murphy, & F. J. Pirozzolo (Eds.) *Multiple intelligences and leadership* (105–118). London: Lawrence Erlbaum.

Bem, S. L. (1974). The measurement of psychological androgyny. *Journal of Consulting and Clinical Psychology, 42,* 155–162.

Boyatzis, R. E. (2006). Using tipping points of emotional intelligence and cognitive competencies to predict financial performance of leaders. *Psicothema, 18,* 124–131.

Brown, D. J. & Keeping, L. M. (2005). Elaborating the construct of transformational leadership: The role of affect. *The Leadership Quarterly, 16,* 245–272.

Brown, F. W. & Moshavi, D. (2005). Transformational leadership and emotional intelligence: A potential pathway for an increased understanding of interpersonal influence. *Journal of Organizational Behavior, 26,* 867–871.

Brown, F. W., Bryant, S. E. & Reilly, M. D. (2006). Does emotional intelligence—as measured by the EQI—influence transformational leadership and/or desirable outcomes? *Leadership & Organization Development Journal, 27,* 330–351.

Burns, J. M. (1978). *Leadership.* New York: Harper and Row.

Candela, C., Barberá, E., Ramos, A. & Sarrió, M. (2002). Inteligencia emocional y género. *Revista Electrónica de Motivación y Emoción, 5* retrieved from http://reme.uji.es/reme/numero10/indexsp.html

Caruso, D. R., Mayer, J. S. & Salovey, P. (2002). Emotional intelligence and emotional leadership. In R. E. Riggio, S. E. Murphy, & F. J. Pirozzolo (Eds.) *Multiple intelligences and leadership* (55–74). London: Lawrence Erlbaum.

Carron, A. V. & Bradley, L. R. (2000). Cohesion: Conceptual and measurement issues. *Small Group Research, 31,* 89–107.

Carron, A. V., Bray, S. R. & Eys, M. A. (2002). Team cohesion and team success in sport. *Journal of Sports Sciences, 20,* 119–126.

Ciarrochi, J., Forgas, J. P. & Mayer, J. D. (2001). *Emotional intelligence in everyday life.* Philadelphia, PA: Psychology Press.

Ciarrochi, J. V., Chang, A. & Caputi, P. (2000). A critical evaluation of the emotional intelligence construct. *Personality & Individual Differences, 28,* 539–561.

Conger, J. A. (1999). Charismatic and transformational leadership in organizations: An insider's perspective on these developing streams of research. *The Leadership Quarterly, 10,* 145–169.

Conger, J. A. & Hunt, J. G. (1999). Charismatic and transformational leadership: Taking stock of the present and future. *Leadership Quarterly, 10,* 121–128.

Conger, J. A. & Kanungo, R. N. (1998). *Charismatic leadership in organizations.* Thousand Oaks, CA: SAGE.

Cooper, R. K. & Sawaf, A. (1997). *Executive EQ: Emotional intelligence in leadership and organizations.* Nueva York.Grosset/ Putman.

Cote, S. & Miners, C. T. H. (2006). Emotional Intelligence, cognitive intelligence and job performance. *Administrative Science Quarterly, 51,* 1–28.

Cuadrado, I. (2004). Valores y rasgos estereotípicos de género de mujeres líderes. *Psicothema, 16,* 279–284.

D'Intino, R. S., Goldsby, M. G., Houghton, J. D. & Neck, C.P. (2007). Self-leadership: A process for entrepreneurial success. *Journal of Leadership and Organizational Studies, 13,* 105–120.

Dasborough, M. T. & Ashkanasy, N. M. (2002). Emotion and attribution of intentionality in leader-member relationships. *The Leadership Quarterly, 13,* 615–634.

Dawda, D. & Hart, S. (2000). Assessing emotional intelligence: reliability and validity of the Bar-On Emotional Quotient Inventory (EQ-I) in university students. *Personality and Individual Differences, 28,* 797–812.

DeCremer, D. & van Knippenberg, D. L. (2002). How do leaders promote cooperation? The effects of charisma and procedural fairness. *Journal of Applied Psychology, 87,* 858–866.

Downey, L. A., Papageorgiou, V. & Stough, C. (2006). Examining the relationship between leadership, emotional intelligence and intuition in senior female managers. *Leadership & Organization Development Journal, 27,* 250–264.

Dries, N. & Pepermans, R. (2007). Using emotional intelligence to identify high potential: A metacompetency perspective. *Leadership and organization development journal, 28,* 749–757.

Eagly, A. H. (1987). *Sex differences in social behavior: A social-role interpretation.* Hillsdale, NJ: Erlbaum.

Eagly, A. H. (2003). More women at the top: The impact of gender roles and leadership style. In U. Pasero (Eds.) *Gender: From costs to benefits* (151–169). Opladen, Wiesbaden, Germany: Westdeutscher Verlag.

Eagly, A. H. (2004). Few women at the top: How role incongruity produces prejudice and the glass ceiling. En D. van Knippenberg & M. A. Hogg (Eds.) Identity, leadership, and power (79–93). London: Sage.

Eagly, A. H. (2007). Female leadership advantage and disadvantage: resolving the contradictions. *Psychology of Women Quarterly, 31,* 1–12.

Eagly, A. H. & Carli, L. L. (2007). *Through the labyrinth: The truth about how women become leaders.* Boston: Harvard University Business School Press.

Eagly, A. H. & Johannesen-Schmidt, M. C. (2001). The leadership styles of women and men. *Journal of Social Issues, 57,* 781–797.

Eagly, A. H., Johannesen-Schmidt, M. C. & van Engen, M. (2003). Transformational, transactional, and laissez-faire: A meta-analysis comparing men and women. *Psychological Bulletin, 129,* 569–591.

Eagly, A. H. & Karau, S. J. (2002). Role congruity theory of prejudice toward female leaders. *Psychological Review, 109,* 573–598.

Extremera, N. & Fernández-Berrocal, P. (2002). Relation of perceived emotional intelligence and health-related quality of life in middle-age women. *Psychological Report, 91,* 47-59.

Extremera, N. & Fernández-Berrocal, P. (2005). Perceived emocional intelligence and life satisfaction: predictive and incremental validity using the Trait-Meta Mood Scale. *Personality and Individual Differences, 39,* 937-948.

Extremera, N., Fernández-Berrocal, P. & Salovey, P. (2006). Spanish version of the Mayer-Salovey-Caruso Emotional Intelligence test (MSCEIY). Version 2.0: Reliabilities, age and gender differences. *Psicothema, 18,* 42–48.

Fernández-Berrocal, P., Extremera, N. & Ramos, N. (2003). Inteligencia emocional y depresión. *Encuentros en Psicología Social, 1,* 251-254.

Fernández-Berrocal, P., Extremera, N. & Ramos, N. (2004). Validity and reliability of the Spanish modified version of the Trait Meta-Mood Scale. *Psychological Reports, 94,* 751-755.

Garcia-Retamero, R. & López-Zafra, E. (2002). Percepción y evaluación de la mujer en liderazgo como explicación de la discriminación de la mujer en puestos de dirección. *Revista de Psicología Social Aplicada, 12,* 21–52.

Garcia-Retamero, R. & López-Zafra, E. (2006a). Congruencia de rol de género y liderazgo: El papel de las atribuciones causales sobre el éxito y el fracaso. *Revista Latinoamericana de Psicologia, 38,* 245–257.

Garcia Retamero, R. & López-Zafra, E. (2006b). Prejudice against women in male-congenial environments: Perceptions of gender role congruity in leadership. *Sex Roles, 55,* 51–61.

Garcia-Retamero, R. & López-Zafra, E. (2009). Causal attributions about feminine and leadership roles: A cross-cultural comparison. *Journal of Cross-Cultural Psychology, 40,* 492–509.

George, J. M. (2000). Emotions and leadership: The role of emotional intelligence. *Human Relations, 53,* 1027–1055.

Gohm, C. L. (2003). Mood regulation and emotional intelligence: individual differences. *Journal of Personality and Social Psychology, 84,* 388-399.

Goleman, D. (1995). *Emotional intelligence.* New York: Bantam Books.

Goleman, D. (1995). *Emotional intelligence.* New York: Bantam Books.

Goleman, D. (1998). *Working with emotional intelligence.* New York: Bantam Books.

Grossman, R. J. (2000). Emotions at work. *Health Forum Journal, 43*, 18–22.

Groves, K. S., McEnrue, M. P. & Shen, W. (2008). Developing and measuring the emotional intelligence of leaders. *Journal of Management Development, 27*, 225–250.

Hackman, M. Z., Furniss, A. H., Hills, M. J. & Paterson, T. J. (1992). Perceptions of gender-role characteristics and transformational and transactional leadership behaviours. *Perceptual and Motor Skills, 75*, 311–319.

Hoogh, A. H., Hartog, D. N. & Koopman, P. L. (2005). Linking the Big-Five factors of personality to charismatic and transactional leadership: Perceived dynamic work environment as a moderator. *Journal of Organizational Behavior, 26*, 839–851.

Houghton, J. D., Bonham, T. W., Neck, C. P. & Singh, K. (2004). The relationship between self-leadership and personality: A comparison of hierarchical factor structures. *Journal of Managerial Psychology, 19*, 427–441.

House, R. J. (1977). A 1976 theory of charismatic leadership. In J. C. Hunt & L. L. Larson (Eds.) *Leadership: The cutting edge* (189–207). Carbondale: Southern Illinois University Press.

House, R. J. & Aditya, R.N. (1997). The social scientific study of leadership: Quo vadis? *Journal of Management, 23*, 409–473.

Hunt, J. G. (1999). Charismatic/transformational leadership's transformation of the field: An historical essay. *The Leadership Quarterly, 10*, 129–144.

Kellet, J. B., Humphrey, R. H. & Sleeth, R. G. (2002). Empathy and complex task performance: Two routes to leadership. *The Leadership Quarterly, 13*, 523–544.

Kellet, J. B., Humphrey, R. H. & Sleeth, R. G. (2006). Empathy and the emergence of task and relations leaders. *The Leadership Quarterly, 17*, 146–162.

Kent, R. L. & Moss, S. E. (1994). Effects of sex and gender role on leader emergence. *Academy of management Journal, 37*, 1335–1346.

Kerr, R., Garvin, J., Heaton, N. & Boyle, E. (2006). Emotional intelligence and leadership effectiveness. *Leadership & Organization Development Journal, 27*, 265–279.

Kirkpatrick, S. A. & Locke, E. A. (1996). Direct and indirect effects of three core charismatic leadership components on performance and attitudes. *Journal of Applied Psychology, 81*, 36–51.

Lam, L. T. & Kirby, S. L. (2002). Is emotional intelligence an advantage? An exploration of the impact of emotional and general intelligence on individual performance. *The Journal of Social Psychology, 142*, 133–143.

Law, K. S., Wong, C. S. & Song, L. J. (2004). The construct and criterion validity of emotional intelligence and its potential utility for management studies. *Journal of Applied Psychology, 89*, 483–496.

Leban, W. & Zulauf, C. (2004). Linking emotional intelligence abilities and transformational leadership styles. *The Leadership & Organization Development Journal, 25*, 554–564.

Levine, J. M. & Moreland, R. L. (1998). Small groups. In D. T. Gilbert, S. T. Fiske, & G. Lindzey (Eds.) *The handbook of social psychology, Vol.2* (415–469). New York: McGraw-Hill.

Lewis, K. M. (2000), When leaders display emotion: how followers respond to negative emotional expression of male and female leaders, *Journal of Organizational Behavior, 21, 2*, 221–34.

Livingstone, H. A. & Day, A. L. (2005). Comparing the construct and criterion-related validity of ability-based and mixed-based measures of emotional intelligence. *Educational and Psychological Measurement, 65,* 851–865.

Lopes, P., Grewal, D., Kadis, J., Gall, M. & Salovey, P. (2006). Evidence that emotional intelligence is related to job performance and affect and attitudes at work. *Psicothema, 18,* 132–138.

López-Zafra, E. (1998). Liderazgo carismático: Un intento de validación convergente al M.L.Q. (Multifactor Leadership Questionnaire). *Revista de Psicología Social, 13,* 211–216.

López-Zafra, E. (2001). ¿Liderazgo carismático en las organizaciones? Elementos para una reflexión sobre el cambio en las relaciones intraorganizacionales. *Revista de Psicología Social, 16,* 97–115.

López-Zafra, E. & Del Olmo, S. M. (1999). Estereotipia de género y liderazgo transformacional en contextos de trabajo típicamente femeninos. *Revista de Psicología Social Aplicada, 9,* 53–71.

López-Zafra, E., Garcia-Retamero, R. & Augusto, J. M. (2008). The impact of transformational leadership, emotional intelligence and group cohesiveness on leadership emergence. *The Journal of Leadership Studies, 3,* 37–49.

López-Zafra, E., Garcia-Retamero, R. & Berrios, M. P. (2009). *Relationship between transformational leadership and emotional intelligence from a gender approach.* Manuscript under review.

López Zafra, E. & Morales, J. F. (1998). La función directiva en los centros docentes: Liderazgo transformacional y género. *Boletín de Psicología, 60,* 15–25.

López-Zafra, E. & Morales, J. F. (1999). Niveles de análisis en el estudio de liderazgo carismático. *Revista de Psicología Social, 14,* 181–198

López-Zafra, E. & Morales, J. F. (2007). Liderazgo democrático y transformacional en las organizaciones: De las perspectivas de Lewin a Bass. En M. P. Berrios & M. M. Ramos (Coord.), *Investigación en psicología Vol. II. Investigación en psicología aplicada* (159–184). Jaén: Servicio de Publicaciones de la Universidad de Jaén.

Lowe, K. B., Kroeck, K. G. & Sivasubramanian, N. (1996). Effectiveness correlates of transformational and transactional leadership: A meta-analytic review of the MLQ literature. *Leadership Quarterly, 7,* 385–426.

Mackenzie, S. B., Podsakoff, P. M. & Rich, G. A. (2001). Transformational and transactional leadership and salesperson performance. *Journal of Academy of Marketing Science, 29,* 115–134.

Mandell, B. & Pherwani, S. (2003). Relationship between emotional intelligence and transformational leadership style: A gender comparison. *Journal of Business and Psychology, 17,* 387–404.

Marques, J. F. (2007). Leadership: Emotional intelligence, passion and...what else? *Journal of Management Development, 26,* 644–651.

Mayer, J. D. & Salovey, P. (1997). What is emotional intelligence? In P. Salovey & D. Sluyter (Eds.) *Emotional development and emotional intelligence: Implications for educators* (3–31). New York: Basic Books.

Mayer, J. D., Caruso, D. R. & Salovey, P. (1999). Emotional intelligence meets traditional standards for intelligence. *Intelligence, 27,* 267–298.

Mayer, J. D., Roberts, R. D. & Barsade, S. G. (2008). Emerging research in emotional intelligence. *Annual Review of Psychology, 59*, 507–536.

Moïra, M., Luminet, O. & Menil, C. (2006). Predicting resistance to stress: Incremental validity of trait emotional intelligence over alexithymia and optimism. *Psicothema, 18*, 79–88.

Molero, F., Cuadrado, I., Navas, M. & Morales, J. F. (2007). Relations and effects of transformational leadership: A comparative analysis with traditional leadership styles. *The Spanish journal of Psychology, 10*, 358–368.

Murray, N. P. (2006). The differential effect of team cohesion and leadership behavior in high school sports. *Individual Differences Research, 4*, 216–225.

Palmer, B., Walls, M., Burgess, Z. & Stough, C. (2001). Emotional intelligence and effective leadership. *Leadership & Organization Development Journal, 22*, 5–10.

Parker, J. D. A., Taylor, G. J. & Bagby, R. M. (2001). The relationship between emotional intelligence and alexithymia. *Personality and Individual Differences, 30*, 107–115.

Prati, L. M., Douglas, C., Ferris, A. P., Ammeter, A. P. & Buckley, M. R. (2003). Emotional intelligence, leadership effectiveness and team outcomes. *The International Journal of Organizational Analysis, 11*, 21–40.

Pescosolido, A. T. (2002). Emergent leaders as managers of group emotion. *The Leadership Quarterly, 13*, 583–600.

Petrides, K. V. & Furham, A. (2000). Gender Differences in Measured and Self-Estimated Trait Emotional Intelligence. Sex Roles: A Journal of Research. *42*, 449-461

Petrides, K.V., Furnham, A. & Martín, G. (2004). Estimates of emotional and psychometric intelligence: Evidence for gender-based stereotypes. *The Journal of Social Psychology, 144*, 149–162.

Porterfield, J. & Kleiner, B. (2005). A new era: Women in leadership. *Equal Opportunities International, 24*, 49–56.

Rose, S. Z. (1995). Professional networks of junior faculty in psychology. *Psychology of Women Quaterly, 9*, 533–547.

Rosete, D. & Ciarrochi, J. (2005). Emotional intelligence and its relationship to workplace performance outcomes of leadership effectiveness. *Leadership & Organization Development Journal, 26*, 388–399.

Salovey, P., Mayer, J. D., Goldman, S., Turvey, C. & Palfai, T. (1995). Emotional attention, clarity, and repair: Exploring emotional intelligence using the Trait Meta-Mood Scale. En J. W. Pennebaker (Eds.) *Emotion, disclosure and health* (125-154). Washington, D. C.: American Psychological Association.

Salovey, P. & Mayer, J. D. (1990). Emotional intelligence. *Imagination, Cognition and Personality, 9*, 185–211.

Salovey, P., Woolery, A., Stroud, L. R. & Epel, E. S. (2002). Perceived emotional intelligence, stress reactivity, and symptom reports: Further explorations using the trait meta-mood scale. *Psychology and Health, 17*, 611–627.

Sivanathan, N. & Fekken, G.C. (2002). Emotional intelligence, moral reasoning and transformational leadership. *Leadership & Organization Development Journal, 23*, 198–204.

Sosik, J. J. & Mergerian, L. E. (1999). Understanding leader emotional intelligence and performance: The role of self-other agreement on transformational leadership perceptions. *Group and Organizational Management, 24*, 367–390.

Srivastava, K. & Bharamanaikar, S. R. (2004). Emotional intelligence and effective leadership behaviour. *Psychological Studies, 49*, 107–113.

Sutarso, P. (1999). Gender differences on the emotional intelligence inventory. The University of Alabama. Retrieved from ProQuest, CD-ROM.

Ugarriza, N. (2001). La evaluación de la inteligencia emocional a través del Inventario de BarOn (I-CE) en una muestra de Lima Metropolitana. Persona. *Revista de la Facultad de Psicología de la Universidad de Lima. 4*, 129–160.

Van Rooy, D. L., Alonso, A. & Viswesvaran, C. (2005). Group differences in emotional intelligence scores: theoretical and practical implications. *Personality and Individual Differences, 38, 3*, 689-700.

Villanueva, J. J. & Sánchez, J. C. (2007). Trait emotional intelligence and leadership self-efficacy: Their relationship with collective efficacy. *The Spanish Journal of Psychology, 10*, 349–357.

Weierter, S. J. M. (1997). Who wants to play "follow the leader"? A theory of charismatic relationships based on routinized charisma and follower characteristics. *Leadership Quarterly, 8*, 171–194.

Wolfradt, U., Felfe, J. & Koster, T. (2002). Self-perceived emotional intelligence and creative personality. *Imagination, Cognition and Personality, 21*, 293–309.

Wong, C. S. & Lang, K. S. (2002). The effects of leader and follower emotional intelligence on performance and attitude: An exploratory study. *The Leadership Quarterly, 13*, 243–274.

In: Feminism and Women in Leadership
Editor: Vicente Nardi, pp. 75-95

ISBN: 978-1-60876-270-5
© 2010 Nova Science Publishers, Inc.

Chapter 4

WHY ARE FEMALE LEADERS MORE VULNERABLE TO BECOMING TARGETS OF PREJUDICE THAN MALE LEADERS? THE MALLEABILITY OF GENDER STEREOTYPES

Rocio Garcia-Retamero[1]* *and Esther López-Zafra*[2]
[1]University of Granada, Max Planck Institute for Human Development
(Berlin; Germany)
[2]University of Jaén (Spain)

ABSTRACT

Our work points out that the prejudice against female leaders stems from gender stereotypes. That is, attributes that are perceived to be typical for men and women emerging from role-bound activities. Recent studies on the malleability of gender stereotypes show that they are flexible, dynamic structures that change with the passage of time. In this book chapter, we analyze people's stereotypic beliefs when evaluating men and women across time. In a study, we examined similarities and differences in beliefs about men and women of the past, present and future in Spain, and focus on the influence of an important demographic variable on these beliefs —the population size of people's location of residence. Results in the study showed that women of the present are estimated to be more masculine than are women of the past, and women of the future are expected to be more masculine than women of the present; whereas men are projected to increase in feminine attributes across years. Perceptions of men and women thus tend to converge with the passage of time. In less populated locations, however, men and women are more gender-stereotyped and, consequently, still shorter of equality than those in more populated areas. Participants who live in less populated, rural areas thus perceived less similarity between women and men's attributes than those who live in more populated, urban locations. We conclude that the study of dynamic gender stereotypes benefits from an extensive research in populations that vary in their demographic

---

* Corresponding author: E-mail: rretamer@ugr.es. Tel: +34 958 246240. Fax: +34 958 246239.

characteristics, and stress the importance of recent movements in rural areas supporting women's participation in the modernization process.

INTRODUCTION

Following the traditional notion of "equal opportunities," which is rooted in the Treaties of Rome (1957) and Amsterdam (1997), directives concerning equal treatment in employment, maternity leave, parental leave, and goods and services should be fully implemented in the European Union. However, recent evidence shows that, even in industrialized societies, fewer women than men progress beyond the middle management (Abele-Brehm, 2000; Eagly, 2004; Eagly & Carli, 2003, 2007; Jacobs, 1999; Ridgeway, 2001; The Economist, 2005). Women face prejudice and discrimination especially in male-dominated areas of employment, due to the perceived incongruency with women's gender role (Eagly, 2007; Eagly & Karau, 2002; Eagly, Karau, & Makhijani, 1995; Garcia-Retamero & López-Zafra, 2006a, 2006b, 2009a, 2009b). Likewise, gender inequality in economic and political participation and decision making remains to this day (Eurostat, 2008; Human Development Report, 2006). This gender gap is mirrored in efforts establishing policies like a "roadmap for equality between women and men" (European Commission, 2006).

Why are women more vulnerable to becoming targets of prejudice than men? We consider that this prejudice stems from *gender stereotypes* —attributes that are perceived to be typical for men and women (Ashmore & Del Boca, 1979; Hamilton, 1981; see also Garcia-Retamero & López-Zafra, 2008; Garcia-Retamero, Müller, & López-Zafra, in press) emerging from role-bound activities (Eagly, 1987; Eagly, Wood, & Diekman, 2000). In this chapter, we analyze people's gender-stereotypic beliefs when evaluating men and women across time.

Various empirical results on gender stereotypes show that attributes such as sensitive and affectionate are considered more typical of women, whereas aggressive and courageous are considered more typical of men (see Williams & Best, 1990; Williams, Satterwhite, & Best, 1999). These attributes about men and women are shared across cultures due to early divisions of labor (Eagly & Wood, 1999; Eagly et al., 2000; Wood & Eagly, 2002): Men's concentration in leadership and other high-power roles leads to the perception that men have agentic characteristics (e.g., self-assertion, dominance); whereas women's concentration in subordinate and care-taking roles leads to the perception that they have communal characteristics (e.g., kindness, supportiveness). Gender stereotypes influence our perceptions letting through only information that is consistent with the stereotypes (Hamilton & Trolier, 1986).

So far, most studies examining gender differences and inequalities between men and women focused on stereotypes at the workplace (e.g., Glick, Larsen, Johnson, & Branstiter, 2005; White & White, 2006), and how these stereotypes influence women's access to leadership positions (e.g., Eagly & Karau, 2002; Garcia-Retamero et al., in press; Powell, Butterfield, & Parent, 2002; Sczesny, Bosak, Neff, & Schyns, 2004). In contrast to previous researchers, who concluded that stereotypes are stable over time (e.g., Hamilton & Trolier, 1986; MacArthur, 1982; Snyder, 1981), recent studies on the malleability of gender stereotypes show that they are rather flexible, dynamic structures (e.g., Diekman & Eagly, 2000; Eagly et al., 2000; Sia, Lord, Blessum, Thomas, & Lepper, 1999; Twenge, 1997, 2001).

In fact, stereotypes are moderated by features of the target, the perceiver, and the context (Deaux & Major, 1987), and change substantially with the passage of time.

There is a fairly well developed literature on how gender stereotypes have evolved over time in different countries. Diekman and Eagly (2000), for instance, examined participants' beliefs about men and women of different time periods in the United States —measured via attributes on the masculine and feminine personality, cognitive, and physical dimension in the past, present, and future. Participants in their studies perceived that women were increasing in their masculine attributes over time; in comparison, men's attributes were perceived to be more stable. Stereotypes about women were thus portrayed to be extremely dynamic; whereas stereotypes about men were portrayed to be rather unchanging. The dynamic aspect of gender stereotypes was also observed in countries such as Brazil, Chile, Germany, and Spain (Diekman, Eagly, Mladinic, & Ferreira, 2005; López-Zafra & Garcia-Retamero, 2009a; López-Zafra, Garcia-Retamero, Diekman, & Eagly, 2008; Wilde & Diekman, 2005).

Interestingly, Wilde and Diekman (2005, pp.195) pointed out that the study of dynamic gender stereotypes would benefit from an extensive research in populations that vary in their demographic characteristics. To our knowledge, however, this suggestion was not investigated so far. In this chapter, we studied the malleability of gender stereotypes over time in Spain, and met the challenge proposed by Wilde and Diekman (2005) by focusing on the influence of an important demographic variable —the population size of participants' location of residence.

Changes in Gender Roles and Social Values in Spain as a Function of Population Size

Taking into account women's progress over the last century (Hyde, 1985), the equalization of men and women is an ongoing process over time —also in Spain. This is reflected in the recent history of Spanish women's rights (Morant, 2006). During the early Franco regime (i.e., in the early 40s), republican legislation was abolished and the former democratic regime destroyed. Strong boundaries within the new regime supported the traditional division of labor between men and women, expecting the latter to take care of the household and have children exclusively. Married women were not allowed to work without her husband's permission and some jobs were even prohibited for them. In addition, salary discrimination and educational differences were common —women had no property rights either. They were only supported when they accepted the law to "patria potestad," the will and authority of the male head of the family (Duran & Gallego, 1986).

Later on —from 1960 onwards—, a strong industrialization process encouraged women's incorporation into the workforce. Women were given equal political, professional and labor rights, which enabled them to contribute to the growth of consumer society and the expanding urban culture, changing and displacing some traditional values (Duran & Gallego, 1986). Women, however, were still excluded from certain professions at that time. In 1975–85, —after the Franco Regime— women found a way to express their needs through feminist groups of the civil society (Valiente, 2003). By 1982, most of the women's legal rights were incorporated into party programs and finally reached the institutions in 1985, especially in the "Instituto de la Mujer" in 1983 (Cousins, 1995; Valiente, 1995). While these changes led to a legal equality of women, other forms of equality between the sexes (e.g., status) still had to be spurred (Camps, 1994).

At the present time, the Organic Law 3/2007, of March 22nd, led to a substantial change in the social structure favoring equalization of men and women in all social contexts (Instituto Andaluz de la Mujer, 2007). Spain, therefore, experienced a noticeable progress in gender equality in a short period of time. Progress in law, however, was faster than that in social roles. Women's unemployment rate in Spain, for instance, is still twice as much compared to men. Women earn 26,3% less than men in Spain yet (Instituto Nacional de Estadística, 2008), and accessorily spend twice as much time than men doing housework (Instituto de la Mujer, 2008). Looking at women's participation regarding higher levels of decision making either at the university (14%), in financial administration (2.8%), or access to political power (29%), one might still refer to an existing glass ceiling (Kanter, 1977; Karsten, 1994). More importantly, the last Global Gender Gap Report in 2008 showed that Spain only holds the 17th position in a ranking within 130 countries of women's participation in public spheres (see Hausmann, Tyson, & Zahidi, 2008).

Crucial changes in social values and norms are also taking place in Spain in recent years (López-Zafra & Garcia-Retamero, 2009b). Traditional values, for instance, are perceived to fade away with time —to a greater extend in highly populated, urban regions than in less populated, rural areas (Marsden, 1996). Religion plays a minor role for young adults and teenagers in urban regions; whereas smaller changes in religious beliefs are observable in rural countryside (Serrano, Godás, Rodríguez, & Mirón, 1997). Spaniards who live in urban regions report stronger post-materialist values (Inglehart, 1997) —such as individual improvement, personal freedom, citizen input in government decisions, and maintaining a clean and healthy environment (Hampel, Boldero, & Holdsworth, 1996)— than those who live in less populated, rural areas. Urban people also have a higher average education level (European Commission, 2000; Royuela & Suriñach, 2005), more women in positions of authority, and a higher percentage of women participating in the labor force (Prados, 1998, 1999); women play a major role in community decision making, and are less exposed to occupational sex segregation as well (Navarro, 1999). In contrast, rural residents are more likely to be of a conservative social and political opinion (Marsden, 1996; Serrano et al., 1997). Yet, rural areas still offer few employment alternatives to unpaid domestic or agricultural work for women (Cuadrado, 1992) —this is expressed in the experience of social closure for women who try to reach higher status positions, for instance, as farmers (Sampedro, 1991).

Taking into account the latest history and recent changes in social values and norms in Spain, it seems very likely that people who live in highly populated, urban regions hold and preserve gender egalitarianism as a social value to a greater extent than those who live in less populated, rural areas. Gender stereotypes, therefore, would be easier to pervade low populated rural areas compared to highly populated, urban locations, independently of the overall increase in similarity between men and women across years. Yet, to our knowledge, there is no empirical data examining this hypothesis. To shed light on this issue, we conducted a study.

Participants in the study lived in regions of Spain that differ substantially in population size. They had to imagine the average woman or man in the present or for a specific time period in the past or future (e.g., 1950 and 2050, respectively), and then estimated the target individual's masculine and feminine attributes. Consistent with Diekman and Eagly (2000), we measured masculine and feminine positive personality and cognitive attributes, which were factor-analytically derived by Cejka and Eagly (1999); and masculine and feminine negative personality attributes, which were drawn from Spence, Helmreich, and Holohan (1979; see also Diekman et al., 2005; López-Zafra et al., 2008; and Wilde & Diekman, 2005 for a similar procedure). Gender-stereotypic dimensions resulted from averaging participants' responses across the attributes.

On the positive personality dimension, the masculine positive personality focuses on self-promotion and individualism and, therefore, is often associated with employees; whereas the feminine positive personality focuses on the relation with other people and tends to be primarily associated with homemakers (Eagly & Steffen, 1984). On the negative personality dimension, the masculine negative personality emphasizes self-aggrandizement and abuse of power; whereas the feminine negative personality emphasizes self-subordination and disagreeable methods of influence. Finally, regarding the cognitive dimension, the masculine cognitive abilities accentuate rationality and mathematical reasoning; whereas the feminine cognitive abilities accentuate intuition and creativity.

HYPOTHESES OF THE STUDY

Hypothesis 1: Changes in Male and Female Stereotypes over Years

The perceived similarity of women and men should increase from the past to the present and from the present to the future. The stereotype of women is expected to be dynamic in the form of increasing masculinity and —to a lesser extent— decreasing femininity. The stereotype of men should be less dynamic —although some change in a feminine direction is expected. Taking into account previous evidence (see Diekman & Eagly, 2000, and López-Zafra & Garcia-Retamero, 2009a), these predictions are held for all dimensions of gender stereotypes and most confidently for the personality dimensions.

Hypothesis 2: Changes in Male and Female Stereotypes as a Function of Population Size

The perceived similarity of men and women is expected to increase with the increasing population size of participants' places of residence. Participants who live in highly populated, urban areas should perceive women as increasing in masculinity and decreasing in femininity to a greater extent than those who live in less populated, rural locations; men, in contrast, are expected to increase in femininity and decrease in masculinity. These predictions are also held for all dimensions of gender stereotypes —again most confidently for the personality dimensions.

Hypothesis 3: Changes in Male and Female Stereotypes over Years as a Function of Population Size

Participants from locations differing in population size should perceive an assimilable increase of similarity between women and men from the past to the present and from the present to the future. That is, variations in perceptions of gender-stereotypic attributes over years should be similar for all participants, regardless of the population size of their place of residence —even when residents from small populations might perceive a greater difference between men and women than residents who live in locations with a higher population size (hypothesis 2).

METHOD

Participants

Three hundred and seventy-one individuals (49% men and 51% women) from eight regions in Spain (i.e., Andalusia, Balearic Islands, Castilla-La Mancha, Castilla-León, Cataluña, Galicia, Madrid, and Valencia) participated in the study. Participants' age ranged from 18 to 40 ($M = 26$, $SD = 8.89$), with 74% holding a secondary level of schooling and 15% a college degree; they were all native and lived in their current residence for at least 15 years.

Surveyors randomly selected participants from two classroom settings or the location where they lived. Participants were informed that there was no obligation to participate, whereby 5 declined. Those who consented received a questionnaire, which was collected approximately 12 minutes later. Participants who completed the questionnaire received a written debriefing.

In the analyses that follow, we split the participants in three groups according to the population size of their residential location. The small-town group includes participants who lived in locations with less than 20.000 inhabitants; the big-town group includes those who lived in locations with more than 20.000, but less than 50.000 inhabitants. Finally, participants in the city group lived in locations with more than 50.000 inhabitants. Table 1 gives an overview of the average population size and the population size of the most and less populated location in each group. The criterion to split participants into groups was determined based on the distribution of population in Spain (Instituto Nacional de Estadística, 2008), which peaked within this interval. Male and female participants were evenly distributed in the population groups.

Table 1. Average Population Size and Population Size of Largest and Smallest Location by Condition

Population size condition	Average Size	Largest Location	Smallest Location
More than 50.000 inhabitants	355,770	2,938,723	58,257
Between 50.000 and 20.000 inhabitants	25,478	37,681	20,060
Less than 20.000 inhabitants	7,273	18,188	213

Procedure

Participants in the study assessed the likelihood that the average woman or man in the present, past, or future would possess each of several gender-stereotypic attributes. For the present year conditions, no specific year was mentioned, whereas for the past and future conditions, a year was specified (i.e., 1950 and 2050, respectively) —resulting in a 2 (sex of target) × 3 (year) × 3 (population size) between-subjects factorial design.

Masculine and feminine positive personality, and cognitive attributes were measured using 7-point scales ranging from "very unlikely" to "very likely." The gender-stereotypic dimensions resulted from averaging participants' responses across the attributes and had high internal consistency —as assessed by alpha-values (see Table 2). After making their estimates, participants were asked to answer demographic questions including information such as age, education, sex, and ethnicity.

Table 2. Items in Gender-Stereotypic Dimensions and Alpha Values

Dimension	Masculine		Feminine	
	English	Spanish	English	Spanish
Positive personality	Adventurous	Atrevido/a	Affectionate	Afectuoso/a
	Dominant	Dominante	Supportive	Compasivo/a
	Competitive	Competitivo/a	Sympathetic	Comprensivo/a
	Daring	Atrevido/a	Gentle	Delicado/a
	Aggressive	Agresivo/a	Sensitive	Sensible
Alpha	.81		.74	
Negative personality	Egotistical	Egocéntrico/a	Fussy	Quisquilloso/a
	Dictatorial	Autoritario/a	Complaining	Protestón/a
	Greedy	Ambicioso/a	Whiny	Quejica
	Arrogant	Arrogante	Nagging	Criticón/a
	Boastful	Pretencioso/a		
Alpha	.72		.73	
Cognitive	Mathematical	Matemático/a	Expressive	Expresivo/a
	Analytical	Analítico/a	Creative	Creativo/a
	Quantitatively skilled	Habilidoso/a	Intuitive	Intuitivo/a
	Good with numbers	Bueno/a con los números	Artistic	Artístico/a
	Good at problem solving	Bueno/a resolviendo problemas	Imaginative	Imaginativo/a
Alpha	.72		.85	

Our questionnaire is partly based on that of Diekman and Eagly (2000). The original questionnaire was translated into Spanish by a native Spanish speaker with excellent knowledge of English. The instrument was then back translated in English by another person of equivalent language skills, and compared with the original English version. Any inconsistencies were resolved by a third native Spanish speaker familiar with the research objectives.

RESULTS

We conducted mixed analyses of variance (ANOVAs) Sex of target × Year × Population size × Gender of dimension (masculine vs. feminine) for each gender-stereotypic dimension (i.e., positive personality, negative personality, and cognitive). We used an alpha level of 0.05 in all analyses. Results of the analyses are reported in Table 3. For all the dependent measures, the inclusion of participants' sex, age, and student/non-student status in the analyses did not systematically influence the pattern of results, which is consistent with previous findings (e.g., Diekman & Eagly, 2000; López-Zafra & Garcia-Retamero, 2009a; Wilde & Diekman, 2005). The main effects of the independent variables are uninformative and should be interpreted in the context of higher order interactions, detailed below.

Table 3. ANOVA Table

Source	df	F ratios for each dimension			
		Positive Personality	Negative Personality	Cognitive	Physical
Sex of target (A)	1	7.23**	8.60**	0.47	0.74
Year (B)	2	28.09***	1.04	38.00***	3.53*
Population size (C)	2	3.68*	1.77	1.12	13.06***
Gender of dimension (D)	1	0.91	0.64	0.64	17.93***
A × B	2	6.35**	7.47***	3.43*	21.22***
A × C	2	4.28*	2.44*	8.25***	0.26
A × D	1	151.00***	153.58***	62.93***	139.25***
B × C	4	1.95	2.05	0.81	0.62
B × D	2	11.86***	9.82***	3.03*	13.07***
C × D	2	11.69***	10.66***	5.53**	4.13*
A × B × C	4	0.21	1.68	0.80	0.73
A × B × D	2	21.47***	20.24***	12.49***	69.94***
A × C × D	2	45.48***	10.04***	4.95**	2.32
B × C × D	4	0.53	0.14	1.79	1.60
A × B × C × D	4	1.37	0.73	1.00	0.17
Within-group error	353				

Note. The within-group error is the mean square error.
*p < .05, **p < .01, ***p < .001

Supporting the perceived convergence of male and female gender-stereotypic attributes with the passage of time (hypothesis 1), the interaction effects between sex of the target and year were significant on all dimensions, $p < .05$. These interactions were moderated by gender of dimension —reflected in the interactions including Sex of target × Year × Gender of dimension, $p < .001$— demonstrating that perceived differences between male and female targets varied over time on the feminine and masculine gender-stereotypic dimensions.

Supporting the perceived convergence of male and female gender-stereotypic attributes with the increasing population size of participants' places of residence (hypothesis 2), the interaction effects between sex of the target and population size were significant on all dimensions, $p < .05$. The significant two-way interactions were moderated by gender of dimension —reflected in the interactions by Sex of target × Population size × Gender of dimension, $p < .01$— showing that perceived differences between male and female targets varied as a function of the residents' population size on the feminine and masculine gender-stereotypic dimensions.

Finally, providing evidence that variations in perceptions of gender-stereotypic attributes over years are similar for all participants —regardless of the residents' population size (hypothesis 3)— the four-way interaction between all variables or interactions that include year and population size were not significant on any dimension, $p > .10$.

In the following, we examined more precisely the above mentioned significant three-way interactions as they have important theoretical implications. We first inspect the Sex of target × Year × Gender of dimension interactions; then, the Sex of target × Population size × Gender of dimension interactions are examined. Results are reported for each dependent variable separately. We conducted trend analyses to describe the shape and direction of the means (Keppel, 1991).

Interaction between Sex of Target, Year, and Gender of Dimension

Positive personality dimension. Participants perceived female targets as increasing substantially in masculine positive personality attributes across years, whereas male targets were perceived as remaining stable. In contrast, participants perceived female targets as stable across years in feminine positive personality attributes and male targets as increasing (see Figure 1). Consistent with these ideas, the significant Target Sex × Year linear interaction in masculine, $F(1, 365) = 88.14, p < .001$, and feminine positive personality, $F(1, 365) = 7.36, p = .01$, indicated that the linear trends over years differed for male and female targets on the positive personality dimensions. Simple effects analyses within levels of target sex revealed only a significant linear increase for female targets in masculine positive personality, $F(1, 190) = 78.62, p < .001$, and for male targets in feminine positive personality, $F(1, 175) = 6.25, p = .013$.

Negative personality dimension. Similar to the previous results, participants perceived female targets as increasing in masculine negative personality attributes across years. Male targets were perceived as remaining stable with the passage of time in masculine negative attributes as well. In contrast to previous results, female targets were perceived as decreasing in feminine negative personality attributes across years, whereas male targets were perceived as increasing (see Figure 2). The significant effects in the trend analyses were a Target Sex × Year linear interaction in masculine, $F(1, 365) = 20.33, p < .001$, and feminine negative personality, $F(1, 365) = 35.26, p < .001$; a linear increase for female targets in masculine negative personality, $F(1, 190) = 26.95, p < .001$, and for male targets in feminine negative personality, $F(1, 175) = 10.06, p = .001$; and a linear decrease for female targets in feminine negative personality, $F(1, 190) = 26.95, p < .001$.

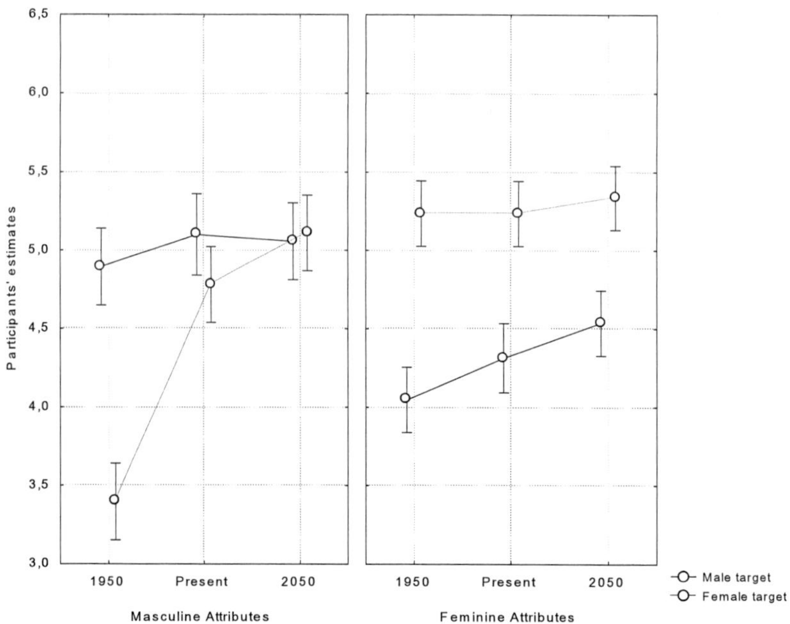

Figure 1. Estimates of the target's masculine and feminine attributes for the positive personality dimension in 1950, present, and 2050. Vertical bars denote .95 confidence intervals.

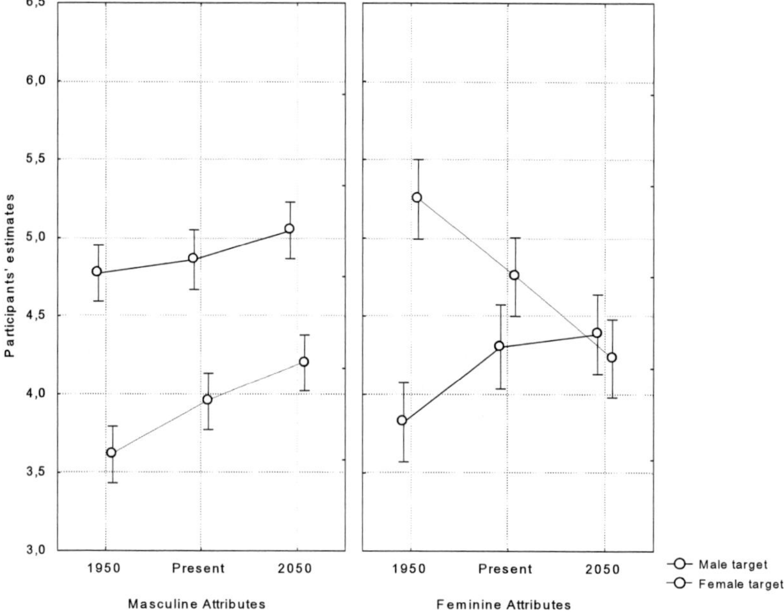

Figure 2. Estimates of the target's masculine and feminine attributes for the negative personality dimension in 1950, present, and 2050. Vertical bars denote .95 confidence intervals.

Cognitive dimension. Both male and female targets were perceived to increase in masculine and feminine cognitive attributes with the passage of time. The increase, however, was larger in female targets on the masculine cognitive dimension and in male targets on the feminine cognitive dimension (see Figure 3). Consistent with this result, the significant effects in the trend analyses were a Target Sex × Year linear interaction in the masculine, $F(1, 365) = 9.73$, $p = .001$, and feminine cognitive dimension, $F(1, 365) = 38.81$, $p < .001$, and a linear increase for male and female targets on both masculine cognitive, $F(1, 175) = 6.48$, $p = .012$ and $F(1, 190) = 52.18$, $p < .001$, respectively, and feminine cognitive dimensions, $F(1, 175) = 35.64$, $p < .001$ and $F(1, 190) = 10.60$, $p = .001$, respectively.

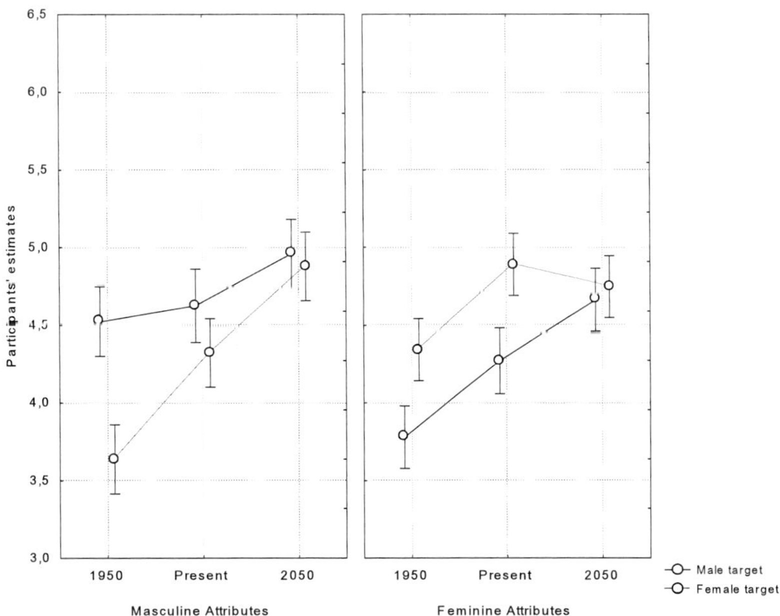

Figure 3. Figure 6. Estimates of the target's masculine and feminine attributes for the cognitive dimension in 1950, present, and 2050. Vertical bars denote .95 confidence intervals.

Interaction between Sex of Target and Population Size

Positive personality dimension. Female targets were perceived to decrease sharply in masculine positive personality attributes with the decrease of the residents' population size, whereas male targets were perceived to increase. On the contrary, female targets were perceived as increasing in feminine positive personality attributes with the decrease of the population size, whereas male targets were perceived as remaining stable (see Figure 4). In line with this result, the Target Sex × Population size linear interaction was significant on both, the masculine, $F(1, 365) = 44.57$, $p < .001$, and feminine positive personality dimension, $F(1, 365) = 15.81$, $p < .001$, indicating differences in linear trends for male and female targets over population size conditions. Simple effects analyses within levels of target sex revealed a significant linear increase for male targets on the masculine positive personality dimension, $F(1, 175) = 21.73$, $p < .001$, and female targets on the feminine positive personality dimension, $F(1, 190) = 69.05$, $p < .001$, and a significant linear decrease for female targets on the masculine positive personality dimension, $F(1, 190) = 24.50$, $p < .001$.

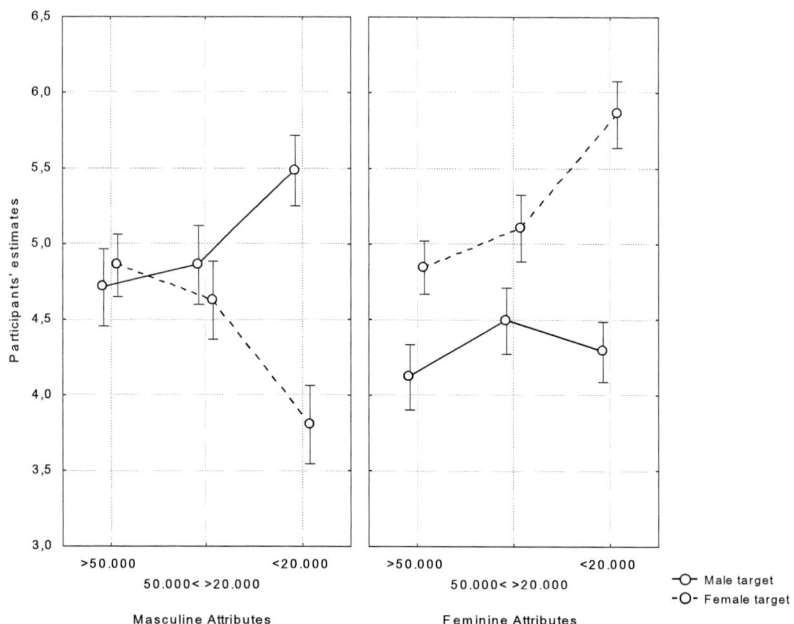

Figure 4. Estimates of the target's masculine and feminine attributes for the positive personality dimension for participants who lived in locations with less than 20.000 inhabitants, beween 20.000 and 50.000 inhabitants, and with more than 50.000 inhabitants. Vertical bars denote .95 confidence intervals.

Negative personality dimension. In line with results on the positive personality dimension, female targets were perceived as decreasing in masculine negative personality and increasing in feminine negative personality with the decrease of the resident's population size. Male targets, however, were perceived to be stable in both dimensions (see Figure 5). The significant effects in the trend analyses were a Target Sex × Population size linear interaction on the masculine, $F(1, 365) = 35.65$, $p < .001$, and feminine negative personality dimension, $F(1, 365) = 5.50$, $p = .02$; a linear decrease for female targets on the masculine negative personality dimension, $F(1, 190) = 37.68$, $p < .001$, and a linear increase for female targets on the feminine negative personality dimension, $F(1, 190) = 5.04$, $p = .03$.

Cognitive dimension. Participants perceived female targets as decreasing substantially in masculine cognitive attributes with the decrease of the population size, whereas male targets were perceived to be stable. Perceptions of male and female targets in feminine cognitive attributes, however, did not vary as a function of the resident's population size, with higher estimates for female than for male targets in all conditions (see Figure 6). Consistent with these ideas, only the Target Sex × Year linear interaction and the linear decrease for female targets on the masculine cognitive dimension were significant, $F(1, 365) = 27.09$, $p < .001$ and $F(1, 190) = 22.59$, $p < .001$, respectively.

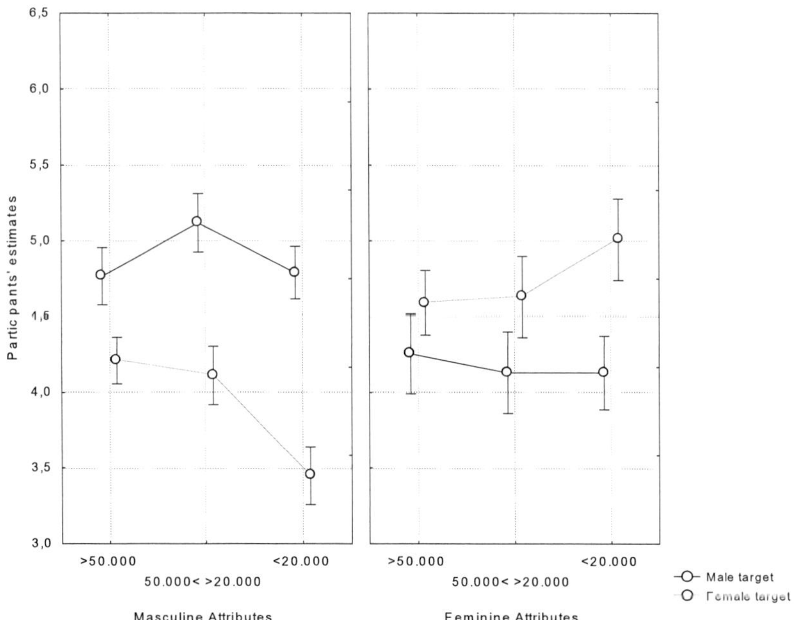

Figure 5. Estimates of the target's masculine and feminine attributes for the negative personality dimension for participants who lived in locations with less than 20.000 inhabitants, beween 20.000 and 50.000 inhabitants, and with more than 50.000 inhabitants. Vertical bars denote .95 confidence intervals.

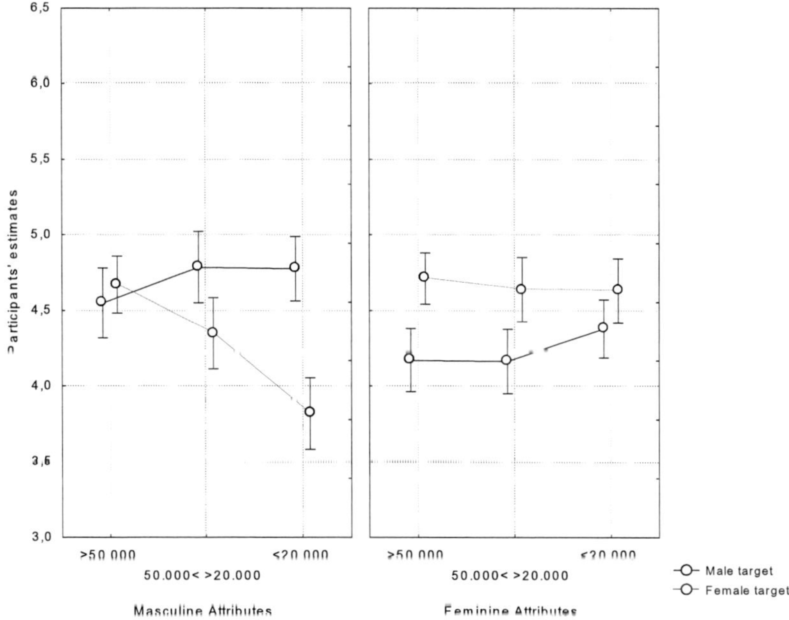

Figure 6. Estimates of the target's masculine and feminine attributes for the cognitive dimension for participants who lived in locations with less than 20.000 inhabitants, beween 20.000 and 50.000 inhabitants, and with more than 50.000 inhabitants. Vertical bars denote .95 confidence intervals.

GENERAL DISCUSSION

In our chapter, we analyzed the malleability of gender stereotypes over time in Spain, and focused on the influence of an important demographic variable —the population size of participants' residence. Results showed that women of the present were estimated to be more masculine than were women of the past, and that women of the future were expected to be more masculine than women of the present —especially in positive personality and cognitive attributes. Men, on the contrary, were believed to remain stable in masculine attributes; although there was a tendency for men to increase in masculine cognitive attributes over the years. Results also revealed that men were estimated to increase in feminine attributes on all dimensions; whereas women were expected to decrease in feminine negative personality, but to remain stable in feminine positive personality attributes. There was also a tendency for women to increase in feminine cognitive attributes over the years. In sum, participants believed that women are becoming more competitive, independent, dictatorial, rational, and mathematical as well as less complaining and sexy over time; whereas men are perceived to become more supportive, affectionate, intuitive, complaining, and gorgeous. Perceptions of men and women, therefore, tend to converge with the passage of time.

Perceptions of Spaniards about women are coherent with those in previous research in other countries such as the United States and Germany (see Diekman & Eagly, 2000; Wilde & Diekman, 2005). Stereotypes about women in all countries thus portrayed women as extremely dynamic (see also Koch, Luft, & Kruse, 2005; Sczesny, Bosak, Diekman, & Twenge, 2007; Twenge, 1997, 2001). Perceptions about men in our study, however, are in contrast to those in previous research —concluding that stereotypes about men are relatively unchanging. Interestingly, men in our study were perceived to increase in their feminine attributes substantially over time —especially from the present to the future. An explanation for this discrepancy could be that men in Spain have started entering roles considered suitable for women only recently (e.g., caretaking; Eurostat, 2006; Garcia-Retamero & López-Zafra, 2009a, 2009b), whereas changes in men's roles toward greater gender equality and less sex segregation in the United States and Germany is an ongoing process since the mid of the 20th century (Abele-Brehm, 2003; Sczesny et al., 2007). Spaniards, therefore, might perceive greater changes in men's feminine attributes than Americans or Germans. In fact, when both men and women are equally responsible for roles that are traditionally perceived suitable for men and women, they perceive themselves as more equal on feminine and masculine attributes (Cast & Bird, 2005; Harris, 1996).

Of special interest in our study is that all participants perceived an increase in the similarity of women's and men's attributes from the past to the present and from the present to the future. Yet, residents from less populated, urban areas (i.e., small regions with less than 20.000 inhabitants) perceived less similarity between women's and men's attributes than those who live in more populated, urban areas. These discrepancies occurred especially in personality attributes —including masculine and feminine attributes on the positive and negative personality dimension. Perceived differences between men and women in low- and highly-populated locations were also confined to cognitive masculine attributes. In sum, residents from less populated, rural areas believed that women are less competitive, independent, dictatorial, rational and quantitatively skilled than those from more populated, urban locations. The former residents also believed that women are more supportive, affectionate, and complaining, whereas men were believed to be more competitive and aggressive. Perceptions of men and women thus tend to converge with the passage of time, but in less populated, rural locations they are still short of equality.

To what extent do people who live in less populated, rural locations have an accurate theory of change in men's and women's gender attributes from the past to the present? Why do their beliefs differ from those who live in highly populated, urban areas? As Diekman and Eagly (2000, pp. 1185) pointed out, gender stereotypes are generally accurate descriptors of average current sex differences (see also Eagly & Diekman, 1997; Hall & Carter, 1999; Swim, 1994), and emerge from role-bound activities (Eagly, 1987). Differences in the division of roles between men and women in high and low populated areas are substantial in Spain (Castañeda, Sánchez, Quintana, & González, 2003; López-Zafra & Garcia-Retamero, 2009b). As lately as in 1998, the land of Spain was considered to be 80% rural, which means that it was mostly integrated by small, low populated towns and villages (Pichler, Shucksmith, Cameron, & Merridew, 2006). The traditional sectoral economy in these locations was mainly based on agriculture (Pichler et al., 2006). The strong male dominance of the Spanish rural labor market (Vaiou, 1996) leads women to remain in low-status positions (Prados, 1998), working as unpaid family assistants to a much greater extent — 13.4% compared to 1.7% in overall Spain— than in highly populated, urban areas (Garcia-Bartolomé, 2001; European Commission, 2000). Other working possibilities are only offered by accepting badly paid periodical jobs in the agro-food industries (Prados, 1998). To overcome the exclusion of the rural labor market, women in low populated areas have to gain a much higher education level compared to urban males and females and they have to be even more competitive and meritocratic (Navarro, 1999) —skills that are difficult to achieve for rural women. In sum, the division of labor between men and women in rural areas emphasizes the difficulties to reach gender equality when women try to enter a male dominated workforce (Mueller, Mulinge, & Glass, 2002.) Rural women, thus, face great obstacles progressing behind a certain level labor inequality, which makes them vulnerable to becoming targets of prejudice. In addition, the low education level of rural women —housewives are generally unschooled or only completed primary education level— also endorses gender stereotypes (see Sayadi & Calatrava-Requena, 2008 for recent evidence). In sum, traditionalist views and roles of men and women in less populated areas are a hindrance for gender equality.

Results in our study extend the literatures on the dynamic gender stereotypes, and are of particular importance for recent movements in rural areas supporting women's participation in the modernization process (Prados, 1999; Sayadi & Calatrava-Requena, 2008). It is important to stress action plans for rural women in Spain —providing possibilities that increase their level of education and promoting awareness for gender stereotypic beliefs and their consequences. Looking at the prognosis of our participants in general, the dynamic of gender stereotypes gives hope that the attitudes of people in small populations are just a retarded starting point for an ongoing movement. Action plans would most likely increase similarity in perceptions of men and women's attributes substantially.

Our research shows that young adults —ranging from 18 to 40— who live in less populated, rural locations have more gender-stereotypic beliefs about men and women than those who live in more populated, urban areas. Our research also proved that stereotypes about social groups are dynamic structures, which presumably reflect changes in women's roles toward greater equality and less sex segregation (Eagly, 1987; Eagly et al., 2000). Our experiment's strengths lie in an informative between-subjects design, a large sample size, and careful execution of the study. Although young adults constitute a relevant population for studying gender-stereotypic perceptions, these participants are younger and of higher education level but with less experience of life than the average population in Spain (Instituto Nacional de Estadística, 2008). It is an open question and an avenue for future research to explore whether people in different cohorts (e.g., older adults or teenagers) show similar gender stereotypes. As our study lacks the measurement of cultural values or gender roles, future research could also account for participants' values such as gender egalitarianism, individual improvement, or personal freedom. Similarly, perceived sex distributions for traditionally male-dominated or female-dominated occupations and household activities could be assessed (see López-Zafra et al., 2008, using a Spanish sample). An interesting research question would also be, whether the population size influences the perceptions of men and women within participants from different countries and to what extent these stereotypic perceptions are related to the modernization progress. Especially the role of women in rural change could benefit from such investigation, as the rural market strongly relies on women (Sayadi & Calatrava-Requena, 2008). The present findings seem to be a promising starting point for a cross-cultural analysis.

REFERENCES

Abele-Brehm, A. E. (2000). A dual-impact model of gender and career-related processes. In T. Eckes & H. M. Trautner (Eds.) *The developmental social psychology of gender* (361–388). Mahwah, NJ: Erlbaum.

Abele-Brehm, A. E. (2003). The dynamics of masculine-agentic and feminine-communal traits: Findings from a prospective study. *Journal of Personality and Social Psychology*, *85*, 768–776.

Ashmore, R. D. & Del Boca, F. K. (1979). Sex stereotypes and implicit personality theory: Toward a cognitive-social psychological conceptualization. *Sex Roles*, *5*, 219–248.

Camps, V. (1994). The changing role of women in Spanish society. *RSA Journal* CXLII:5452.

Cast, A. D. & Bird, S. R. (2005). Participation in 'non-traditional' spheres and the perspective-taking of husbands and wives. *Social Psychology Quarterly*, *68*, 143–159.

Castañeda, J., Sánchez, C., Quintana, D. & González, T. (2003). Razonamiento predictivo y contenidos sesgados: Un estudio con personas mayores de hábitat rural y urbano (Predictive reasoning and biased content: A study with older adults from rural/urban hábitat). *Cognitiva*, *15*, 67–82.

Cejka, M. A. & Eagly, A. H. (1999). Gender-stereotypic images of occupations correspond to the sex segregation of employment. *Personality and Social Psychology Bulletin*, *25*, 413–423.

Cousins, C. (1995). Women and social policy in Spain: The development of a gendered welfare regime. *Journal of European Social Policy*, *5*, 175–197.

Cuadrado, M. (1992). El desarrollo del mundo rural en España" (The development of rural Spain). *Informe Preliminar*, 1 & 2. IRYDA, Madrid.

Deaux, K. & Major, B. (1987). Putting gender into context: An interactive model of gender-related behavior. *Psychological Review, 94*, 369–389.

Diekman, A. B. & Eagly, A. H. (2000). Stereotypes as dynamic constructs: Women and men of the past, present, and future. *Personality and Social Psychology Bulletin, 26*, 1171–1188.

Diekman, A. B., Eagly, A. H., Mladinic, A. & Ferreira, M. C. (2005). Dynamic stereotypes about women and men in Latin America and the United States. *Journal of Cross-Cultural Psychology, 36*, 209–226.

Duran, M. A. & Gallego, M. T. (1986). The women's movement in Spain and the new Spanish democracy. In Daherup D. (Eds.) *The new women's movement: Feminism and political power in Europe and the USA* (200–216). London: Sage.

Eagly, A. H. (1987). *Sex differences in social behavior: A social-role interpretation.* Hillsdale, NJ: Lawrence Erlbaum.

Eagly, A. H. (2004). Few women at the top: How role incongruity produces prejudice and the glass ceiling. In van Knippenberg D. & Hogg M. A. (Eds.) *Identity, Leadership, and Power* (79–93). London: Sage.

Eagly, A. H. (2007). Female leadership advantage and disadvantage: Resolving the contradictions. *Psychology of Women Quarterly, 31*, 1–12.

Eagly, A. H. & Carli, L. L. (2003). The female leadership advantage: An evaluation of the evidence. *The Leadership Quarterly, 14*, 807–834.

Eagly, A. H. & Carli, L. L. (2007). *Through the labyrinth: The truth about how women become leaders.* Boston: Harvard University Business School Press.

Eagly, A. H. & Diekman, A. B. (1997). The accuracy of gender stereotypes: A dilemma for feminism. *Revue Internationale de Psychologie Sociale/International Review of Social Psychology, 10*, 11–30.

Eagly, A. H. & Karau, S. J. (2002). Role congruity theory of prejudice toward female leaders. *Psychological Review, 109*, 573–598.

Eagly, A. H., Karau, S. J. & Makhijani, M. G. (1995). Gender and the effectiveness of leaders: A meta-analysis. *Psychological Bulletin, 117*, 125–145.

Eagly, A. H. & Steffen, V. J. (1984). Gender stereotypes stem from the distribution of women and men into social roles. *Journal of Personality and Social Psychology, 46*, 735–754.

Eagly, A. H. & Wood, W. (1999). The origins of sex differences in human behavior: Evolved dispositions versus social roles. *American Psychologist, 54*, 408–423.

Eagly, A. H., Wood, W. & Diekman, A. B. (2000). Social role theory of sex differences and similarities: A current appraisal. Eckes T. & Trautner H. M. (Eds.) *The developmental social psychology of gender* (123–174). Mahwah, NJ: Erlbaum.

European Commission (2000). *Women active in rural development —Assuring the future of rural Europe.* Luxembourg: Office for Official Publications of the European Communities. Retrieved November 14, 2008 from http://ec.europa.eu/agriculture/publi/women/broch_en.pdf.

European Commission (2006). *Gender mainstreaming. A roadmap for equality between women and men 2006-2010. DG Employment, social affairs and equal opportunities, gender equality unit.* Retrieved October 14, 2008, from http://europa.eu.int/comm/employment_social/gender_equality/gender_mainstreaming/roadmap_en.html

Eurostat (2006). *8 March 2006: International women's day. A statistical view of the life of women and men in the EU25.* Retrieved April 10, 2006, from http://epp.eurostat.cec.eu.int/pls/portal/docs/PAGE/PGP_PRD_CAT_PREREL/PGE_CAT_PREREL_YEAR_2006/PGE_CAT_PREREL_YEAR_2006_MONTH_03/3-06032006-EN-BP1.PDF.

Eurostat (2008). *8 March 2008: International women's day. A third of managers are women.* Retrieved November 12, 2008, from http://epp.eurostat.ec.europa.eu/pls/portal/docs/PAGE/PGP_PRD_CAT_PREREL/PGE_CAT_PREREL_YEAR_2008/PGE_CAT_PREREL_YEAR_2008_MONTH_03/1-06032008-EN-AP.PDF

Garcia-Bartolomé, J. M. (2001). Mujeres, explotación familiar agraria y desarrollo rural (Women, familiar agricultural explotation and rural development). In *Jornadas para agentes de desarrollo local* (18). Cuenca: Diputación de Cuenca.

Garcia-Retamero, R. & López-Zafra, E. (2006a). Congruencia de rol de género y liderazgo: El papel de las atribuciones causales sobre el éxito y el fracaso" (Congruency between leadership and gender roles: Notes on causal attributions about success and failure). *Revista Latinoamericana de Psicología, 38,* 245–257.

Garcia-Retamero, R. & López-Zafra, E. (2006b). Prejudice against women in male-congenial environments: Perceptions of gender role congruity in leadership. *Sex Roles, 55,* 51–61.

Garcia-Retamero, R. & López-Zafra, E. (2008). Atribuciones causales sobre éxito y fracaso y percepción del liderazgo en la mujer (Causal attributions about success and failure, and perceptions of leadership in women). *Estudios de Psicología, 15,* 273–287.

Garcia-Retamero, R. & López-Zafra, E. (2009a). Causal attributions about feminine and leadership roles: A cross-cultural comparison. *Journal of Cross-Cultural Psychology, 40,* 492–509.

Garcia-Retamero, R. & López-Zafra, E. (2009b). Causal attributions about success and failure in female leaders. In J. H. Urlich & B. T. Cosell (Eds.), Handbook of *gender roles: Conflicts, attitudes and behaviors* (169–188). Hauppauge, New York: Nova.

Garcia-Retamero, R., Müller, S. M. & López-Zafra, E. (in press). The influence of gender stereotypes on causal attributions about successful leadership. *The International Journal of Psychology Research.*

Glick, P., Larsen, S., Johnson, C. & Branstiter, H. (2005). Evaluations of sexy women in low- and high-status jobs. *Psychology of Women Quarterly, 29,* 389–395.

Hall, J. A. & Carter, J. D. (1999). Gender-stereotype accuracy as an individual difference. *Journal of Personality and Social Psychology, 77,* 350–359.

Hamilton, D. L. (1981). *Cognitive processes in stereotyping and inter-group behavior.* Hillsdale, NJ: Erlbaum.

Hamilton, D. L. & Trolier, T. K. (1986). Stereotypes and stereotyping: An overview of the cognitive approach. In Dovidio, J. F. & Gaertner S. L (Eds.) *Prejudice, discrimination, and racism* (127–163). New York: Academic Press.

Hampel, B., Boldero, J. & Holdsworth, R. (1996). Gender patterns in environmental consciousness among adolescents. *Journal of Sociology, 32,* 58–71.

Harris, A. C. (1996). African American and Anglo-American gender identities: An empirical study. *Journal of Black Psychology, 22,* 182–194.

Hausmann, R., Tyson, L. D. & Zahidi, S. (2008). *The global gender gap report 2008.* Geneva: World Economic Forum.

Human Development Report (2006). *Beyond scarcity: Power, poverty and the global water crisis.* Retrieved November 30, 2006, from http://hdr.undp.org/hdr2006/pdfs/report /HDR06-complete.pdf

Hyde, J. S. (1985). *Half the human experience: The psychology of women* (3rd ed.). Lexington, MA: Heath.

Inglehart, R. (1997). *Modernization and postmodernization: Cultural, economic, and political change in 43 societies.* Princeton, NJ: Princeton University Press.

Instituto Andaluz de la Mujer (2007). Ley Orgánica para la igualdad efectiva de mujeres y hombres" (Framework Law for an effective equality between women and men). *Artículo 14: Una perspectiva de género: Boletín de información y análisis jurídico.* 24, Mayo de 2007.

Instituto de la Mujer (2008). *Mujeres y hombres en España 2007* (Men and women in Spain in 2007). Retrieved November 15, 2008 from http://www.mtas.es/mujer/mujeres/ estud_inves/index.htm.

Instituto Nacional de Estadística (2008). *Cifras oficiales de población* (Official population data). Retrieved November 11, 2008, from http://www.ine.es/inebmenu/ mnu_cifraspob.htm.

Jacobs, J. A. (1999). The sex segregation of occupations: Prospects for the 21st century. In Powell G. N. (Eds.) *Handbook of gender and work* (125–144). London: Sage.

Kanter, R. M. (1977). *Men and women of the corporation.* New York: Basic Books

Karsten, M. F. (1994). *Management and gender: Issues and attitudes.* Westport, Connecticut: Praeger.

Keppel, G. (1991). *Design and analysis: A researcher's handbook.* Englewood Cliffs, NJ: Prentice Hall.

Koch, S. C., Luft, R. & Kruse, L. (2005). Women and leadership —20 years later: A semantic connotation study. *Social Science Information, 44,* 9–39.

López-Zafra, E. & Garcia-Retamero, R. (2009a). *Perceptions about the dynamic aspect of gender stereotypes in Spain.* Manuscript under review.

López-Zafra, E. & Garcia-Retamero, R. (2009b). *Situación de las mujeres respecto a posiciones de liderazgo* (Women's roles in leadership positions). Jaén: Servicio de publicaciones de la Universidad de Jaén.

López Zafra, E., Garcia-Retamero, R., Diekman, A. B. & Eagly, A. H. (2008). Dinámica de estereotipos de género y poder: Un estudio transcultural (The dynamic of gender stereotypes and power: A cross-cultural study). *Revista de Psicología Social, 23,* 213–219.

MacArthur, L. Z. (1982). Judging a book by its cover: A cognitive analysis of the relationship between physical appearance and stereotyping. In Hastorf, A. H. & Isen, A. M. (Eds.) *Cognitive social psychology* (149–212). New York: Elsevier Science.

Marsden, T. K. (1996). Rural geography trend report: The social and political bases of rural restructuring. *Progress in Human Geography, 20,* 246–258.

Morant, I. (2006). *Historia de las mujeres en España y América Latina* (The history of women in Spain and Latin America). Madrid: Cátedra.

Mueller, C. W., Mulinge, M. & Glass, J. (2002). *Interactional processes and gender workplace inequalities.* Social Psychology Quarterly, *65, 163–185.*

Navarro, C. J. (1999). Women and social mobility in rural Spain. *Sociologia Ruralis, 39*, 222–235.

Pichler, F., Shucksmith, M., Cameron, S. & Merridew, T. (2006). *First European quality of life survey: Urban–rural differences*. Luxembourg: Office for Official Publications of the European Communities. Retrieved November 14, 2008 from http://www.eurofound. europa.eu/pubdocs/2006/63/en/1/ef0663en.pdf.

Powell, G. N., Butterfield, D. A. & Parent, J. D. (2002). Gender and managerial stereotypes: Have the times changed? *Journal of Management, 28*, 177–193.

Prados, M. J. (1998). *Rural women's participation in decision-making in Spain*. Paper presented at the Ninth Session of the Working Party on Women and the Family in Rural Development, Yerevan, Armenia, 30th September – 3rd October, 1998. Retrieved November 9, 2008 from http://www.fao.org/unfao/bodies/eca/wpw/9wpwspa.htm

Prados, M. J. (1999). Andalusian women and their participation in rural tourist trade. *Geojournal, 48*, 253–258.

Ridgeway, C. L. (2001). Gender, status, and leadership. *Journal of Social Issues, 57*, 637–656.

Royuela, V. & Suriñach, J. (2005). Constituents of quality of life and urban size. *Social indicators research, 74*, 549–572.

Sampedro, M. R. (1991). El mercado de trabajo en el medio rural: Una aproximación a través del género (The labor market in rural environments: A gendered approach). *Política y Sociedad, 8*, 25–33.

Sayadi, S. & Calatrava-Requena, J. (2008). Gender needs awareness and gender asymmetry: An analysis of a rural women survey in mountainous areas of south-eastern Spain. *Spanish Journal of Agricultural Research, 6*, 453–468.

Sczesny, S., Bosak, J., Diekman, A. B. & Twenge, J. M. (2007). Dynamics of sex-role stereotypes. In Kashima, Y. Fiedler, K. & Freytag, P. (Eds.) *Stereotype Dynamics: Language-Based Approaches to the Formation, Maintenance, and Transformation of Stereotypes* (135–161). Mahwah, NJ: Lawrence Erlbaum.

Sczesny, S., Bosak, J., Neff, D. & Schyns, B. (2004). Gender stereotypes and the attribution of leadership traits: A crosscultural comparison. *Sex Roles, 51*, 631–645.

Serrano, G., Godás, A., Rodríguez, D. & Mirón, L. (1997). A psychological profile of Spanish adolescents. *Psychology in Spain, 1*, 90–103.

Sia, T. L., Lord, C. G., Blessum, K. A., Thomas, J. C. & Lepper, M. R. (1999). Activation of exemplars in the process of assessing social category attitudes. *Journal of Personality and Social Psychology, 76*, 517–532.

Snyder, M. (1981). On the self-perpetuating nature of social stereotypes. In Hamilton, D. L. (ed.), *Cognitive processes in stereotyping and inter-group behavior* (183–212). Hillsdale, NJ: Erlbaum.

Spence, J. T., Helmreich, R. L. & Holahan, C. K. (1979). Negative and positive components of psychological masculinity and femininity and their relationships to self-reports of neurotic and acting out behaviors. *Journal of Personality and Social Psychology, 37*, 1673–1682.

Swim, J. K. (1994). Perceived versus meta-analytic effect sizes: An assessment of the accuracy of gender stereotypes. *Journal of Personality and Social Psychology, 66*, 21–26.

The Economist (2005). *The conundrum of the glass ceiling, 376 (8436)*, 67–69.

Treaty of Amsterdam (1997). Retrieved October 28, 2008, from http://www.eurotreaties.com/amsterdamtreaty.pdf.

Treaty of Rome (1957). Retrieved October 28, 2008, from http://www.treatyofrome.com/

Twenge, J. M. (1997). Changes in masculine and feminine traits over time: A meta-analysis. *Sex Roles, 36*, 305–325.

Twenge, J. M. (2001). Changes in women's assertiveness in response to status and roles: A cross-temporal meta-analysis, 1931-1993. *Journal of Personality and Social Psychology, 81*, 133–145.

Vaiou, D. (1996). Women's work and everyday life in southern Europe in the context of European integration. In Garcia-Ramon, M. D. & Monk, J. (Eds.) *Women of the European union. The politics of work and daily life* (61–73). London: Routledge.

Valiente, C. (1995). The power of persuasion: The instituto de la mujer in Spain. In McBride Stetson, D. & Mazur, A. G. (Eds.) *Comparative state feminism* (221–236). Thousand Oaks: Sage.

Valiente, C. (2003). The feminist movement and the reconfigured state in Spain (1970s-2000). In Banaszak, L. A. Beckwith, K. & Rucht, D. (Eds.) *Women's movements facing the reconfigured state* (30–47). New York: Cambridge University Press.

White, M. J. & White, G. G. (2006). Implicit and explicit occupational gender stereotypes. *Sex Roles, 55*, 259–266.

Wilde, A. & Dickman, A. B. (2005). Cross-cultural similarities and differences in dynamic stereotypes: A comparison between Germany and the United States. *Psychology of Women Quarterly, 29*, 188–196.

Williams, J. E. & Best, D. L. (1990). *Measuring sex stereotypes: A multination study*. Beverly Hills, CA: Sage.

Williams, J. E., Satterwhite, R. C. & Best, D. L. (1999). Pancultural gender stereotypes revisited: The five factor model. *Sex Roles, 40*, 513–525.

Wood, W. & Eagly, A. H. (2002). A cross-cultural analysis of the behavior of women and men: Implications for the origins of sex differences. *Psychological Bulletin, 128*, 699–727.

Chapter 5

GENDER AND ETHICS IN QUALITATIVE INTERVIEWING: RESEARCH RELATIONSHIPS IN THE CONTEXT OF A STUDY OF INFERTILITY IN PORTUGAL

Helena Machado [a] *and Susana Silva* [b]

[a] Research Centre for the Social Sciences and Department of Sociology,
University of Minho, Portugal
[b] Department of Hygiene and Epidemiology, Institute of Public Health (ISPUP) and
Cardiovascular R&D Unit, University of Porto Medical School, Portugal

ABSTRACT

This chapter seeks to understand the role of gender relations and gender identities in the context of doing qualitative research and their impacts in the ethics of conducting qualitative interviewing. This discussion is informed by the research experience of two female researchers related with two different studies, with a particular focus on the process of conducting qualitative interviews with women and men in Portugal who had been medically diagnosed with infertility. Our aim is to focus on two main topics related to gender and ethics in the research relationships, in the context of studying infertility. First, the gender of the participant in the study: should we have interviewed women, men or couples? Should the interviewer be a woman or a man? Second, the construction of local ethics: is there a need for local ethical guidelines for researchers who use qualitative research in infertility? We will explore the emotions that we have experienced when doing qualitative research about infertility, illustrating that with empirical examples from our fieldwork. Those feelings were particularly acute due to two main factors: in the presence of social and gender inequalities (e.g., socioeconomic, professional and geographic inequalities in the access to fertility drugs for ovarian stimulation and women's physical and emotional discomfort within the fertility treatments); and by the fact that one of the researchers was confronted by some of the participants in the study with questions about her own fertility and her fulfillment of the role of being a mother. We call for a feminist research methods training program that takes into account the social, cultural, ethical and professional local contexts where the daily research relationship occurs.

INTRODUCTION

This paper seeks to understand the role of gender relations and gender identities in the context of doing qualitative research and their impacts in the ethics of conducting qualitative interviewing. This discussion is informed by the research experience of two female researchers related with two different studies, with a particular focus on the process of conducting qualitative interviews with women and men in Portugal who had been medically diagnosed with infertility. We have developed two studies about infertility, independent of each other: Silva has conducted an analysis of processes of mutual shaping between medicine, technology, law and gender (Silva, 2008a), through the performing of interviews with women and men who have gone through personal experiences of medically assisted reproduction. She has conducted, transcribed and analysed the interviews herself. Machado participated in a study about the ways in which infertility is a condition that can compromise both individuals' and families' sense of well-being and the extent to which this varies according to different gendered expectations (Machado & Remoaldo, 2008). She was a member of an interdisciplinary team and a young female researcher was hired to conduct interviews, under the supervision of senior researchers. This meant that Machado didn't interact with the individuals who participated in the study, but she was involved in content analysis of the data gathered with the interviews. In addition she was asked to participate in the process of selecting the interviewer, having to decide the gender of the person to hire. The type and level of involvement in the conduct of qualitative interviews was different for Silva and Machado. However, we believe that both shared some common concerns relative to the issues of gender and ethics in qualitative interviewing in the context of infertility. Thus, we have decided to produce a joint paper with the results of our mutual reflexivity.

We join the call for an embodied research (Reich, 2003; Dickson-Swift *et al.*, 2009) and an ethics-in-context approach in sociology (Riessman, 2005). It means that the research relationships in the infertility studies domain are constructed on the basis of gender identities and social relationships in which women and men live and act (Crow & Pope, 2008) and that researchers' emotions and feelings should enter into reflections about research ethics. Researchers can face many challenges and carry emotional costs while undertaking qualitative research, and feminist research methods may be particularly influential on them (*e.g.* Campbell, 2002; Johnson & Clarke, 2003; Dickson-Swift *et al.*, 2007, 2009; Sampson *et al.*, 2008). The research experiences reported here aim to contribute to the sparse empirical work around these dilemmas, namely at the following levels: disclosure and reciprocity, listening to untold stories, reflexivity and management of emotions.

In this chapter our aim is to focus on two main topics related to gender and ethics in the research relationships, in the context of studying women's and men's accounts on infertility or involuntary childlessness. The first issue concerns the gender of the participant in that sort of study. Should we have interviewed women, men or couples? Should the interviewer be a woman or a man? In the two studies that are the basis of our discussion about the role of gender relations and gender identities in doing qualitative research and their impacts in the ethics of interviewing, most of the men who participated were interviewed together with their wives, and the interviewers were females. Is it possible that this context of interview might have restrained the male participants' speeches and emotional repertoires? This might be the case, if we take into consideration that men tend to be socialized to silence their emotions and anxieties, in particular in the presence of their wives, as a way of being protective of their female companions (Webb & Daniluck, 1999; Throsby & Gill, 2004; Machado & Remoaldo, 2008; Silva & Machado, 2008). This context of interview supports the understanding of the processes by which the social relationships and gender identities are deployed to construct meanings and to provide significance to personal experiences in the context of infertility (Hertz, 1995; Walzer & Oles, 2003).

The construction of local ethics is our second subject of reflection. Is there a need for local ethical guidelines for researchers who use qualitative research in infertility? The regulatory frameworks, legislation provisions and guidelines for ethical scientific procedures and guidance have been constructed worldwide over the last four decades (Montgomery & Oliver, 2009). However, those ethical considerations neglect the emotional costs that emerge from doing qualitative research about the experiences within infertility. We will explore the emotions that we have experienced when doing qualitative research about infertility, illustrating "ethically important moments" (Guillemin & Gillam, 2004) in doing research with empirical examples proceeding from our fieldwork. Those significant emotions and feelings were particularly acute due to two main factors: in the presence of social and gender inequalities (*e.g,.* socioeconomic, professional and geographic inequalities in the access to fertility drugs for ovarian stimulation and women's physical and emotional discomfort within the infertility treatments); and the fact that Silva was confronted by some of the participants in her study of infertility with questions about her own fertility and her personal fulfillment in the role of being a mother.

The Sociological Studies of Infertility in Portugal

The first sociological studies undertaken in Portugal about infertility concern two academic works: one MA thesis on Sociology of Family and one PhD thesis on Sociology, whose titles could be translated into English as "Women call the storks: Family, procreation and bioethics in the public space" (Garcia, 1995), and "Infertility and medically assisted reproduction in Portugal: From private problems to public issues" (Augusto, 2004). In the first case, Garcia analysed the ethical, normative and juridical construction of the social uses of assisted reproductive technologies in Portugal. In the second case, Augusto identified the main frameworks in which the production of meanings and claims of expertise about infertility were produced in Portugal, drawing on interviews with doctors and couples involved in fertility treatments. Besides the two mentioned studies, the Research Group on Science, Technology and Society (Center for Social Studies, School of Economics, University of Coimbra, Portugal) has undertaken work about the regulation of "reprogenetics"[1], with a particular emphasis on the emergence of new social actors and new forms of public participation in this domain (Nunes & Matias, 2004; Santos & Nunes, 2006).

More recently, the authors of this text have studied the social images of infertility in Portugal from the understanding of the experiences and representations of infertile couples, based on two different studies, in which each researcher was involved. Machado was a

---

[1] In this context, the concept of reprogenetics comprises the research on human genetic, nuclear transfer and stem cell technologies, preimplantations genetic profiling, human embryonic stem cell alteration and germ line therapy (Nunes & Matias, 2004).

member of an interdisciplinary team (involving one geographer, one sociologist, and three physicians), whose research aim was to analyse the clinical, sociocultural and economic dimensions taken into account by infertile contemporary couples of a Northwestern Portuguese municipality, Guimarães[2] (Machado & Remoaldo, 2008; Remoaldo & Machado, 2008). Silva carried out a PhD thesis concerned with the recent processes of mutual shaping of medicine, technology, law and gender within the assisted reproductive technologies in Portugal, with a primary focus on interactions between expert and lay knowledge, informed consent and rhetoric devices related to donation of eggs, sperm and embryos[3] (Silva, 2008a, 2008b; Silva & Machado, 2008, 2009a, 2009b).

To map out a relevant social issue which remains clearly under-studied in Portugal, such as the usually silenced women's and men's accounts of their experiences of infertility or involuntary childlessness, requires time, patience and determination; and calls for the combination of a variety of methods. In the two linked studies on infertility in Portugal in which this chapter is grounded, we used a qualitative and interpretative approach (Olshansky, 1996; Alderson, 2001; Becker & Bryman, 2004; Liamputtong & Ezzy, 2005), based on forty-five semi-structured interviews to women and men who had been medically diagnosed with infertility. These studies gathered the participation of nineteen heterosseuxual couples, twenty-five women and one man, taking place between June 2005 and February 2006. The participants in these studies were all Portuguese, heterosexual, married and white. The most common age group was the 30 to 34 years of age, with the lowest limit of the age range being a woman of 26 and the upper limit a man of 54. When it comes to family income, twelve of the forty-five couples had less than 1000€/month and fourteen made 2500€ or more a month. The modal group regarding level of education was the individuals with six years of education, in women (n=14) as well as in men (n=12). Eleven women and four men had a university degree.

These two studies were funded by the Foundation for Science and Technology (FCT - Portuguese Ministry of Science, Technology and Higher Education). When we submitted to FCT these qualitative research proposals we stated our engagement in informative and mutually respectful interactions (Sandelowski & Barroso, 2003), and explained the benefits to those individuals participating in our studies (Dickson-Swift *et al.*, 2007: 328). These proposals were evaluated by a panel of international and national experts, who implicitly approved their ethical scientific norms and conducts. We didn't need to obtain approval from a research ethics committee for conducting these studies on patients' accounts on infertility. This facilitative approach to ethics review may be seen as an attempt to engage and support qualitative researchers in their studies, while respecting legal and professional ethical guidelines (Connolly & Reid, 2007). In the end of 2008 the FCT opened a call for projects in all scientific domains, and it was the first time that principal investigators were asked to sign a Declaration of Intent that takes into account the European regulations concerning the donation, procurement, testing, processing, preservation, storage and distribution of human tissues and cells. The spread of 'ethical guidelines' from medical to social research is an

---

[2] The project *The characterization of infertility in Guimarães (Northwest of Portugal)*, coordinate by the geographer Paula Remoaldo, was funded by the Portuguese Foundation for Science and Technology (POCTI/DEM/44483/2002) and it was developed between June 2004 and October 2005.

[3] Silva's PhD thesis entitled *Doctors, jurists and lay people: a study of the social images of the medically assisted reproduction*, got a grant from the Portuguese Foundation for Science and Technology and was developed between April 2004 and July 2008 (doctoral fellowship SFRH/BD/10396/2002).

important issue affecting contemporary sociological relationships in United Kingdom (Aldred, 2008), but at the present time that is not a major concern in Portuguese sociological academia.

The institutional ethical guidelines that frame the professional and research activities of the sociologists working in Portugal are twofold. First, the Act on the Protection of Personal Data (Act 67/98 of 26 October), that transposed into the Portuguese legislation the European norms on the protection of people with regard to the processing of personal data and on the free movement of such data. The National Commission of Data Protection is the Portuguese Authority endowed with the power to supervise and monitor compliance with the laws and regulations in the area of personal data protection. Second, The Code of Ethics of the Portuguese Sociological Association that is very similar to the Code of Ethics of the International Sociological Association. These ethical codes serve only as general guidelines and tend to focus on the researcher-researched dyad (Aldred, 2008) and attend primarily to one side of the dialogue in developing guidelines for human subjects' protection – the researched protection and risk management concerns (Connolly & Reid, 2007). However, conducting qualitative interviews can unsettle a researcher, who may experience emotions that are sometimes difficult to bear (Riessman, 2005), and can involve complex and shifting social and political relations with a focus on gender, power and organizations (Aldred, 2008), as highlighted by feminist critics over the past few decades (*e.g.* Oakley, 1981; Tang, 2002).

The Gender of the Participant in the Study

Relatively little work has been done to get inside the men's accounts of their experiences of infertility and involuntary childlessness (Thorsby & Gill, 2004). Llyod (1996: 433-435) analysed the arguments used both by women, men and researchers to justify the lack of participation of men in studies of infertility. He concluded that this absence of information had two main meanings: women and men have gender identities that shape their different reactions to infertility, seen as a problem especially by women; and hegemonic societal norms and values link male fertility with male virility, and sexual performance (also see Webb & Daniluk, 1999; Thorsby & Gill, 2004).

In our research experience, we faced the sub-representation of the men's discourses; while in the study conducted by Silva only one man was interviewed alone, in the study that has involved the participation of Machado, all men were interviewed in couple. In the study conducted by Silva the interviewer was herself, a woman in her early thirties; while in the study in which Machado has participated the team has decided to hire a female interviewer, in her late twenties. Machado had to interview a man and a woman who applied to the position of interviewer in the study of infertility. She decided to hire a woman by assuming that the interaction between the interviewer and potential respondents would be facilitated insofar as most studies on the subject of infertility have been mostly directed to middle and high class female participants, thus reproducing the stereotyped infertile patient: middle or upper-middle class white women, in her thirties (Cussins 1996). Is it possible that this context of interview might have restrained the male participants' speeches and emotional repertoires? Probably this might be the case. In both studies, men seem to develop a positive reconstruction regarding the 'threat' of infertility, reconfiguring some comically situations associated with the medical and technical procedures involved in the fertility treatments, through the redefinition of life priorities and by deleting their emotions (Machado & Remoaldo, 2008; Silva & Machado, 2008). Female researchers conducting interviews with couples about their accounts of infertility may offer a potentially strong basis to understand the processes by which the social relationships and gender identities are deployed to construct meanings and to provide significance to personal experiences in the context of infertility or involuntary childlessness (Hertz, 1995).

Both women and men have subjectivities and emotional lives that they bring to research relationships (Riessman, 2005: 476). For instance, one female interviewee talked about her perceptions concerning her husband' feelings within fertility treatments — according to the narrative of this woman, these treatments "disturbed" her husband, who felt a "little frustration" for being father of an IVF child. This female interviewee stated that this was not an issue of conversation between the couple, and invited her own husband to talk about his feelings in the course of the interview, showing that gender norms are among the cultural values that mediate how women and men talk about their experiences of fertility treatments (*e.g.*, Becker, 2000; Inhorn & Balen, 2002; Thompson, 2005):

> She: I think that it [IVF] disturbs him. He doesn't talk about it with me. He tries to take these things for fun. (…) Personally, I think that he feels a little frustration for not making the child in the normal way. (…) I would like to hear him talk about it. (…)
> He: I had not properly imagined that my sons would happen like that, do you understand? And, for me, it was the moment of making love and, as a consequence, the birth of a child.

At the end of an interview with a couple, the thirty-three-years-old white man said good-bye to the female interviewer and when he was alone with her he said that he would like to talk without the presence of his younger wife. Silva asked him why he didn't speak in front of his wife and he answered: *She is already so fragile. I need to protect her.* This male interviewee seems to silence his emotions and anxieties in the presence of his wife, as a way of protecting her, but he opens the door to talk about them with another woman—the interviewer. Unfortunately, Silva didn't have the opportunity to conduct this second interview, because the male interviewee emailed her 15 days after the first interview, saying that his wife was pregnant without any fertility treatment. According to his words, due to this confirmed pregnancy a second individual interview was no longer relevant. When Silva read this e-mail, she asked herself why that pregnancy is used as an argument to cancel an individual interview about men's experience of infertility, and her first thought was that it was possible that this male interviewee disclosed information that he may regret (Oakley, 1981; Kavle, 1996: 116).

Silva still remembers an acute feeling of exhaustion in the end of an individual interview with a woman who was crying uncontrollably during the first five minutes of the interview. This research relationship was well succeed because it was possible to establish an empathy between interviewer and interviewee, grounded on mutual understanding and availability to look at and heard the interviewee. This female interviewee became so upset that Silva turned off the tape recorder and gave her hand to the interviewee. As many others qualitative researchers, we think that it is very important to respond to the interviewees as human beings, touching them and offering support (Dickson-Swift *et al.*, 2007: 336). After these intense emotional moments, the female interviewee justified her reaction, saying that she wanted to believe that she will be a mother of a biological child despite her age, highlighting the distinction between women and men in this domain:

> For me, this is a kind of delicate issue. (...) Why? I am 36 years-old and I still have not lost hope. (...) Do you understand? That's it! Because there is a clock and if we aren't on time, the time finishes! (...) That must be different for a man. Women have that timing: it happens or after [the time] it's over. (...) I have never talked about this. (...) If I do it [talk about fertility treatments], it means that I don´t have any hope. Do you understand me?

Silva raised two main concerns related to the research relationship in this situation: she enters into the female interviewee's life at a time of anxiety and stress, and it was the first time that this female interviewee talks about her experience of infertility (Liamputtong & Ezzy, 2005; Dickson-Swift *et al.*, 2007). We must also reflect about the impact of the personal characteristics of the interviewer on the discourse of this interviewee (*e.g.* Haraway, 1991; Tang, 2002; Ortiz, 2005). Like the interviewee, the interviewer was a woman in her thirties, who may also felt the burden of the female age and the need to foster hope (elements that "should be different" for men). Silva believes that her gender helped the female interviewee to feel understood. Being a female interviewer was important in developing this collaborative relationship, and in gaining acceptance into this woman' private world. Unlike the interviewee — a civil engineering —, the interviewer was a social scientist interested in the study of the experiences of infertile couples in Portugal, who should understand the differences between the male and female views and feelings within the fertility treatments. The social image of the researcher was constructed on the grounds of a woman in the reproductive age, whose study aims to help the infertile couples.

Like Silva, Machado also felt that the young researcher that conducted the interviewees was perceived as a person who could help the interviewees (Easterday *et al.*, 1991; Malin, 2002). This perception was grounded on the analysis of the interviewees' answers to the last two questions of the interview schedule: "What do you think about this interview?", and "Do you want to ask me anything else?". The interview process was described by most respondents as an opportunity to express feelings often concealed. In addition, the interview was seen as a sign that "someone" is interested by the problem of infertile couples in Portugal. At the same time that the researcher was perceived as someone who could also help infertile couples through dissemination of results, some of the interviewees have reconstructed that possibility as a way of turning active agents in helping other couples who share the same situation. One male interviewee has described his joy to participate in the study referring to it as a 'moral' imperative:

> I was very pleased to have been contacted for this study. This is an issue that concerns me very closely. I must confess that I think this is a very important study, and I had a moral obligation to participate. I thought that if I participate I might be helping someone who is in the same circumstances.

It also happened the disappointment with the interview from the part of two of the interviewed couples. One of the female interviewees described her frustration with the interview this way: "We thought you would offer us financial and medical support, anything that could help to solve our problem".

How to respond to what interviewees have said about their expectations towards our studies? We now look at this issue in turn.

Facing Social and Gender Inequalities

The interviewees' choices between public or private IVF clinics depended on economic, social and organizational elements, namely the following ones: the financial costs involved in the treatment; when the couple expected to start the treatment (some Portuguese public IVF clinics had a long waiting list); the kind of medical care they wished; the availability of psychological support; and their place of residence. The interviewees reported practices which they have developed to minimize the inefficiencies of the Portuguese health system concerning the fertility treatments' domain, such as: buying medication in Spain (where the fertility drugs were cheaper); benefiting from a health professional subsystem that financed fertility drugs or treatments; or choosing a clinic with ethical guidelines which were seen as more adequate to their own values. This last option was mentioned mainly in cases when the couple wanted to undergo a fertility treatment, under the condition that the medical intervention wouldn't cause cryopreservation of surplus embryos. The discourses of the interviewees about cryopreservation of embryos were usually accompanied by strong emotions (Silva & Machado, 2009b). In the course of one of the interviews with a couple, both man and woman referred to that fact that they didn't know what happened with two cryopreserved embryos they have originated eight years ago. They also added that any day it could happen that they would see someone similar to them in the street and they would wonder if that person could be the result of the implementation of one of those embryos in the uterus of an unknown woman. Together we reflected on the urgent need to regulate the fates of the human embryos in Portugal[4], and on the uncertainties that characterize the medical and technical procedures within the fertility treatments.

The accounts that we heard from the interviewers tended to correspond to stereotypical gender expectations. The female interviewees frequently used linguistic expressions of uncertainty, probability, blame and dependency. In order to ensure the confirmation of a successful pregnancy, women, and to a lesser extent men, experienced a disciplinary regime based on a sort of reproductive and sexual asceticism. This ruling of female embodiment is based on cultural representations of the physical capital of women as inexorably linked to their genetic capital, and also to men's genetic capital and reproductive track. Therefore, women and in particular their uterus become privileged spaces for classification and evaluation of women as "good" or "bad" reproductive bodies, as opposed to the prevailing vision of men who are never really "bad" reproductive beings (Ettorre, 2007). Either women or men have gender identities that structure their experiences and emotions in infertility treatments. These gendered identities are strongly rooted in some cultural assumptions such as the fact that women show more availability to medical assessment and seek advice and/or medical treatment sooner than men, the idea that it is the woman who has to publicly justify the absence of children and the (re)production of the stereotypes that women are physically

---

[4] When we conducted the interviews, there wasn't a legal framework on assisted reproductive technologies in Portugal. In July 2006 it became legal to donate 'surplus' or 'spare' embryos for another couple or for scientific research. In both situations, the IVF couples have to consent it expressly in writing.

and emotionally fragile human beings, unstable and moved by a natural impulse towards motherhood, and that men are strong and should silence their emotions (Machado & Remoaldo, 2008; Silva & Machado, 2008).

When we were confronted with a set of social and gender inequalities in access and use of medical care in the context of treatment of infertility, in Portugal, we felt the weight of sharing human experiences characterized by social injustices, physical and psychological suffering and stigmatization (Morse & Field, 1995). In a context in which "lay" citizens tended not to be represented in spaces of public debate and decision, we felt the heavy social responsibility to disseminate the experiences and views of women and men who attempted to conceive through medical assisted reproduction and to propose a set of measures that can help to achieve social justice and equal citizenship. This motivation – 'giving voice' to the 'voiceless' (in particular women) — strongly drives the feminist research agenda (Sampson *et al.*, 2008: 924).

We think that it is important to conceive local and global interventions in order to prevent the marketing of reproductive health and to invest on medical and technical procedures that respect women's bodies. In the case of Portugal, this means to guarantee an equal accessibility to fertility drugs for ovarian stimulation; to resist to the privatization of reproductive health care and to assure its quality and efficacy; and to promote affordable simplified reproductive technologies methods (Ombelet, 2008). It is also important to highlight how men can be incorporated in roles supportive of women's social well-being and reproductive health, revealing the male affectivity, the male emotions, and men's co-responsibility in shared projects of parenting.

Normative Reproduction: A Fertile Married Woman and a Healthy Biological Child

The interviewees' discourses reproduced the dominant expectations and cultural beliefs regarding the normal boundaries of expected social behaviours concerning motherhood and fatherhood, that is, couples who are able to conceive and/or generate a healthy child with whom they maintain bio-genetic ties. The reluctance in adopting a child with certain characteristics (for example, older children, children with health problems, non-caucasian children, or even the adoption of two or more children simultaneously) tended to be framed by the interviewees in a context where their personal rights regarding procreation were found to prevail, as well as a possible reflection of a dominant cultural belief which promotes the child's status as the property of adults and not as desired company (Strickler, 1992. 125). One of the interviewed women, for example, had adopted a child and emphasized throughout the interview the importance that this was a healthy child. At the end of the interview she asked Silva if she had any children of her own, to which she replied affirmatively. Confronted with this answer, the interviewee wanted to know if everything went well and if the interviewer had waited "a long time" for her child:

> Respondent: When they are your own biological children and they are born, we are not going to reject your own children for being handicapped or for having other problems. (...) Since I'm already adopting a child, I would rather have a perfect child, because any mother, if

she knows she is going to have a handicapped child, she would not want it right? We all want our children to be perfect. (...)

Interviewer: Would you like to ask me anything?

Respondent: I see that you are married [points to the ring on my left hand]. Do you have children?

Interviewer: Yes, I have one who will be two-years-old in November.

Respondent: But did it all go well? Didn't it take you too long waiting? [to reach a pregnancy]

Interviewer: It all went well.

In this sequence of questions it became evident to Silva the double standing she was assuming at that moment: the standing as a researcher and, simultaneously, the one of woman-wife-mother, whose adequacy to dominant reproductive behaviours was being assessed. If Silva appeared to correspond to one of the expectations of the idealized profile of a woman – she was married because she wore a ring on her left ring finger, two other fundamental elements seemed to be lacking: being able to conceive and give birth to a healthy child, with whom she maintained a bio-genetic tie. While Silva studied other people's reproduction and fertility, her own were equally present and questionable and it can be perceived as a context that ensures reciprocity in the research relationship (Liamputtong & Ezzy, 2005). However, when confronted with the sense of normative reproduction in the research relationship, several contradictory feelings emerged. Until this day Silva isn't sure if she should have said to the interviewee that "all went well" with the birth of her first child. In fact, the ultra-sound of the second trimester pregnancy exam revealed that her child's kidneys were dilated with what appeared to be multicystic dysplasia, which could have been life-threatening. The doctors detected a bilateral hydronephrosis when the child was 3 days old and submitted him to a surgical procedure at 10 days of age. At the time this interview was made, Silva took her son to frequent medical exams, some of them invasive and painful, for both of them. To collect data while married woman and mother of an unhealthy biological child had a significant impact on analyses the social images about normative reproduction (Reich, 2003).

At the present time, Silva is happy to talk about this personal aspect of her life, but when she conducted this qualitative interview, she intensely hated the stigmatized nature of how others projected meanings onto her baby's behaviors, mainly related to his *unhealthy* condition. At that time, Silva felt uncomfortable to share her personal story and she thought that her own research participant did not want to hear it. In this particular research relationship Silva applied an embodied interpretation that touches both 'head'/'thinking' and 'heart'/'feelings' aspects of emotion work (Todres & Galvin, 2008; Dickson-Swift *et al.*, 2009), and she 'makes problematic' issues that are problematic in her life (Lofland & Lofland, 1995: 13). Both women — the interviewer and the interviewee — display multiple meanings of intensive mothering (Bell, 2004), in ways that reveal how their embodied motherhood is mediated through dominant cultural and biomedical discourses about a healthy biological child.

Silva suffered a lot with the decision she took concerning to silence her personal story within the birth of her first child, due two main motives: she was asking to the interviewees to talk about their personal experiences, but she didn't want to share her lived experience; and some feminist writers advocate researchers' self-disclosure as good research practice (Oakley,

1981; Dickson-Swift *et al.*, 2007: 332-334). Silva felt very lonely in this particular decision-making process and formal ethical guidelines seem of limited help to sustain or not sustain her decision. She realized that she needed to know how to protect herself when undertaking qualitative interviewees with infertile women and men (Sampson *et al.*, 2008: 930).

CONCLUSION

In this chapter we conclude that it is important to conceive a feminist research methods training program that takes into account the social, cultural, ethical and professional local contexts where the daily research relationships occur. Via research relationships in the context of a study of infertility in Portugal we have learned ethical ways of conducting qualitative interviewing (Adams, 2008), developing a "relational ethics" (Ellis, 2007) and an "ethics of care" (Parry, 2004) where we act from our emotions and rationales and take responsibility for the consequences of our actions.

Drawing on Guillemin and Gillam (2004) reflexion, we think that it is important to use both "procedural ethics" and "ethics in practice" for dealing with "ethically important moments" in qualitative research. In our studies, some personal characteristics of the female interviewees could be beneficial as well as distressing to conduct interviews with women and men who conceived or tried to conceive a biological child by fertility treatments in Portugal — being a white married woman, sociologist and in her thirties seems to be beneficial, but being a mother of a unhealthy biological child was very disturbing.

We have intended to understand the ways in which research relationships within the study of infertility relate to social and individual constructions of well-being (Machado & Remoaldo, 2008), which in turn disclose articulated relations with social and cultural contexts of gender roles and conjugality, based on processes of essentialization of the yearning to procreate a healthy child, and mostly aimed at women.

ACKNOWLEDGMENTS

The two research projects upon which this chapter is based were funded by the Foundation for Science and Technology, Portuguese Ministry of Science, Technology and Higher Education (doctoral fellowship SFRH/BD/10396/2002 and research project POCTI/DEM/44483/2002).

REFERENCES

Act 67/98 of 26 October. *Data Protection Act.* http://www.cnpd.pt/english/bin/legislation/Law6798EN.HTM

Adams, T. E. (2008). A review of narrative ethics. *Qualitative Inquiry, 14(2),* 175-194.

Alderson, P. (2001). *On doing qualitative research linked to ethical healthcare.* London: The Wellcome Trust.

Aldred, R. (2008). Ethical and political issues in contemporary research relationships. *Sociology*, *42(5)*, 887-903.

Augusto, A. (2004). *Infertilidade e reprodução medicamente assistida em Portugal: Dos problemas privados aos assuntos públicos* [Infertility and medically assisted reproduction in Portugal: from private problems to public issues]. Covilhã, Universidade da Beira Interior, Portugal: PhD thesis in Sociology.

Becker, G. (2000). *The elusive embryo: How women and men approach new reproductive technologies*. Berkeley: University of California Press.

Becker, S. & Bryman, A. (Eds.) (2004). *Understanding research for social policy and practice: Themes, methods and approaches*. Policy Press: Bristol.

Bell, S. E. (2004). Intensive performances of mothering: a sociological perspective. *Qualitative Research*, *4(1)*, 45-75.

Campbell, R. (2002). *Emotionally involved: The impact of researching rape*. New York: Routledge.

Connolly, K. & Reid, A. (2007). Ethics review for qualitative inquiry: Adopting a values-based, facilitative approach. *Qualitative Inquiry*, *13(7)*, 1031-1047.

Crow, G. & Pope, C. (2008). Editorial foreword: The future of the research relationship. *Sociology*, *42(5)*, 813-819.

Cussins, C. (1996). Ontological choreography: agency through objectification in infertility clinics. *Social Studies of Science*, *26(3)*, 575-610.

Dickson-Swift, V. James, E. L. Kippen, S. & Liamputtong, P. (2007). Doing sensitive research: What challenges do qualitative researchers face? *Qualitative research*, *7(3)*, 327-353.

Dickson-Swift, V. James, E. L. Kippen, S. & Liamputtong, P. (2009). Researching sensitive topics: Qualitative research as emotion work. *Qualitative research*, *9(1)*, 61-79.

Easterday, L. Papademas, D. Schorr, L. & Valentine, C. (1991). The making of a female researcher: Role problems in fieldwork. In: R. Burgess (Eds). *Field research: A sourcebook and field manual* (62-67). London & New York: Routledge.

Ellis, C. (2007). Telling secrets, revealing lives: Relational ethics in research with intimate others. *Qualitative Inquiry*, *13(1)*, 3-29.

Ettorre, E. (2007). Genomics, gender and genetic capital: The need for an embodied ethics of reproduction. *Advances in medical sociology: Bioethical issues, sociological perspectives*, *9*, 245-261.

Garcia, J. L. (1995). *As mulheres telefonam às cegonhas: Família, procriação e bioética no espaço público* [Women call the storks: Family, procreation and bioethics in the public space]. Lisboa, ISCTE, Portugal: MA thesis in Sociology.

Guillemin, M. & Gillam, L. (2004). Ethics, reflexivity, and "ethically important moments" in research. *Qualitative Inquiry*, *10(2)*, 261-280.

Haraway, D. (1991). *Simians, cyborgs, and women: The reinvention of nature*. London: Free Association Books.

Hedgecoe, A. (2008). Research ethics review and the sociological research relationship. *Sociology*, *42(5)*, 873-886.

Hertz, R. (1995). Separate but simultaneous interviewing of husbands and wives: making sense of their stories. *Qualitative inquiry*, *1(4)*, 429-451.

Inhorn, M. & Balen, F. V. (2002). *Infertility around the globe: New thinking on childlessness, gender and reproductive technologies*. Berkeley: University of California Press.

Johnson, B. & Clarke, J. (2003). Collecting sensitive data: The impact on researchers. *Qualitative health research, 13*, 421-434.

Kvale, S. (1996). *Interviews: An introduction to qualitative research interviewing.* Thousand Oaks, CA: Sage Publications.

Liamputtong, P. & Ezzy, D. (2005). *Qualitative research methods.* South Melbourne: Oxford University Press.

Lloyd, M. (1996). Condemned to be meaningful: Non-response in studies of men and infertility. *Sociology of Health & Illness, 18(4)*, 433-454.

Lofland, J. & Lofland, J. (1995). *Analyzing social settings: A guide to qualitative observation and analysis.* Belmont, CA: Wadsworth Publishing.

Machado, H. & Remoaldo, P. (2008). Incomplete women and strong men: Accounts of infertility as a gendered construction of well-being. In: B. Harris, L. Gálvez, & H. Machado (Eds.) *Gender and well-being: Historical and contemporary perspectives.* Aldershot, Hampshire: Ashgate Publishing (forthcoming July 2009).

Malin, M. (2002). Made in Finland: Infertility doctors' representations of children. *Critical Public Health, 12(4)*, 291-308.

Montgomery, K. & Oliver, A. L. (2009). Shifts in guidelines for ethical scientific conduct: how public and private organizations create and change norms of research integrity. *Social Studies of Science, 39(1)*, 137-155.

Morse, J. M. & Field, P. A. (1995). *Qualitative research methods for health professionals.* Thousand Oaks, CA: Sage Publications.

Nunes, J. A. & Matias, M. (2004). *A regulatory void? Reprogenetics in Portugal* [report]. http://www.ces.uc.pt/nucleos/nects/media/documentos/STAGE_relatorio_1.PDF.

Oakley, A. (1981). Interviewing women: a contradiction in terms? In: H. Roberts (Eds.) *Doing feminist research* (30-61). London: Routledge & Kegan Paul.

Olshansky, E. F. (1996). Theoretical issues in building a grounded theory: Application of an example of a program of research on infertility. *Qualitative health research, 6(3)*, 394-405.

Ombelet, W. (2008). False perceptions and common misunderstandings surrounding the subject of infertility in developing countries. *European Society of Human Reproduction and Embryology Special Task Force on 'Developing Countries and Infertility', 1*, 8-11.

Ortiz, S. M. (2005). The ethnographic process of gender management: Doing the "right" masculinity with wives of professional athletes. *Qualitative Inquiry, 11(2)*, 265-290.

Parry, D. C. (2004). Understanding women's lived experiences with infertility. Five short stories. *Qualitative Inquiry, 10(6)*, 909-922.

Portuguese Sociological Association (s/d). *Código Deontológico* [Code of Ethics]. http://www.aps.pt/?area=000&marea=001&PHPSESSID=3332219f31eba1c161013aff61a520f3

Reich, J. A (2003). Pregnant with possibility: Reflections on embodiment, access, and inclusion in field research. *Qualitative sociology, 26(3)*, 351-367.

Remoaldo, P. & Machado, H. (2008). *O sofrimento oculto: Causas, cenários e vivências da infertilidade* [The hidden suffering: Causes, sceneries and experiences of infertility]. Porto, Portugal: Edições Afrontamento.

Riessman, C. K. (2005). Exporting ethics: A narrative about research in South India. *Health: An interdisciplinary journal for the social study of health, illness and medicine, 9(4)*, 473-490.

Sampson, H. Bloor, M. & Fincham, B. (2008). A price worth paying?: Considering the 'cost' of reflexive research methods and the influence of feminist ways of 'doing'. *Sociology, 42(5)*, 919-933.

Sandelowski, M. & Barroso, J. (2003). Writing the proposal for a qualitative research methodology Project. *Qualitative health research, 13(6)*, 781-820.

Santos, B. S. & Nunes, J. A. (2006). *Reinventing democracy: grassroots movements in Portugal*. London & New York: Routledge.

Silva, S. (2008a). *Médicos, juristas e "leigos": um estudo das representações sociais sobre a reprodução medicamente assistida* [Doctors, jurists and lay people: a study of the social images of the medically assisted reproduction]. Porto, Faculdade de Letras da Universidade do Porto, Portugal: PhD thesis in Sociology.

Silva, S. (2008b). Consentir incertezas: O consentimento informado e a (des)regulação das tecnologias de reprodução assistida [Consenting to uncertainties: Informed consent and (de)regulation of assisted reproductive technologies]. *Cadernos de Saúde Pública, 24(3)*, 525-534.

Silva, S. & Machado, H. (2008). The diagnosis of infertility: Patients' classification processes and feelings. *Medical Sociology online, 3(1)*, 4-14.

Silva, S. & Machado, H. (2009a). Trust, morality and altruism in the donation of biological material – the case of Portugal. *New genetics and society, 28(2)*, 103-118.

Silva, S. & Machado, H. (2009b). A compreensão jurídica, médica e "leiga" do embrião em Portugal: um alinhamento com a biologia? [The juridical, medical and "lay" understanding of embryo in Portugal: an alignment with biology?]. *Interface – Comunicação, Saúde, Educação, 13(30)*, 31-43.

Strickler, J. (1992). The new reproductive technology: Problem or solution?. *Sociology of Health & Illness, 14(1)*, 111-132.

Tang, N. (2002). Interviewer and interviewee relationships between women. *Sociology, 36(3)*, 703-721.

Thompson, C. (2005). *Making parents: The ontological choreography of reproductive technologies*. Cambridge, Massachusetts: The MIT Press.

Thorsby, K. & Gill, R. (2004). "It's different for men": Masculinity and IVF. *Men and Masculinities, 6(4)*, 330-348.

Todres, L. & Galvin, K. (2008). Embodied interpretation: A novel way of evocatively re-presenting meanings in phenomenological research. *Qualitative research, 8(5)*, 568-583.

Walzer, S. & Oles, T. P. (2003). Accounting for divorce: Gender and uncoupling narratives. *Qualitative Sociology, 26(3)*, 331-349.

Webb, R. & Daniluk, J. (1999). The end of the line: Infertile men's experiences of being unable to produce a child. *Men and Masculinities, 2(1)*, 6-25.

In: Feminism and Women in Leadership
Editor: Vicente Nardi, pp. 111-125

ISBN: 978-1-60876-270-5
© 2010 Nova Science Publishers, Inc.

Chapter 6

THE GENDER GAP IN PATENTING: A FEMINIST ISSUE PREVENTING ECONOMIC EQUALITY

Sue V. Rosser
Georgia Institute of Technology, Atlanta, Georgia, USA

ABSTRACT

In the United States, Japan, and many European countries, most research universities are placing increasing emphasis upon innovation, technology transfer and applied research. In all countries, across all sectors and in all fields, the percentage of women obtaining patents is not only less than their male counterparts but it is less than the percentage of women in science, technology, engineering, and mathematics (STEM) in the field in the country.

This raises several questions: First, what is the evidence that women aren't obtaining patents at the same rate as their male counterparts? Second, is this a feminist issue? Finally, what can we apply from feminist phase theories to close this gender gap in patenting?

What other problems and losses result from the boys' club that excludes women and results in a gender gap in patenting? First, women who are scientists lose. Second, science experiences a loss in attracting more individuals with creative ideas. Third, society loses because of fewer products.

Overall, both nationally and internationally, the gender gap in patents has shown some signs of closing over time. These studies provide some evidence for progression through the stages. Reaching the stage of inclusion seems distant, although some fields and sectors, such as the biotech start-ups, appear to be closer to inclusion.

INTRODUCTION

More than a year ago, a young male faculty member in a different department made me aware of a new issue, critical for women in science, of which I had previously been ignorant. When he first brought the issue of gender and patents to my attention, my reactions ranged from how boring to who cares? Fortunately the new faculty member was persistent, bringing up the issue again at a reception, when he bumped into me in the hall, and finally when he made an appointment to discuss it with me.

On some level, I wondered if my resistance came from the realization that a gender gap in patents would mean that women had been left out of the leading edge of science yet again. After more than 30 years of studying issues of women, science and technology, and working actively on the national and local levels (Rosser and O'Neil, 2002) to implement programs to increase the numbers of women scientists and engineers, I couldn't bear to recognize the old pattern of women achieving parity in one area, just as the men lead the shift to a new, different arena.

As a dean, of course, I felt obligated to take the research interests of my faculty member seriously. The more I looked into the gender gap in patents, the more I began to see that it represents a very critical issue for women in science today. Although I didn't know very much about patents, as a dean at a research I technological institution, I was keenly aware of the increasing significance of technology transfer and commercialization of science. In the United States, Japan, and many European countries, most research universities are placing increasing emphasis upon innovation and applied research. This results in blurring of boundaries between academia and industry. Technology transfer and licensing offices and increased percentages of total research funding coming from industry, as well as conflict of interest policies that spell out ethical ways for faculty to commercialize the products that result from their federally funded research conducted at the university mark the evidence of the commercialization of science and this blurring. Even the most distant faculty colleagues in humanities and fine arts become aware of the trend when they read about the unanimous 2006 decision of Texas A& M University to include inventions in tenure and promotion decisions (Zaragoza, 2008), serve on a university tenure and promotion committee where a lengthy discussion emerges over how much weight patents should be given compared to peer-reviewed publications in a promotion decision or when they serve on the committee to determine how to modify existing policies on sabbaticals and research leaves for faculty who wish to take one or more years away from the classroom for a "start-up" company.

Most faculty also recognize the drivers for this trend towards applied research and increasingly closer relationships between the corporate world and academia. The exciting work emerging from new interdisciplinary fields such as biotechnology, nanotechnology, and information technology have spawned many of these stimulating intellectual relationships. Those very names suggest the application (technology) to basic science discoveries in molecular biology, materials, and computer science. These new fields have experienced remarkable growth. For example, patents in information technologies have shown a five-fold increase from the early eighties (1980-1985) to the early 21st C. (2000-2005) (Ashcraft and Breitzman, 2007).

De-funding of higher education, particularly by state legislatures, has forced public institutions into closer relationships with corporations. Relatively flat funding from the federal government for research and education in physical sciences and engineering until President Bush's proposed 2009 budget, combined with recent flattening of the National Institutes of Health (NIH) budget after its doubling from 1998-2003 to support health and bioscience provide further impetus for the university—industry relationship. The economic crash beginning in 2008 has led to budget cuts for universities that will ultimately impact research productivity; the results of the Stimulus Package remain to be seen.

Spurred by several reports produced by the National Science Board (NSB, 2008), the National Academies (2007) and the Council on Competitiveness (2005), the U.S. Congress has begun to recognize science, technology and innovation as crucial keys for insuring the competitive edge of the United States in the global economy. The tightening on visa restrictions in the wake of September 11 underlined the dependence of the U.S. science and technological enterprise on students from other countries and professionals who are immigrants on H-1B visas. Globalization and the flattening of the world described by Thomas Friedman uncovered the possibilities for loss of U.S. innovative competitiveness. In August, 2007, The U.S. Congress held hearings on future directions for science and technology in general and on ways to improve the 1980 Bayh-Dole Act in particular, to rebalance incentives for patents, transfer, and licensing between corporations and universities. The focus on patents reflects their significance as a measure of innovation.

Not only corporate funding but also much of the current funding available from federal agencies now goes to fund applied research, commercialization, and technology transfer. The funding plus the bonuses, stock options, and hefty salaries paid to scientists serving on advisory boards to start-up companies means that a gender gap in patents signals the old story of women again being left behind since patents are a primary indicator of technology transfer.

WOMEN IN SCIENCE AND TECHNOLOGY

Just as globalization, constraints brought on by September 11, and new interdisciplinary fields in science and technology have increased focus on commercialization of science and innovation in the United States, they have also brought renewed attention back to issues of women in science and technology. Reports released from the National Academies of Science (2007) such as *Rising Above the Gathering Storm,* as well as *Innovate America* (The Council on Competitiveness, 2005), and *Science and Engineering Indicators* (National Science Board, 2008) spell out the anticipated workforce shortage. They also underline the extent to which the U.S. science and engineering workforce have depended upon students from other countries to provide well-qualified and motivated graduate students and immigrant scientists and engineers to keep both U.S. industrial and academic science staffed. September 11, 2001 not only caused entry problems via H-1B and student visas, but it also changed the desire of many scientists, engineers, and students to come to the United States. The projected dearth of scientists and engineers resulting from the decrease in immigrant scientists causes the focus to shift to underutilized sources within the U.S. population to fill the gap. Women represent the largest underutilized source.

During the last three decades, the overall percentage of women receiving degrees in science, technology, engineering, and mathematics (STEM) has increased dramatically. This dramatic increase tends to mask at least three other aspects of the demographics of the science and technology workforce. First, when the data are presented as U.S. and immigrant scientists only, not disaggregated by gender, they mask the decrease in the U.S. white men, the traditional group from which the U.S. has drawn its STEM workforce, that has occurred during the last decades. In the United States, women currently earn more of the bachelors and masters degrees than men (See Table 1). In 2004, women earned 57.6% of the bachelor's degrees in all fields (NSF, 2007) and 59.1% of all master's degrees. Beginning in 2000, women also earned more of the bachelors degrees in science and engineering (S&E) , although they earned only 43.6% of the master's degrees in science and engineering. In 2004, women earned 60% of the PhDs in non-science and engineering fields, but only 44% of the PhDs in science and engineering received by U.S. citizens and permanent residents.

Second, the aggregated data mask the wide variance of women's participation among fields in STEM. Major gender differences occur in distribution of the genders across the disciplines. Overall, at the bachelor's level, women earn the majority of the degrees in the non-science and engineering fields such as humanities, education, and fine arts, and in the S&E fields of psychology, the social sciences, and biological sciences. Men earn most of the degrees in the physical sciences, earth, atmospheric, and ocean sciences, mathematics and statistics, computer sciences and engineering (NSF, 2007).

At the level of the master's degree, women earned the majority of degrees in 2004 not only in non-science and engineering fields, but also in biological sciences, psychology, and the social sciences. Women earned less than half of the master's degrees in earth, atmospheric, and ocean sciences, mathematics and statistics, physical sciences, computer sciences and engineering (NSF, 2007).

Women still earned less than half of the science and engineering Ph.D. degrees in 2004 in all fields except psychology and a few social sciences such as anthropology, history of science, and sociology. Women earned 46.3% of the PhDs in biological sciences. Unfortunately, the social and life sciences represent areas with constant or decreasing numbers of tenure-track positions and relatively tight federal funding, leading to intense competition.

In short, in many of the social sciences and the life sciences, women have reached parity in the percentages of degrees received. In other areas such as the geosciences, as well as mathematics and physical sciences, the percentages of women continue to increase, although they have not approached parity. In contrast, in engineering and computer sciences, the percentages of women have reached a plateau or dropped during the last decade. Unfortunately, these STEM areas, particularly computer science and engineering, represent the fast-growing areas with the greatest workforce demand in our increasingly technological society.

Finally, aggregated data mask the attrition of women at every phase of the educational and career STEM pipeline. Despite grades and other academic attainments equal to or surpassing those of the men who remain in STEM, more women leave science and engineering compared to their male counterparts. This results in very few women in senior and leadership positions in the STEM workforce. In academia in the United States, at four year institutions in 2004, women made up 41.0% of assistant professors, 31.1% of associate professors, and 17.6% of full professors (See Table 2) in science and engineering. For example at the top 50 PhD-granting institutions in chemistry, women accounted for 21% of assistant professors, 22% of associate professors, and only 10% of full professors (Marasco, 2006). These sorts of institutions are the ones where most innovation and patenting occur in academia, although industry emphasizes patenting much more than academia.

Juxtaposing the increasing emphasis of global science and technology on innovation with the data on gender participation in the science and technology workforce reveals an additional issue of potential consequence both for women scientists and engineers as well as for the competitiveness of the U.S. The percentage of women granted patents ranks significantly lower than that of their male peers. Not only is the percentage of women obtaining patents lower than men, but it also ranks very low relative to the percentage of women in the STEM disciplines.

Table 1. Women as a Percentage of Degree Recipients in 2004 by Major Discipline and Group

	All Fields	All Science & Engineering	Psychology	Social Sciences	Biology	Physical Sciences	Geosciences	Math/Statistics	Engineering	Computer Science
Percentage of Bachelor's degrees received by women	57.6	50.4	77.8	54.2	62.5	42.1	42.2	45.9	20.5	25.1
Percentage of MS degrees received by women	59.1	43.6	78.1	55.9	58.6	37.5	44.6	45.4	21.1	31.2
Percentage of Ph.D. degrees received by women	45.3	44	67.3	44	46.3	25.9	33.9	28.4	17.6	20.5

Source: NSF 2007 Table C-2 for BS, F2 for Masters, F2 for doctoral.

Table 2. Percentage of Women Doctoral Scientists and Engineers in Academic Institutions by Field and Rank in 2003

	All Science & Engineering	Psychology	Social Sciences	Biology/ Life Sciences	Physical Sciences	Engineering	Math & Statistics	Computer Science
Assistant Professor	41.0	63.1	48.4	38.4	24.5	16.0	29.2	23.3
Associate Professor	31.1	52.5	35.5	29.4	19.2	11.9	15.9	19.9
Full Professor	17.6	30.8	21.4	19.0	6.8	3.8	9.2	12.3
Total (includes Instructor/Lecturer)	29.8	50.0	32.8	32.1	14.8	10.3	17.1	18.3

Source: Commission on Professionals in Science and Technology (CPST), 2007.

Curiosity drove me to explore the gender gap data in different disciplines, sectors, and countries. The evidence proved overwhelming. In every discipline, including those such as biology, in which women had begun to approach parity, whether government, academic or private sector, and in all countries, the gender gap remained substantial.

MEASURES OF PRODUCTIVITY: PATENTS AND PUBLICATIONS OBTAINED BY U.S. WOMEN

Quantifying gender and patents becomes a difficult exercise, fraught with problems. Many patents bear the names of several individuals, often including lawyers and other individuals who work for the company but who have little to do with the invention itself. Some counts include all patents with at least one woman inventor. For example, a 2007 study from the National Center for Women and Information Technology reported that from 1980-2005, approximately 9% of U.S.-invented IT patents had at least one female inventor. Others use fractional counts. When the fraction of the patent that can be counted as female is calculated, the overall percentage of female U.S.-invented IT patents drops to 4.7%, although the fractional percentage has increased from 1.7% in 1980 to 6.1% in 2005 (Ashcraft & Breitzman, 2007). This positive increase in percentage of patents by women occurred during a period when the percentage of women employed in IT decreased slightly from 32% in 1983 to 27% in 2005 (Ashcraft & Breitzman, 2007). Nonetheless, these data underline that 93.9% of U.S. origin patents come from men who constitute around 70% of the U.S. IT workforce. The percentage of U.S. origin patents obtained by women in IT ranks well below their percentage in the IT workforce.

Although women are closer to parity in numbers and percentages in the life sciences, a similar gender gap pattern found in other fields with regard to patenting appears to occur in the life sciences (Ding et al., 2006). A study of over 1,000 recipients of NIH training grants in cellular and molecular biology revealed that 30% of men compared to 14% of women recipients had patented (Bunker Whittington and Smith-Doerr, 2005). In contrast, this same study revealed that women's patents are more frequently cited than those of the men, suggesting a similar pattern to that found in earlier studies of publication rates in which men published more than women but that women's publications were cited more frequently (Long, 1993). A study restricted to a sample of 4,227 life science faculty found that 5.65% of the women while 13.0% of the men held at least one patent, despite no significant differences in publication patterns (Thursby & Thursby, 2005). The lower percentage of women obtaining patents appears to hold across sectors of government, academia and industry, (Stephan & El-Ganainy, 2007; U.S. Patent and Trademark Office, 2003) with the exception of science-based network firms in the biotechnology industry (Whittington & Smith-Doerr, 2008) where women are equally as likely as men to become involved in patenting but do not patent as frequently as men.

Women also tend to have lower publication rates than men, but the gender disparities in publication rates are not as significant as those for patents. For the United States, Xie and Shauman (2003) document that women publish at about 70% to 80% of the rate of men, based on 1988 and 1993 data bases. In her study of tenured or tenure-track faculty in doctoral granting departments in computer science, chemistry, electrical engineering, microbiology and physics in 1993-1994, Fox (2005) found that men are twice as likely as women to publish 20 or more papers, while women are almost twice as likely as men to publish zero or one paper. Murray and Graham (2006) found that men at "Big School" had higher total publication counts (82 vs 55) and higher publication counts per year (3.7 vs 2.6) than women, although these were not statistically significant; however, the citation counts per paper were very similar (42 for men vs. 41 for women). The significant difference between men and women was that men published 16% of their publications jointly with industry, while women published only 6% jointly with industry (Murray & Graham, 2006, Table 1).

An additional issue, not exactly paralleled in citation counts for papers, arises surrounding quality or impact of patents. Patents are obtained both to protect new inventions or ideas, as well as in business to prevent others from using or developing linked components critical to the basic operation of the invention. It is the latter type of patent, particularly common in computing, that many claim are "junk patents" that are "putting too many patents of dubious merit in the hands of people who can use them to drag companies and other inventors to court" (Tessler, 2008, p. 1). One possible way to read the higher citation count for women's patents is to assume that women hold fewer patents of "dubious merit" compared to men.

INTERNATIONAL COMPARISONS OF PATENTS OBTAINED BY WOMEN

Unfortunately, the gender gap also appears to hold internationally. Since patent offices do not record the gender of inventors for each patent (Ashcraft & Breitzman, 2007), relying on names makes determination of gender difficult in some instances, particularly for gender-ambiguous names (Chris) or for names commonly applied to women in some countries and men in others (Jean in the U.S. compared to France). Using complicated and labor-intensive techniques, researchers have evolved methodologies to match gender with patents for large databases internationally. This reliance on names constitutes a further complication to studying the gender gap in patents. Ashcraft and Breitzman (2007) compared female IT patenting rates in the United States and Japan. Naldi and Prenti (2002) used large data bases to study gender differences in patenting and publications in the United Kingdom, France, Germany, Italy, Spain, and Sweden in biology, biomedical research, chemistry, clinical medicine, earth and space, engineering, mathematics, and physics. Frietsch et al (2007) studied gender differences in patenting and publications in those same fields and in those same six countries plus eight others: Australia, Austria, Belgium, Denmark, Ireland, New Zealand, Switzerland, and the United States.

Using the Scopus database that covers more than 15,000 peer-reviewed journals in the life sciences, health sciences, physical sciences, and social sciences, Freitsch (2007) found that the share of female authors varied by country between 21.5% (Switzerland) through 28.3% (U.S.) to 38.6% (Italy). He also found considerable variation by field, with biology (33.9%), bio-medicine (32.2%) and medicine (28.3%) having the largest share of female authors, while engineering (20.4%), physics (18.1%) and mathematics (16.3%) had the least. Chemistry (25.3%) and geosciences (21.8%) were intermediate. His data of share of female authors by discipline and country, suggest that women publish somewhat less than men in each field but that women's publication rates are significantly higher than their patenting rates in all countries and all fields.

All these studies document that in all of these countries in all of the different areas, the percentage of women obtaining patents is significantly lower than that of their male counterparts. Considerable variation exists among the technological fields with pharmaceutical (24.1%) and basic chemicals (12.5%) tending to have higher percentages of patents obtained by women and machine-tools (2.3%) and energy machinery (1.9%) having lower percentages in 2001 (Frietsch et al, 2007). Within the IT industry, some variation occurred among subcategories, with women obtaining about 8% (fractional count) of the computer software patents in the U.S. and about 6% (fractional count) of patents in other fields such as hardware, semiconductors, communications, and peripherals. Relatively the same subcategory distributions held for Japanese women, but at lower percentages overall, since Japanese women obtained about 3.0-3.6% (fractional count) of patents overall but 5.6% (fractional count) of the software patents.

As suggested by the comparison of U.S. and Japanese women in IT, considerable differences in the percentage of women obtaining patents occur among countries. The study of patenting in 14 countries (Frietsch et al., 2007) documented that in general the percentage of women's patenting has increased during the past decade in all countries. However, substantial variations exist among countries, even within Europe. Australia (13.7%), Spain (17.5%), and New Zealand (14.0%) rank highest; Switzerland (7.4%), Germany (5.9%) and Austria (4.5%) rank lowest. The U.S. (11.1%), Sweden (9.3%), and Denmark (11.4%) rank somewhere in the middle with regard to percentage of women obtaining patents (Frietsch, et al., 2007). In all countries, the percentage of women obtaining patents is less than the percentage of women in the STEM workforce.

Issues surrounding quantification, quality, and association of some names with a particular gender might raise doubts if the gender gap in patents were small or not evident in all sectors, disciplines, or countries. But the gap is substantial. In short, in all countries across all sectors and in all fields, the percentage of women obtaining patents is not only less than their male counterparts but it is less than the percentage of women in STEM in the field in the country. This raises the questions of whether this a feminist issue and what can be applied from women's studies and gender studies to close this gender gap in patenting?

IS THIS A FEMINIST ISSUE?

Gender discounting of women's scientific work by industry, greater comfort level of venture capitalists with men than women, fewer opportunities for commercialization open to women, broader and more varied collegial networks available to men, and a boy's club atmosphere imply exclusion and being locked out, if not actual discrimination against women in commercialization of science. These suggest that the gender gap in patents is a feminist issue.

Both in the U.S. and internationally, the focus for scientific research has shifted from basic to applied research and innovation, for which one of the primary indicators is patents granted. If women scientists and engineers are not obtaining patents at rates comparable to their participation in the STEM workforce and at significantly lower rates than their male peers, then women are not participating in the new areas and directions for science and technology. This hurts women scientists and engineers who are left out of the leading edge work in innovation. Women are then not seen as leaders in their field which hurts women financially and in their professional advancement. Commercialization of science can be extremely lucrative, if the patent results in a product that is developed, brought to market, and successful. Since patents "count" as a marker of success, similar to publications, and may even be required for some bonuses and "fellow" status in some industries, women's small percentages of patents also inhibit their professional advancement. Very few women obtaining patents hurts scientific innovation, technology, and competitiveness overall. Although men dominate patenting in all fields, some relative gender differences in fields of patents exist.

TIMING AND A MODEL TO CLOSE THE GENDER GAP

In another paper, (Rosser, 2009), I discuss possible reasons, including some policy recommendations, to address the gender gap. This chapter focuses on the timing: Why was the gap discovered so recently? Now that we've noticed, when, if ever, will the gap be closed? Since the commercialization of science only began to explode in academia in the 1970s and was particularly fueled by the passage of the Bayh-Dole Act in 1980, encouraging academics to claim intellectual property and work with universities to license these rights to firms, in some ways it is not surprising that the "gender gap" has relatively recently been identified (Ding et al., 2005, 2006; Bunker Whittington & Smith Doerr, 2005) and that researchers are only beginning to explore the dimensions of the gap across different fields, sectors, and countries (Ashcraft & Breitzman, 2007; Frietsch et. al 2007, Naldi, 2002, 2004).

To someone like me, who has focused on women in science, women's studies, and curriculum transformation for more than thirty years, it smacks of a familiar pattern: Women are excluded until someone "discovers" their absence. Then women become integrated over time in what can be described as a series of stages or phases.

In *Female Friendly Science* (1990), I proposed a five-stage model for curriculum transformation to aid in including more information on women and men of color. Built on models developed by feminist scholars working in other disciplines (McIntosh, 1984; Schuster & Van Dyne, 1985; Tetreault, 1985), the following model is specific for science and mathematics:

Stage 1. Absence of women not noted. This is the traditional approach to science and the curriculum from the perspective of the white, Eurocentric, middle- to upper-class male in which the absence of women is not noted. The assumption is that gender affects neither who becomes a scientist nor the science produced.

Stage 2. Women as an add-on. Recognition that most scientists are male and that science may reflect a masculine perspective on the physical, natural world. A few exceptional women such as Nobel laureates who have achieved the highest success as defined by the traditional standards of the discipline may be accepted in the scientific community and included in the curriculum.

Stage 3. Women as a problem. Barriers that prevent women from entering science are identified. Women are recognized as a problem, anomaly, or absence from science and the curriculum. Women may be seen as victims, as protesters, or as deprived or defective variants, who deviate from the white, middle-to upper-class norm of the male scientist.

Stage 4. Women as the focus. Women scientists and their unique contributions are sought. The extent to which the role of women has been overlooked, misunderstood, or attributed to male colleagues throughout the history of science is explored to determine women's scientific achievements. Questions are asked about new perspectives that might result when women become the focus in topics chosen for study. New methods may be used and language in which data and theories are described may shift, improving the quality of science.

Stage 5. Inclusive science. Scientists, scientific research and science curriculum are redefined and reconstructed to include diversity in terms of gender, as well as race, class, age and other factors.

Thinking of the stage model and its possibilities for explaining phenomena of curriculum drew my attention to the possibility of its application to the gender gap in patents. My junior colleague's interest in the reasons for, and parameters surrounding, the gender gap in patents coupled with several recent high profile studies (Ashcraft & Breitzman, 2007; Ding, et. Al., 2006; Murray & Graham, 2007; Stephan & El Gananiy, 2007) focused on the women's low rates of patenting suggest that we are moving towards stage 3, centering on barriers or problems that prevent women from patenting. A recent article on the dearth of women in high positions in Silicon Valley (Ross, 2008) exemplifies the problem stage. The article states that "almost one-third of women at the 'middle-level' of their high-tech careers are planning to quit primarily because of perceived barriers to advancement." (Ross, 2008).

The time when commercialization and technology transfer began to take off in the late 1970s to the early 1980s until the "discovery" of the gender gap in about 2004-2005 constitutes stage 1, when the absence of women is not noted. Occasional articles highlighting star women who patent at high rates exemplify stage 2, exceptional women who patent at the same rates under the same conditions as men in male-dominated fields. Stephanie Louise Kwolek, the inventor of Kevlar, a synthetic material used in bullet-proof vests that is five times stronger than the same weight as steel, who worked as a chemist at DuPont, obtaining 28 patents during her 40 year career (About.com.Inventors, 2009) exemplifies such a stage 2 woman. A recent spate of attention to the gender gap as demonstrated by publications, NSF-funded projects, and conference presentations begins to encroach on Stage 4: Focus on the Gender Gap, although it seems unlikely that more than a few individuals have reached Stage 4.

In short, most scientists, engineers and academia have not noticed the gender gap and remain in stage 1. Even individuals involved in technology transfer appear unaware of the absence of women until it's brought to their attention. Once they think about it, they typically agree that very few women patent in the fields with which they are familiar. After some thought, they'll often mention one or two women in their field who do obtain patents, exemplifying stage 2. Most will then begin to move to stage 3 when they wonder what prevents women from patenting at the same rate as men. The recent study from Stanford's Clayman Institute and the Anita Borg Institute titled, *Climbing the Technical Ladder: Obstacles and Solutions for Mid-level Women in Technology* (Simard, et. Al., 2008) highlights the problem aspect of this stage 3.

A gender gap also seems to apply in the recognition of the gender gap in patents. Men and women outside of fields where technology transfer and commercialization occur are equally ignorant of the gender gap in patents. In fields where technology transfer and commercialization are prevalent, men appear much less aware of the gender gap than women. Most women in these same fields are completely aware of the gap and immediately articulate the number of women who patent in their particular area and their personal theories about why women do not patent at the same rate as men. In contrast, men in those same fields typically state that they were unaware of the gap, deny its existence, or declare that it may exist elsewhere but not in their laboratory or department (Rosser, 2009).

IMPLICATIONS FOR CLOSING THE GENDER GAP

What are the implications of stage theory for technology transfer? What will it mean for closing the gender gap in patenting?

A stage or phase theory implies that the final stage of inclusion won't be reached without taking the time to go through each of the earlier stages. Evidence of narrowing the gender gap among younger cohorts of women suggests progression through the stages. First, the numbers and percentages of women obtaining patents have increased over time. Overall, the U.S. Patent and Trademark Office reports that the percentage of U.S. origin patents in all categories which include at least one woman inventor has increased from 3.7% (1977-1988) to 10.9% in 2002, and that the number of U.S. origin patents that include at least one woman inventor has also been increasing (U.S. Patent and Trademark Office, 2003). From 1977-2002, women inventors showed the greatest participation in U.S. origin patents in design (11.5%) and plant (11.7%) patenting. By 2002, 12.9% of the design patents and 21.2% of the plant patents had at least one woman inventor. In 2002, 19.6% of chemical utility patents had at least one woman inventor, but electrical (7.0%) and mechanical (7.8%) utility patents with one woman inventor ranked much lower.

Second, younger women are patenting more than senior women colleagues. In a study at "Big School, only 23% of women faculty had patented, while 74% of men faculty held at least one patent. Among the younger cohort the gap is less; in the "entire population of junior faculty, 44% of men have been granted patents compared to only 11% of women". (Murray & Graham, 2007).

Third, limited evidence suggests that women are becoming involved with patenting at the same rates as their male peers in some venues. In a study of science-based network firms in the biotechnology industry, Whittington and Smith-Doerr (2008) documented that women were as likely as men to become involved in patenting, although the women were still patenting less frequently than the men.

Overall, both nationally and internationally, the gender gap in patents has shown some signs of closing over time. These studies provide some evidence for progression through the stages. Reaching stage 5 of inclusion seems distant, although some fields and sectors, such as the biotech start-ups, appear to be closer to inclusion.

In order to reach inclusion (stage 5), not only will all disciplines, but all sectors and individuals involved, have to pass through these stages. As I worked in projects on curricular transformation occurring in the sciences, I recognized that the phases applied to more than curriculum. These stages describe steps of personal development through which individuals progress as they become aware of biases due to gender and race in curriculum and pedagogy.

In an early book (Rosser, 1986), I suggested that an individual must progress personally through, or at least to, a stage of development before he or she can develop curriculum and pedagogical techniques at that stage. For example, a faculty member cannot teach a stage 5, inclusive course in which the primary focus shifts from the white male experience to include women, men of color, and disabled persons, if she or he is only at the add-on phase (stage 2) in her or his own thinking.

Just as phase theory may be applied to personal development and transformation toward inclusion as well as curriculum, it also may be applied to programs, departments, institutions, and/or agencies. As is the case with individuals, even with a well-conceived (stage 5) plan for diversity and inclusion and the best of intentions on the part of all faculty, staff, and/or employees, a university cannot jump from stage 1 to 5 without going through the intermediate stages. Moving an entire department and curriculum towards gender inclusion is difficult. Transforming an entire college or university has proved a long-term challenge.

Technology transfer and commercialization involve interactions with many individuals outside the university from a variety of sectors with quite different cultures from that of academia. Corporations and their boards, venture capitalists, marketing specialists, and angel funders, in addition to students, men and women faculty, and technology transfer personnel in universities will all need to progress through these stages to close the gender gap. Not only is the group involved in technology transfer very large and diverse in terms of backgrounds and expertise, but different components and individuals hold competing interests and cultures.

More significant than understanding the stage theory and process is the desire of each individual and each group, as well as that of corporate power and elite educational institutions, to want to close the gender gap. Since technology transfer and patenting involve substantial amounts of money, such a desire cannot be taken for granted. Indeed, one study of the gender gap noted that part of the appeal of technology transfer for some academics may have been to create an elite male-only club: As Stephan and El-Ganainy suggest, "entrepreneurial science opened the possibility of having a 'boys' club' when it emerged on campuses in the late 1970s" just at the time when larger numbers of women and underrepresented minorities were entering academic science (Stephan & El-Ganainy, 2007, p. 486.)

Besides the obvious issues of fairness and discrimination, what other problems and losses result from the boys' club that excludes women and results in a gender gap in patenting? First, women who are scientists lose. Studies (Stephan & El-Ganainy, 2007) document that women scientists, compared to their male peers have fewer graduate students and post-docs and smaller, less diverse collegial networks. Compared to their male peers, women are asked less frequently to consult, serve on scientific advisory boards, and have their work discounted more frequently by industry (Murray & Graham, 2007). This means that women scientists lose out not only on higher salaries, stock options, awards and promotions, but also on opportunities to work in some of the most cutting edge fields on the frontiers of science such as information technology, biotechnology, and nanotechnology.

Second, science loses in attracting more individuals with creative ideas. Fewer women are attracted to science because of the perceived chilly atmosphere of exclusion (Rosser, 2004). As indicated in the recent Clayman Institute and Anita Borg Study (Simard, et.al, 2008), perceived barriers and obstacles cause women either not to enter the field, drop-out or switch mid-career.

Third, society loses because of fewer products. Very few women obtaining patents hurts scientific innovation, technology, and competitiveness overall. Although men dominate patenting in all fields, some relative gender differences in fields of patents exist. Since ideas for patents often arise in areas with which the innovators have experiences, it is not surprising that studies of the patents obtained by women (Macdonald, 1992) and of women inventors document that women invent more technologies related to reproduction or children. Women also have invented many technologies for the home (a patented house that cleans itself, using 68 separate devices), and for caretaking, particularly of children (disposable diapers and the pull-down-from-the-wall baby-changing stations found in public restrooms). Small numbers of women patenting suggests fewer products to solve problems and facilitate daily life for women and children in particular. If more women were involved in commercialization, imagine the new, useful products to benefit society that might be developed. Simultaneously, increasing the percentage of women scientists and engineers who patent is also likely to increase their economic equality as technology transfer and commercialization of science increase in the U.S. and globally.

REFERENCES

About. com. Inventors. (200). "Patent Point to Ponder—Mothers of Invention Part 3: Women Fighting germs, stronger than steel, and Nearly Me." http://inventors.about.com/library/inventors/blkidprimer6_12w3.htm. Retrieved 1/12/09.

Ashcraft, Catherine. & Breitzman, Anthony. (2007). *Who Invents IT? An Analysis of Women's Participation in Information Technology Patenting.* Boulder, CO: National Center for Women in Technology (NCWIT).

Bunker Whittington, Kjersten. & Smith Doerr, Laurel (2005). "Gender and commercial science: Women's patenting in the life sciences." *Journal of Technology Transfer, 30:* 355-370.

Council on Competitiveness. (2005). *Innovate America: National Innovation Initiative Summit and Report.* Washington, D.C.: Council on Competitiveness.

Ding, Waverly, Murray, Fiona, & Stuart, Toby. (2006). "Gender differences in patenting in the academic life sciences". *Science, 313* (5787) 665-667.

Fox, Mary Frank. (2005). "Gender, family characteristics, and publication productivity among Scientists." *Social Studies of Science, 35(1),* 131-150.

Frietsch, Rainer, Haller, Inna, Vrohlings, Melanie, & Grupp, Hariolf. (2007). "*Battle of The Sexes? Main areas of gender-specific technological and scientific activities in industrialized countries*". Unpublished paper presented at Georgia Tech, October 16, 2007.

Long, S. (1993). "Women in Science. Part 1. The Productivity Puzzle". *Essays of an Information Scientist, 15,* 248.

Macdonald, Anne. (1992). *Feminine Ingenuity: Women and invention in America.* New York: Ballantine Books.

Marasco, C. A. (2006). "Women faculty gain little ground." *Chemical and Engineering News 84,* 58-59.

McIntosh, P. (1984). "The study of women: Processes of personal and curricular revision." *The Forum for Liberal Education, 6(5)*, 2-4.

Murray, F. & Graham, L. (2007). "Buying and selling science: Gender stratification in commercial science." *Industrial and Corporate Change Special Issue on Technology Transfer 16(4)*, 657-689.

Naldi, Fulvio & Prenti, Ilaria Vannini (2002). *Scientific and Technological Performance by Gender. A feasibility study on patents and biometric indicators.* Luxembourg: European Union Commission.

Naldi, F. & Parenti, I. (2004). "Performance by Gender." http://ec.europa.eu/research/infocentre/export/success/article_721_en.html. (Retrieved 4/13/09).

National Academy of Sciences. (2007). *Rising above the Gathering Storm.*

National Science Board. (2008). *Science and Engineering Indicators.* www.nsf.gov/sbe/srs/seind08/ Retrieved May 19, 2008.

National Science Foundation. (2007). *Women, Minorities, and Persons with Disabilities.* Washington, DC: National Science Foundation. http://www.nsf.gov/statistics/women. Retrieved May 15, 2008.

Ross, A. S. (2008). "Few women at the top in Silicon Valley". *San Francisco Chronicle,* (November 24, 2008), D-1.

Rosser, S. V. (1990). *Female Friendly Science.* Elmsford, NY: Pergamon Press.

Rosser, S. V. (2009). "Is Technology Transfer a Feminist Issue?" *NWSA Journal 21* (2), 65-84.

Rosser, S. V. (1986). *Teaching Science and Health from a Feminist Perspective: A Practical Guide.* Elmsford, NY: Pergamon Press.

Rosser, S. V. (2004). *The Science Glass Ceiling: Academic Women Scientists and their Struggle to Succeed.* New York: Routledge.

Rosser, S. V. & O'Neil, E. L. (2002). "Funding for women's programs at NSF: Using individual POWRE approaches for institutions to ADVANCE". *Journal of Women and Minorities in Science and Engineering. 8(3-4)*, 327-345.

Schuster, M. & Van Dyne, S. (1985). *Women's Place in the Academy: Transforming the Liberal Arts Curriculum.* Totowa, NJ: Rowman & Allanheld.

Simard, C. Henderson, A. D. Gilmartin, S. Schiebinger, L. & Whitney, T. (2008). *Climbing the Technical Ladder: Obstacles and Solutions for Mid-level Women in Technology.* Palo Alto, CA: Michelle Clayman Institute for Gender Research and the Anita Borg Institute.

Stephan, P. & El-Ganainy, A. (2007). "The entrepreneurial puzzle: Explaining the Gender gap." *Journal of Technology Transfer 32*, 475-487.

Tessler, Joelle. (2008). "Program turns to online masses to improve patents". http://www.sfgate.com/cgi-bin/article.cgi?f=/n/a/2008/09/14financia...

Tetreault, M. K. (1985). "Stages of thinking about women: An experience-derived evaluation model." *Journal of Higher Education, 5(4)*, 368-384.

Thursby, J. & Thursby, M. (2005). "Gender patterns of research and licensing activity of science and engineering faculty." *Journal of Technology Transfer 30*, 343-353.

U.S. Patent & Trademark Office. (2003). *U.S. Patenting by Women.* Washington, DC: U.S. Patent and Trademark Office.

Whittington, K. B. & Smith-Doerr, L. (2008). "Women inventors in context: Disparities in patenting across academia and industry. *Gender and Society 22*, 194.

Xie, Y. & Shauman, K. (2003). *Women in Science.* Boston: Harvard University Press.

Zaragoza, S. (2008). "State want added path to tenure at Texas universities." *Austin Business Journal.* (Feb. 8, 2008). http://austin.bizjournals.com/austin/stories/2008/02/11/stroy5.html.

In: Feminism and Women in Leadership
Editor: Vicente Nardi, pp. 127-143

ISBN: 978-1-60876-270-5
© 2010 Nova Science Publishers, Inc.

Chapter 7

WOMEN'S LEADERSHIP IN PLANT BIOTECHNOLOGY AND RELATED SCIENCES

Georgina Kosturkova and Krasimira Tasheva
Department of Plant Biotechnology, Institute of Genetics,
Bulgarian Academy of Sciences 1113 Sofia, Bulgaria

ABSTRACT

Plant Biotechnology in Bulgaria has thirty five years of history. After the establishment of the first laboratory of *in vitro* cultures in the Institute of Genetics of the Bulgarian Academy of Sciences in the middle 1970's similar laboratories were organized in more than twenty other research institutes and universities. Major part of the personnel are women occupying different positions: head of units, project/group leaders, senior scientists, research and technical assistants. Many Bulgarian women working in this sphere have developed good scientific career contributing to development of many aspects of plant biotechnology. Leadership of women will be discussed in context of their participation in projects, outstanding research, tuition, expertise and motives to deal with plant biotechnology on the background of gender activities in biological sciences. The latter were compared with physical and mathematical sciences traditionally attracting more men. Survey was carried on three levels: (i) research organizations/institutes; (ii) research groups; (iii) researchers

INTRODUCTION

Biotechnology is every where in our life and is a frontier area in scientific development. Its boom started in the middle of the XXth century and spread over all living organisms – microorganisms, plants, animals and man. It emerged from different sciences like microbiology, biochemistry, molecular biology, genetics, breeding and medicine and with its multidisciplinary character entered various important for our life spheres like food and agriculture, pharmacy and health, chemistry and ecology. Biotechnology was delegated with great hopes to cope with such 'hot topics' as food security, lethal diseases, global warming and renewable energy. However, biotechnology is also expected to satisfy whims like choosing the sex or the eyes color of our babies. Along with its undisputable success of new products, new drugs and vaccines, new plant varieties and animal breeds, new efficient techniques and methods contributing for our sustainable development, biotechnology raises some social and ethical challenges which proved to be of greater concern to women than the men. It is not only because women are taking more care about food and health, but because female body became an object of some of the most advanced biotechnologies like 'test tube babies' or embryo transfers or utilization of human embryonic stem cells. "Scientists are called upon to take on greater responsibility with regard to the outcomes of their studies: the statement that science is neutral, while only its application can be judged in the light of social values, is no longer valid" and "Achieving gender equity is the first essential step for women to be able to pay an active role in producing, controlling and orienting biotechnologies" (Molfino and Zucco 2008).

Nowadays more women are employed and have higher positions, more have university education and are entering science. Many of them occupy high professional levels allowing them to manage and shape knowledge. However, still there are gender differences in choice of research field and sector of employment. In European Union states the lowest proportion (about one fifth) of female researchers is in engineering and technology while natural, agricultural and medical sciences are more attractive to women representing around 30 %, 40 % and 50 %, respectively. In Bulgaria there is no marked difference between these three areas where half of the research positions are occupied by women (European Commission 2006). Biotechnology as multidisciplinary area has its place and role in all of above mentioned scientific fields and women have their particular role and place in biotechnology.

Biotechnology in

Here, the leadership of women in one very small part of biotechnology (plant biotechnology) will be discussed. In Bulgaria, the basis of plant biotechnology was laid in the mid seventies of the last century. At present, there are more than 20 laboratories and groups in the major research organizations (the Bulgarian Academy of Sciences and the Agricultural Academy) and universities with dominant female presence (Kosturkova 2008).

METHODOLOGY

Leadership of women in biotechnology was examined on the background of gender activities in biological sciences. The latter were compared with physical and mathematical sciences which traditionally attract more men. Survey was carried on three levels: (i) research organizations/institutes; (ii) research groups; (iii) researchers. Parallel was made between participation of women and men in scientific fields which traditionally are preferred by women (like biology) and men (physics and mathematics). The survey included twenty four research institutes from the Bulgarian Academy of Sciences (Table 1): fourteen in biological sciences; seven in physical sciences and three in mathematical sciences to make the compared groups almost equal in members. Data present gender activities in governing bodies and boards taking decisions.

Table 1. List of the research institutes of the Bulgarian Academy of Sciences under survey.

	Institute's name	web address
	Biological Sciences	
1	Institute of Molecular Biology	http://www.bio21.bas.bg/imb/
2	Institute of Genetics	http://ig.bas.bg/
3	Institute of Neurobiology	http://www.bio.bas.bg/neurobiology/
4	Institute of Plant Physiology	http://www.bio21.bas.bg/ipp/
5	Institute of Experimental Morphology and Anthropology with Museum	http://www.iema.bas.bg/
6	Institute of Microbiology	http://www.microbio.bas.bg/
7	Institute of Botany	http://www.bio.bas.bg/botany/
8	Institute of Zoology	http://www.zoology.bas.bg/
9	Forest Research Institute	http://www.fribas.org/
10	Institute of Experimental Pathology and Parasitology	http://www.iepp.bas.bg/
11	Institute of Biology and Immunology of Reproduction	http://ibir.bas.bg/
12	Institute of Biophysics	http://www.bio21.bas.bg/
13	Centre of Biomedical Engineering	http://www.clbme.bas.bg/
14	Central Laboratory of General Ecology	http://www.ecolab.bas.bg/
	Physical Sciences	
1	Institute of Nuclear Research and Nuclear Energetics	http://www.inrne.bas.bg/
2	Institute of Solid State Physics "Georgi Nadjakov"	http://www.issp.bas.bg/
3	Institute of Electronics "Acad. Emil Djakov"	http://www.ie-bas.dir.bg/
4	Institute of Astronomy	http://www.astro.bas.bg/
5	Central Laboratory of Solar energy and new energy sources	http://www.senes.bas.bg/
6	Central Laboratory of Optical Storage and Processing of Information	http://www.optics.bas.bg/
7	Central Laboratory of Applied Physics	http://www.clap-bas.com/
	Mathematical Sciences	
1	Institute of Mathematics and Informatics	http://www.math.bas.bg/
2	Institute of Mechanics	http://www.imbm.bas.bg/
3	Institute for Parallel Processing	http://www.bas.bg/clpp/

One of the groups consists of biologists who have graduated university thirty years ago in 1978. This group was chosen because its representatives have equal start in their career development in research institutes (mainly from the Bulgarian Academy of Sciences) and universities (mainly University of Sofia).

The Department of Biotechnology of the Institute of Genetics was chosen because: (i) it is within the structure of the Bulgarian Academy of Sciences; (ii) it was the first Bulgarian plant *in vitro* laboratory with "career" little bit longer than 30 years (established in 1974); (iii) the author Dr. Kosturkova is a representative of the biologists' group graduated in 1978 and is working in the Department of Plant Biotechnology for 31 years. Data were collected from published sources and by personal interviews.

PARTICIPATION OF FEMALE AND MALE SCIENTISTS IN RESEARCH ACTIVITIES OF BIOLOGICAL, PHYSICAL AND MATHEMATICAL INSTITUTES

The Bulgarian Academy of Sciences (BAS) is the biggest research center with 3 680 scientists (employees) working in more than 70 institutes and specialized laboratories and units in all scientific fields. Founded 140 years ago its mission is to "develop science in conformity with the universal human values and with the country's national interests" and to promote "enhancement of intellectual and material wealth of the Bulgarian people" (www.bas.bg). BAS has been an attractive place for scientific career, both, for men and women.

Biological institutes compose one of the biggest groups of research units and here they are compared with two smaller groups - that of physical and mathematical sciences. Concerning staff members there is significant difference between the examined groups (Figure 1). The portion of women is 63 % for biological institutes and reciprocal of 37 % and 40 % for physical and mathematical institutes, respectively. On this gender background women's leadership is expressed only by the position of scientific secretary representing 78 % and 86 % in biological and physical sciences and complete dominancy of men in mathematical sciences. Director's positions are occupied by women only in 14 % of biological units while in all physical and mathematical institutes this leading position is occupied by men. Dominancy of men could be seen in all managing and decision taking bodies. Male managing boards prevail in 57 % of biological institutes and in 100 % of physical and mathematical institutes. The portion of women members of boards is 38 %, 6 % and 12 % for biological, physical and mathematical sciences, respectively. Similar is the case of scientific committees where the number of men predominates to that of women – 80 % for physical and mathematical sciences and 48 % for biological sciences. In most of the cases chairmen of the committees are men also. The majority of Head of departments and research groups are men too – 54 % for biological sciences and 77 % for physical and mathematical sciences.

The Institute of Genetics is not an exception. Though the staff is predominantly female with women researchers four times more than their male colleagues, the director and the both deputy directors are men. Like most of the biology institutes the scientific secretary and half part of the heads of departments are women. However, female leaders of research groups and projects predominate.

CAREER DEVELOPMNET OF WOMEN AND MEN GRADUATED 30 YEARS AGO

Thirty years ago, in 1978, about ninety students were granted master degree in biology by the University of Sofia. Almost 40 % of them has chosen career of scientists, with relative portion of women to men being 40 % to 60 %. However, during this 30 years period one third of men has left science because of different reasons (financial being the major one). At present this ratio is almost equal (nine women and eleven men) for scientists working in

Bulgaria. Career development and scientific activities of two groups of equal number (eight women and eight men who provided data) were included in the survey.

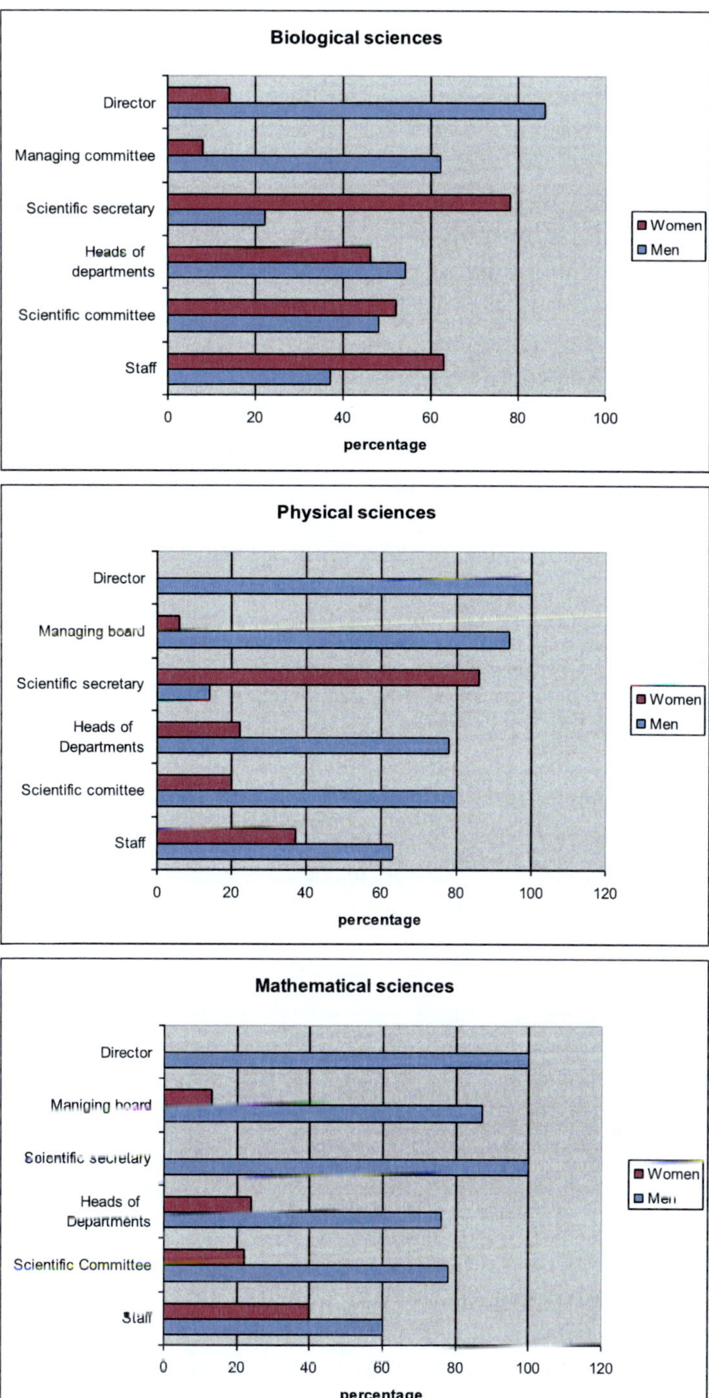

Figure 1. Relative portion of women and men in management activities in academic research institutes in biological, physical and mathematical sciences.

These scientists work in different biological areas: algology (Benderliev et al. 2004, 2005); biochemistry (Angelov 2008); biotechnology (Kosturkova 2006, 2008); botany (Tonkov et al. 2008a,b); ecology (Lyubenova 2005, 2006); genetics and breeding (Dimanov 2003, Kosturkova 2006); human health (Vangelova 2008, Vangelova and Israel 2005, Vangelova et al. 2006); microbiology (Vasileva-Tonkova et al. 2007, 2008); molecular biology (Detcheva and Grancharov 2006a,b, Decheva et al. 2002, Stoilov et al. 2000, 2002); plant physiology (Stancheva et al. 2004, 2006); zoology (Dimitrov et al. 2007, Kalchev et al. 2006, 2007, 2008).

Career development of women and men follows similar pattern respective to the state laws for higher education and scientific degrees, as well as, the Constitution declaring general prohibition of gender discrimination. A successful first step for research career is a doctorate. All representatives of the group were Ph.D students in Bulgaria or abroad (60 %) are Ph.D with small difference in the mean values of the period of getting the doctor degree (8 years for men and 9 years for women). However, the shortest and the longest period for women was 5 and 11 years, while for men it was 7 and 16 years after graduation (Figure 2). Here should be mentioned that the Ph.D fellowship is three to four years (and most of the students manage to have viva for this period) but here was recorded the year when one becomes a doctor.

Another successful first step was to get a position of researcher or assistant in institute or university, respectively. Half of the women were appointed for the lowest IIIrd grade of researcher (equivalent to university assistant) after a period of 5 to 9 years (mean value of 7 years) while one third of the men had the same positions after 1 to 9 years (mean value of 5 years), respectively. The higher position of researcher IInd grade (or senior assistant) was occupied by women after a period of 8 to14 years (mean value of 10.3) and by men after a period of 4 to10 years (mean value of 7.3 years). Promotion to the next position of researcher I[st] grade (or chief assistant) took place after a period of 11 to 19 years (mean value 14.3 years) for women and 8 to 17 years (mean value 12.1 years). The position of senior researcher and an associate professor was reached by 62 % of women and 88 % of men after a period of 20-29 years (mean 25 years) and 11-27 years (mean 22.8 years), respectively. Only one men succeeded to have DSc. degree and to become a full professor after career of 30 and 31 years, respectively.

Gender differences could be observed concerning some criteria for successful research work. Compared to their male colleagues women have greater number of publications (55 % of the whole share) but less citation (44 %). Women are as active as men in project coordination (49 % of all projects) though they participate in less projects (42 %). Women tutored and trained more Ph.D and MSc. students (62 %) while less of them (40 %) were selected as experts in different organizations (Figure 3). No one of the female representatives of the group have been elected for high administrative and managing position like director or head of department, while 30 % of the male colleagues have been occupying such positions.

Concerning family life – all representatives of the group are married (on the average of 27 years), most of them having two children (average 1.8 and 1.6 for women and men, respectively). Men in their majority (about 90 %) declare that family duties do not disturb their working obligations while that is true only for 33 % of the women.

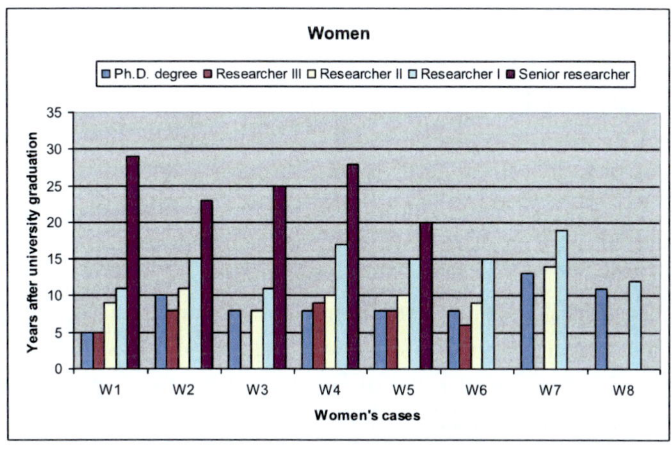

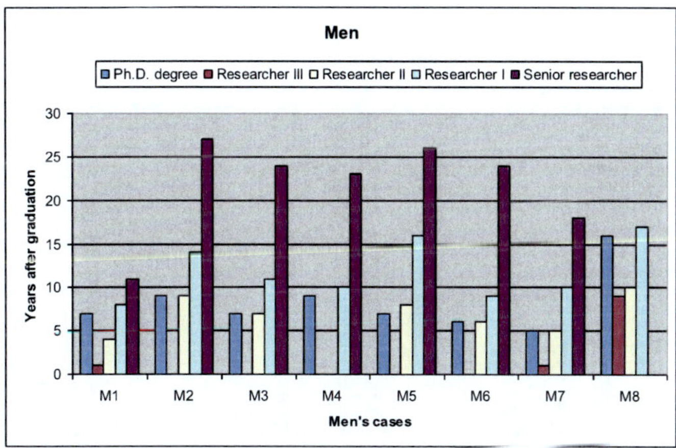

Figure 2. Career development of women and men graduated Faculty of Biology of the University of Sofia thirty years ago.

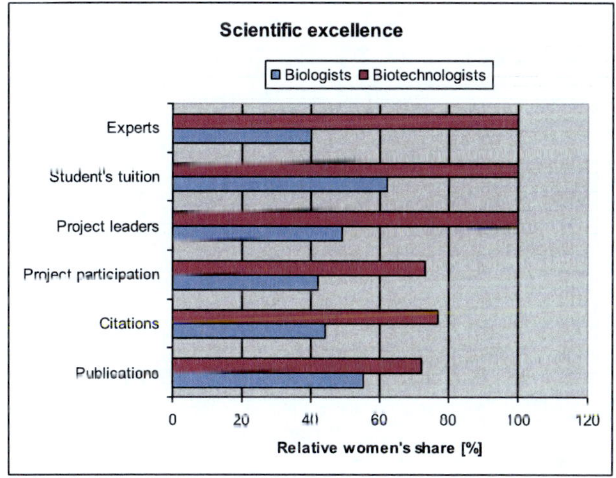

Figure 3. Comparison of scientific excellence of female and male researchers in biology and biotechnology.

LEADERSHIP OF WOMEN IN PLANT BIOTECHNOLOGY

The Laboratory of Plant Tissue Cultures of the Institute of Genetics, Bulgarian Academy of Sciences (BAS) was founded in 1974 laying the basis of plant biotechnology development in Bulgaria. Participation of women in all scientific and management activities is remarkable for this period of thirty five years (Figure 4). The total staff (researchers, assistants and technicians) portion of women was always larger varying from 70 % to 89 %. Female scientists prevailed during the whole period representing from 50% to 77 %. During the first 10 years the number of male senior researchers was bigger (67 %) but later female senior researchers prevailed starting from 60 % in 1985, reaching 100 % in 1995 and keeping this percentage till now. The position of Head of Department was occupied by women in half of this 35 years period. Senior researchers have been members of the institute's Scientific Committee.

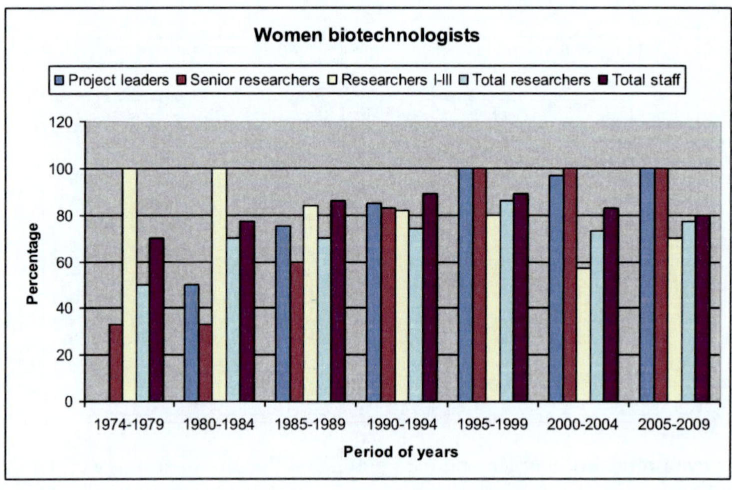

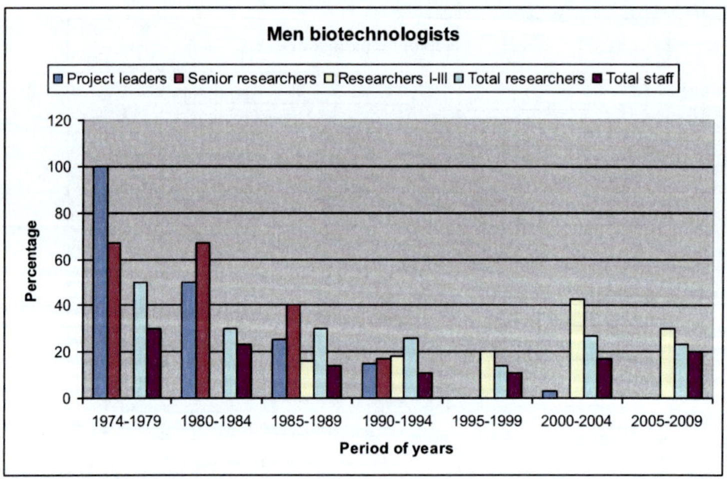

Figure 4. Participation of women and men in research and management activities of the Department of Plant Biotechnology of the Institute of Genetics at the Bulgarian Academy of Sciences

Publishing productivity and participation in projects was twice bigger of women (regarding only present members of the department). Students' tuition and expertise have been also female activities.

Women have been excellent project leaders managing from 50 % to 85 % of the national and international projects during the period from 1980 to 1995 and practically 100 % of the projects for the last 15 years. During the last five years women have been principle investigators of 12 projects in several areas of application of plant *in vitro* cultures in biotechnology, genetics, breeding and ecology.

A major part of the research was dedicated to the global problem of plant response to biotic and abiotic stress under *in vitro* and *in vivo* conditions, screening and selection of tolerant plants to unfavorable conditions like drought, salinity, heavy metals pollution, herbicides and diseases (Kosturkova and Delinick, 2007, Kosturkova et al. 2001, 2003, 2006, 2008, Nedev et al. 2003, Noveva et al. 2006). Another important area is enrichment of gene fund by development of new plant forms applying biotechnology techniques (Kosturkova et al. 2005a, Mehandjiev et al 2006, Nedev 2008, Nikova et al. 2004, 2005, Rodeva et al. 2005). Significant investigations have been made on propagation *in vitro* of valuable, endangered and medicinal plants for protection of biodiversity and utilization of alternative methods for secondary substances production (Petrova et al. 2005, 2006a,b, Tahseva et al. 2005). Complement molecular analysis have been an important part of the investigations (Kosturkova et al. 2003, Landjeva et al. 2004, Petrova et al. 2006a, Sakthivelu et al. 2008a). However, the first step for the successful application of biotechnology is the development of *in vitro* techniques, methods and manipulations (Kosturkova 2005, Kosturkova et al. 2005b, Nedev et al. 2007, Sakthivelu 2008a, Zayova et al. 2008) to which considerable efforts have been dedicated throughout the whole life of the department (Dryanova and Ganeva 1997/1998a,b, Kosturkova 1993, Kosturkova et al. 1997, Tasheva et al. 2003, Zagorska et. al. 1998).

WHY WOMEN ARE SUCCESSFUL IN BIOTECHNOLOGY

Previously Kosturkova has written "The answer after 30 years of experience in most of the spheres of *in vitro* and DNA techniques could be the following - biotechnology work is specific and needs: skilled hands and quick fingers; gentle action and tenderness; patience and persistency; curiosity and watchfulness; imagination and creativity, dedication and love. In addition, to manage several things simultaneously. All these are traditionally attributes of women." (Kosturkova 2008). Presently this view is supported by biotechnologists from the both genders (Figure 5) who do not differ significantly in their perception for the personal features one needs to be successful in plant *in vitro* cultures and manipulations. Women answers are distributed almost equally between "skillfulness" (19 %), "watchfulness" (17 %), "patience" (17 %), "persistency" (16 %), "creativity" (16 %) and "inventiveness" (15 %) with narrow borders (4 %) of fluctuations. Men put in different order of priority these personal characteristics: "persistency" (21.2 %), "watchfulness" (19 %), "skillfulness" (17 %), "patience" (15.3 %), "inventiveness" (13.7 %) and "patience" (15.3 %) with variations of importance within 7 %. The leading for women is "skillfulness" which is important to operate with very tiny objects (isolated from the plant cells and tissues) with precise hand and fingers movement following strict procedures with sophisticated instrumentation. "Watchfulness" is a prerequisite for the experiments where a lot of empirism exists in explant cell and tissue development in controlled *in vitro* conditions. The process from cell to whole plant regeneration (recovery) is a long one and needs quite a big "patience" and "persistence". Similar is the case with genetic manipulations when new forms are created and selected. For the latter a big portion of imagination and inventive mind are necessary to go deep in cell processes and to change the mechanisms of its development.

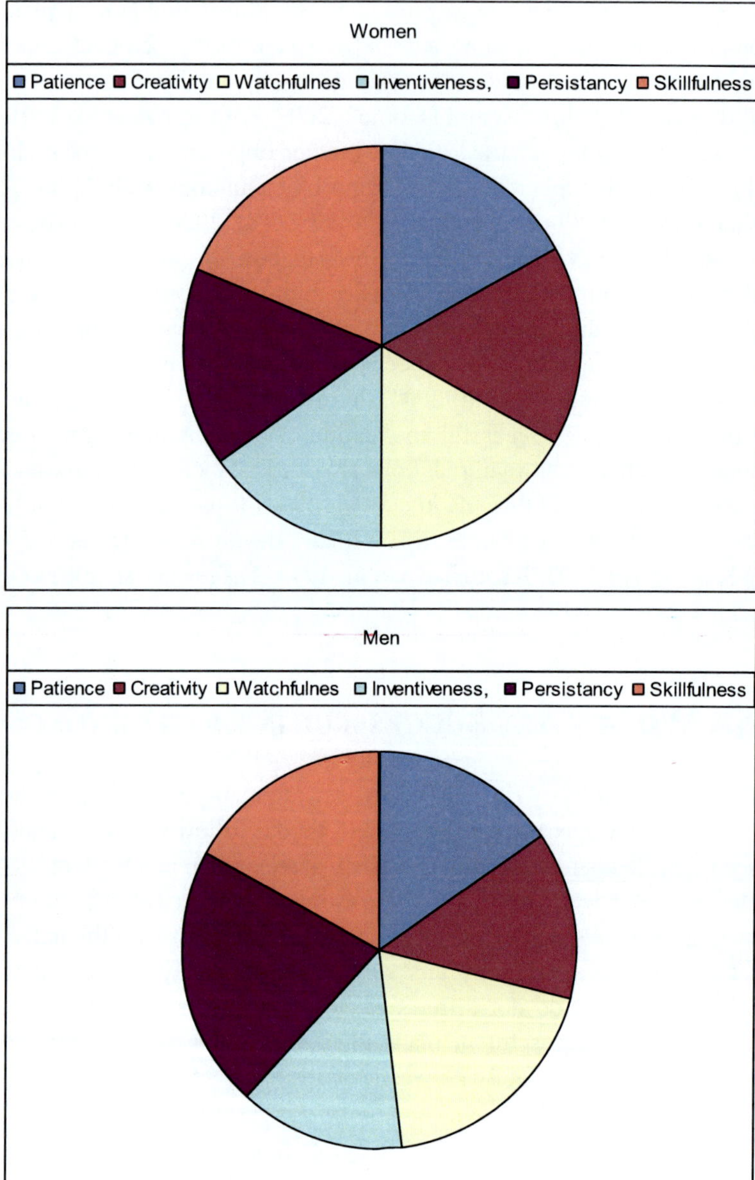

Figure 5. Gender perception for the importance of different personal features for successful plant biotechnology work

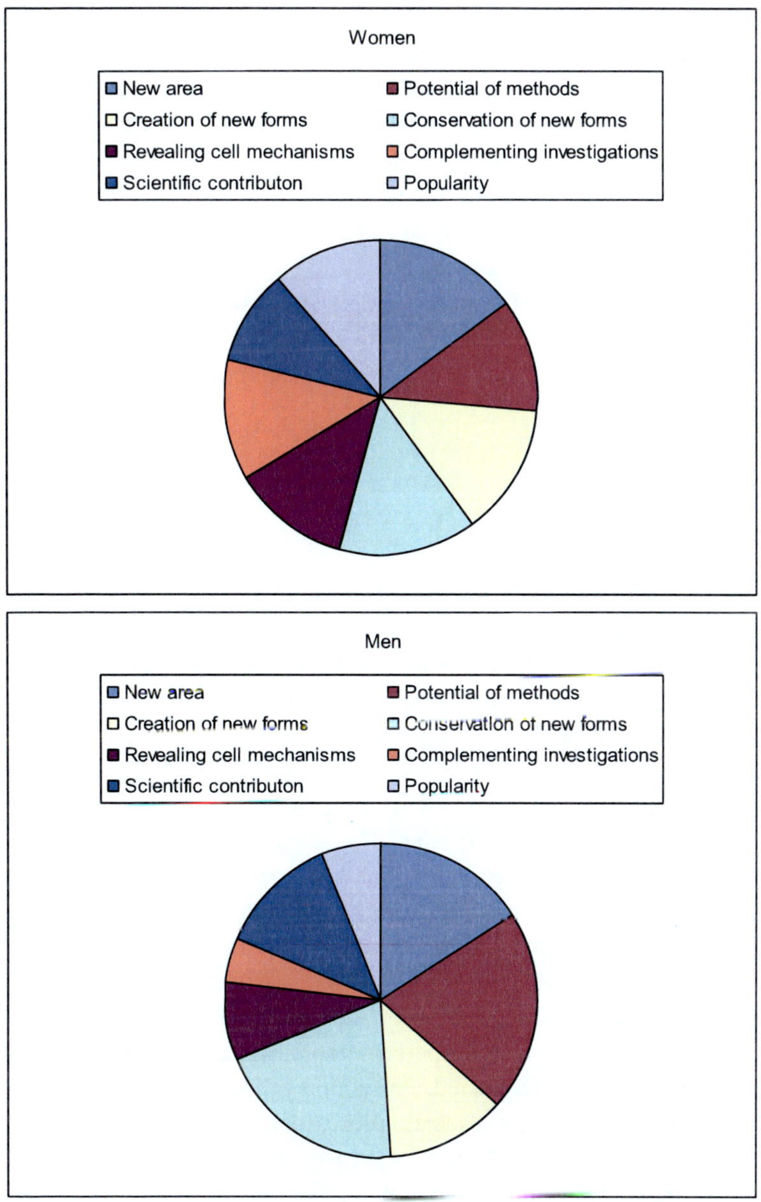

Figure 6. Gender attitude to what is attractive in plant biotechnology

Concerning the attractiveness of biotechnology, the opinion of two gender groups of biotechnologists was studied, too (Figure 5). Plant *in vitro* cultures starting their development in the middle of the previous century still are considered "new field" and are attractive area equally for women and men (15 % and 16 % respectively). Initially great expectations were delegated to the application of *in vitro* techniques and manipulations in fundamental and applied science. At present the "potentials of the methods" still is worship, though, less by women (11.5 %) than men (20.8 %). However, the latter high value is in contrast to the low one (4.8 %) representing the use of biotechnology methods as "complementing other investigations" of men. Women are keen to use additionally the new methods (12.4 %).

"Possibility to create new valuable forms" is almost equally evaluated by female (13.4 %) and male (12 %) scientists. The small difference coincides with that one in perception for the importance of creativity (Figure 6) what confirms the role of women in giving life. Opinion of women (14.4 %) and men (19.7 %) differs about the "possibility for conservation of valuable forms". Perhaps the latter is accepted as an antipode to possibility for creating of new forms. The possibility of *in vitro* methods to be utilized in "revealing the mechanisms of development" is recognized more by women (12 %) than the men (8.2 %). That could be explained with the traditional curiosity of the "tender" half of the mankind and its role in giving birth and raising children. The both genders have similar attitude (expressed by 10 % and 12.5 %) to the "possibility for contribution in science" and self expression but women see greater "possibility for popularity" than men (11.3 % compared to 6 %) in the career of a biotechnologist.

CONCLUSION

In Bulgaria, like in many other countries there is marked gender difference in choice of research field. A large proportion of female scientists are employed in areas where 'research and development expenditure is lowest' (European Commission 2005). The 'scissors' diagram of relative distribution of women and men at the different levels of seniority within the employment hierarchy could describe many research institutes.

Representation of women in top positions even in traditionally more 'feminised' fields of science (like biology) and scientific boards is still insufficient illustrating the gender bias in decision taking and policy making processes. This conclusion is supported by the figures in the group of biologists who graduated in 1978 and had equal start in scientific life. There are no female representatives in senior administrative positions while three of the men were in managing boards as directors and heads. It is difficult to define if the evaluation of the scientific excellence is gender dependent, or neutral as it is claimed. However, it seems that women prepare their Ph.D thesis for shorter period and are granted doctor degree at average one year earlier than the men. Twenty percent more women occupy the lowest grade of research position for 2 years longer period. Promotion to the next levels takes 2-3 years more for women. At present, seniority (or associate professorship) is reached by 26 % less women for 2 years longer period. No one of the women is a doctor of sciences or a full professor. Though women are underrepresented in administrative positions and expert committees they realize themselves as project leaders and students tutors. Reconciling professional and private life is still difficult for majority of female scientists like in many other countries (European Commission 2005) though it is likely that women with families also mange to pass the necessary long qualification even in international research area.

Contrasting to the above observations is the case with the women's leadership in the field of plant biotechnology. Female researchers overpass the male ones in all scientific criteria surveyed here (publication production, citations, coordination and participation in projects, expertise and tuition). Promotion through all career steps from the lowest level of researcher IIIrd grade (or assistant) to the highest reached level of senior researcher (associate professor) is two years on average shorter for female biotechnologists compared to female biologists included in this survey.

Looking for the motivation of women to choose *in vitro* cultures and genetic manipulations for scientific realization marked gender differences were not observed in the attitude and perception to biotechnology. Similar survey in Hungary (Acsady and Ferencz 2008) reveals that attitudes towards biotechnology are not significantly determined by gender and women are almost as optimistic as men that biotechnology and genetic engineering will improve our way of life. Analogically there are no clear margins in the perception of what personal features are important for the success of the work. However, discussing about the quality of women scientists it was pointed that they are 'very good in keeping a research team cooperative, in showing a high degree of responsibility in their research, and in controlling their egos better than men'. "They want to express their creativity and curiosity in exploring unknown areas of science, they want to elaborate theories and feel to comply with their wishes of self-fulfilment." (Molfino and Zucco 2008)

ACKNOWLEDGMENTS

The authors thank their colleagues from the Department of Plant Biotechnology of the Institute of Genetics - Dr. E. Zayova, T. Nedev, M. Petrova, Ph. Phillipov. Preparation of this paper was possible with the support of biologists graduated 1978 and presently working at the Academy of Sciences (Dr. G. Angelov, Dr. N. Atanasov, Dr. R. Dencheva, Dr. R. Kalchev, Dr. P. Pilarski, Dr. I. Stancheva and Dr. E. Vasileva), University of Sofia (Dr. M. Lyubenova and prof. S. Tonkov) and in other institutes (Dr. D. Dimanov and Dr. K. Vangelova). Biotechnology research was possible with the financial support of the National Scientific Fund to more than 15 projects (CC1201 still active).

REFERENCES

Angelov, G. (2008). Heavy metal pollution in Boatin reserve (Bulgaria). *Turk. J. Bot.,32,* 155-160.

Acsady, J. & Ferencz, Z. Perception and Attitudes Towards Biotechnology in Hungary. In: Molfino F. & Zucco F. (Eds.) *Women in Biotechnology. Creating interfaces.* Berlin: Springer; 2008, 93-106.

Benderliev, K., vanova, N. & Pilarski, P. (2004). Singlet oxygen and other reactive oxygen species are involved in regulation of release of iron-binding chelators from *Scenedesmus* cells, *Biologia Plantarum 47, 4,* 523-526.

Benderliev, K., Ivanova, N. & Pilarski, P. (2005). Reactive oxygen species regulate iron uptake in *Scenedesmus incrassatulus*. Gen. *Appl. Plant Physiol* 30, 3-4, 85 94.

Detcheva, R. & Grancharov, K. (2006a). Synergistic effect of geldanamycin and cisplatin on F4N leukaemia cells. *Compt. rend. Acad. Bulg. Sci., 59, (10),* 1063-1066.

Detcheva, R. & Grancharov, K. (2006b) Role of Hsp90 for the resistance of F4N cells towards cisplatin. *Compt. rend. Acad. Bulg. Sci., 59, (3),* 313-316.

Detcheva, R., Kenderov, A., Russinova, A., Spassovska, N., Kolev, K. & Grancharov, K. (2002). Correlation between HSP90 Induction Kinetics in Murine Leukemia Cells and the

Amount of Cisplatin over a Wide Range of Cytostatic Concentrations. *Zeitschrift für Naturforsch., 57c*, 407-411.

Dimanov, D. (2003). Hereditability, correlative and regression coefficients of some quantitative characters in somaclonal Oriental tobacco progenies. *Genetics and Breeding, 32*, 3-4, 11-15.

Dimitrov, H., Chassovnikarova, T. & Atanasov, N. (2007). Species diversity and structure of terrestrial small mammal assemblages in different vegetation types in Strandzha Mountain (Southeast Bulgaria). *Ecology&Safety. International Scientific Publications, 1*, 268-276.

Dryanova, A. & Ganeva, G. (1996/1997a). Callus induction and plant regeneration of wheat lines with disomic addition of rye chromosomes. Genetics & Breeding (Sf) *28, 3*, 3-9.

Dryanova, A. & Ganeva, G. (1996/1997b). In vitro regeneration system from immature embryos of different ploid genotypes triticale. Genetics & Breeding (Sf) *28, 2*, 36-42.

European Commission. Women and Science. Excellence and Innovation – Gender Quality in Science. Brussels: 2005

European Commission. Women and Science. Statistics and Indicators. She Figures. Brussels: 2006

Kalchev, R., Tsavkova, V. & Stoyanova, S. (2005). Small-scale distribution, accuracy determination and comparability of abundance and diversity of phytoplankton in two Bulgarian reservoirs. *Phytologia Balcanica, 11 (1)*, 25-32.

Kalchev, R., Terziisky, D., Stoeva, A. & Grozev, G. (2006). Nutrients and other chemical variables, related to plankton primary production in fertilized and control fishponds. *Bulgarian Journal of Agricultural Science, 2*, 226-235.

Kalchev, R., Vasilev, V., Hiebaum, G., Tzavkova V. & Pehlivanov, L. (2007). Recovery of the Srebarna Lake - experience and perspectives. *J. of Balkan Ecology, 10 (2)*, 117-130.

Kosturkova, G. (2008). Contribution of Bulgarian Women to Plant Biotechnology: Institute of Genetics Case. In: Molfino F. & Zucco F. (Eds.) *Women in Biotechnology. Creating interfaces.* Berlin: Springer, 107-117.

Kosturkova G. P. (1993). Protoplast cultures of alfalfa and their application in genetic manipulations *in vitro. Biotechnology & Biotechnological Equipment, 2*, 40-42.

Kosturkova, G. P. (2005). *In vitro* development of various soybean (*Glycine max*) explants from mature seeds. *"Breeding and Technological Aspects in Production and Processing of Soybean and Other Legume Crops". Scientific Reports of the Jubilee Scientific conference*, 8-9 Sept. 2005, Pavlikeni, 94-99.

Kosturkova, G. P. (2006). Report on *Plant Breeding and Biotechnology. Survey in Bulgaria.* Rome, Italy: FAO. http:apps3.fao.org/wiews/wiews.jsp

Kosturkova, G. Angelov, G. Rodeva, R. & Mehandjiev, A. (2003). *In vitro* modeling of biotic stress - higher resistance of pea cultures to *Phoma medicaginis* culture filtrates. *Proc. V^{th} Int. Symposium "BioProcesses"*, 186-189.

Kosturkova, G. & Delinick, A. (2007). Development of Plant Model to Study Biological Effects of Nanodilutions. *International Electronic Journal BIOAUTOMATION, 8*, S1, 184-192.

Kosturkova, G., Dimitrova, M. & Mehandjiev, A. (2005a). *In vitro* organogenic potential of new mutant lines of pea (*P. sativum*). *Plant Science (Bg), 42, 3*, 222-225.

Kosturkova, G., Mehandjiev, A., Tasheva, K., Dimitrova, M., Rodeva, R. & Mihov, M. (2005b). Establishment of long-term organogenic cultures of pea for crop improvement programs. *Proc. COST Action 843 Conf., Slovakia,* 66-68.

Kosturkova, G., Mehandjiev, A. D., Dobreva, I. & Tsvetkova, V. (1997). Regeneration systems from immature embryos of Bulgarian pea genotypes. *Plant Cell, Tissue and Organ Cultures, 48,* 139-142.

Kosturkova, G., Nedev, T. & Dimitrova, M. (2006). Application of callus cultures of soybean (*Glycine max*) to study abiotic stress factors. *Field Crops Studies (Bg), 3, 2,* 245-249.

Kosturkova, G., Rodeva, R. & Mehandjiev, A. (2001). *In vitro* selection systems for *Ascochyta pisi* and herbicide higher tolerance of pea. in "Towards the sustainable Production of Healthy Food Feed and Novel Products" (Eds.) AEP, *Proceedings of 4th European Conference on Grain legumes, 8-12 July. Cracow, Poland,* 158-159.

Kosturkova, G., Todorova, R., Sakthivelu, G., Akitha Devi, M. K., Giridhar, P., Rajasekaran, T. & Ravishankar, G. (2008). Response of Bulgarian and Indian soybean genotypes to drought and water deficiency in field and laboratory conditions. *Journal of General and Applied Plant Physiology, 34,* 3-4, 239-250.

Landjeva, S., Angelov, G., Nenova, V., Merakchijska, M. & Ganeva, G. (2004). Seedling growth and peroxidase responses to excess copper in wheat-*Aegilops geniculata* chromosome addition and substitution lines. *Genetics and Breeding, 33 (3-4),* 11-19.

Lyubenova, M., Ganeva, Y., Chipilska, L., Hadjieva, P. & Chanev, Chr. (2006). Biological Active Components of Chenopodium botrys L. Phytomass. *Journal of Balkan Ecology, Vol. 9, No 3,* 289-295.

Lyubenova, M. & Asenova, A. (2005). Indicatory Significance of Early and Late Wood of *Pinus sylvestris* L. and *Pinus nigra* Arn. Located in Sofia Region, Bulgaria. *Journal of Balkan Ecology, vol. 8, N 1,* 47-55.

Mehandjiev, A., Kosturkova, G. & Mihov, M. (2001). Enrichment of *Pisum sativum* gene resources through combined use of physical and chemical mutagens. *Israel J. Plant Science, 49,* 279-284

Mehandjiev, A., Mihov, M., Noveva, S., Rodeva, R. & Kosturkova, G. (2006). Some results from the investigations in genetic improvement of pea (*Pisum sativum* L.). *Field Crops Studies (Bg), 3, 3,* 397-403.

Molfino F. & Zucco F. Women in Biotechnology. Creating interfaces. Berlin: Springer; 2008.

Nedev, T., Dimitrov, B., Kruleva, M., Krapchev, B. & Necheva, D. (2003). Screening of Herbicide Resistance in Maize Calli *in vitro. Maize Genetics Cooperation Newsletter, 77,* 72-74.

Nedev, T., Krapchev, B. & Vassilevska-Ivanova, R. (2008). Capacity for Callus formation in Inbred Lines and F$_1$ Hybrids of Sweet Corn (*Zea Mays* L.) *Comptes rendus de l'Acad. bulgare des Sciences. 61, 2,* 197-202.

Nedev, T., Todorova, R., Kosturkova, G., Akitha Devi, M. K., Sakthivelu, G., Giridhar, P., Rajasekaran, & T. Ravishankar, G. (2007). Variation in *in vitro* morphogenic response to growth regulators in soybean genotypes from India and Bulgaria. *International Electronic Journal BIOAUTOMATION, 8, S1,* 193-200.

Nikova, V., Pundeva, R., Vladova, R. & Petkova, A. (2004). Application of tissue culture method to overcome the complete sterility of F$_1$ hybrid *Nicotiana plumbaginifolia* Viviani x *N. tabacum* L. *Israel J. Plant Science. 52,* 45-49.

Nikova, V., Vladova, R., Pundeva, R., Petkova, A. & Philipov, Ph. (2005). Overcoming the complete sterility of interspecific hybrids between *Nicotiana sylvestris* Speg.& Comes and N. *tabacum* L. via tissue culture methods. *Genetics & Breeding, 34, 3-4,* 23-31.

Noveva, S., Lazarova, N., Kosturkova, G. & Mehandjiev, A. (2006). Study of toxicity of heavy metals in pea (*Pisum sativum* L.) using different methods. *Field Crops Studies (Bg), 3, 3,* 405-413.

Petrova, M., Stoilova, T. S. & Zagorska, N. (2006a). Isoenzyme and protein patterns of *in vitro* micropropagated plantlets of *Gentiana lutea* L. after application of various growth regulators. *Biotechnol. & Biotechnol. Eq., 20, 1,* 15-19.

Petrova, M., Tasheva, K., Zagorska, N. & Evstatieva, L. (2005). *In vitro* propagation of *Arnica montana* L. *Comptes Rendus de l'Academie bulgare des Sciences, 58, 1,* 67 – 72.

Petrova, M., Zagorska, N., Tasheva, K. & Evstatieva, L. (2006b). *In vitro* propagation of *Gentiana lutea* L. *Genetics & Breeding, 35, 1-2,* 63-68.

Rodeva, R., Kosturkova, G. & Mehandjiev, A. (2005). Searching for resistance to ascochyta blight in pea by conventional and biotechnological methods and approaches. *Plant Science (Bg) 42, 3,* 226-230.

Sakthivelu, G., Akitha Devi, M. K., Giridhar, P., Rajasekaran, T., Ravishankar, G. A., Nedev, T. & Kosturkova, G. P. (2008a). Drought induced alterations in growth, osmotic potential and in vitro regeneration of soybean cultivars. *Journal of General and Applied Plant Physiology, SI, 34, 1-2,* 103-112.

Sakthivelu, G., Akita Devi, M. K., Giridhar, P., Rajasekaran, T., Ravishankar, G., Nikolova, M. T., Angelov, G., Todorova, R. & Kosturkova, G. (2008b). Isoflavone composition, phenol content, and antioxidant activity of soybean seeds from India and Bulgaria. G. *Journal of Agricultural and Food Chemistry, 56, 6,* 2090-2095.

Stancheva, I., Mitova, I. & Petkova, Z. (2004). Effects of different nitrogen fertilizer sources on the yield, nitrate content and other physiological parameters in garden beans. *Environ. Experimental Botany, 52,* 277-282.

Stancheva, I., Youssef, A. G., Geneva, M., Iliev, L. & Georgiev, G. (2008). Regulation of milk thistle (Silybum marianum L.) growth, seed yield and silymarin content with fertilization and thidiazuron application, *The Europ. J. Plant Sci. Biotech., 2 (1), 94-98.*

Stoilov, L., Darroudi, F., Meschini, R., Van Der Schans, G., Mullenders, L. H. F. & Natarajan A. T. (2000). Inhibition of repair of of X-ray induced DNA double-strand breaks in human blood lymphocytes exposed to sodium butyrate. *Int. J. Rad. Biol., 76 (11),* 1485-1491.

Stoilov, L., Wojcik, A., Giri, A. & Obe, G. (2002). SCE formation after exposure of CHO cells pre-labelled with BrdU or biotin-dUTP to various DNA damaging agents. *Mutagenesis, 17(5),* 399-403.

Tasheva, K., Petrova, M., Zagorska, N. & Georgieva, E. (2005). Micropropagation *In Vitro* of *Rhodiola rosea* L. *Proc. COST Action 843 Conference, Slovakia,* 69 –70.

Tasheva, K., Zagorska, N., Dimitrov, B. & Evstatieva, L. (2003). *In vitro* cultivation of *Rhodiola rosea* L. (2003). *Proceedings of the International Scientific Conference "75 years Institute of Forestry", BAS,* Sofia, October, 161-165.

Tonkov, S., Bozilova, E., Marinova, E. & Jüngner, H. (2008a). History of vegetation and landscape during the last 4000 years in the area of Straldzha mire (southeastern Bulgaria) – *Phytologia Balcanica,14 (2),* 185-191.

Tonkov, S., Bozilova, E., Possnert, G. & Velcev, A. (2008b). A contribution to the postglacial vegetation history of the Rila Mountains, Bulgaria: the pollen record of Lake Trilistnika. – *Quaternary International, vol. 190, 1*, 58-70.

Vangelova, K. (2008). Variations of cortisol, fatigue and sleep disturbances in sound engineers: effect of job task and fast backward-rotating shifts. *Rev. Environ. Health, 23 (1)*, 83-89.

Vangelova, K. & Israel M. (2005). Variations of melatonin and stress hormones under extended shifts and radiofrequency electromagnetic radiation. *Rev. Environ. Health, 20 (2)*, 151-161.

Vangelova, K., Deyanov, C. & Israel M. (2006). Cardiovascular risk under radiofrequency electromagnetic radiation. Int. *J. Hyg. Environ. Health, 209*, 133 - 138.

Vasileva-Tonkova, E., Galabova, D., Stoimenova, E. & Lalchev, Z. (2008). Characterization of bacterial isolates from industrial wastewater according to probable modes of hexadecane uptake. *Microbiol. Res. 163*, 481-486.

Vasileva-Tonkova, E., Nustorova, M. & Gushterova, A. (2007). New Protein Hydrolysates from Collagen Wastes Used as Peptone for Bacterial Growth. *Current Microbiol. 54*, 54-57.

Zagorska, N., Shtereva, L., Dimitrov, B. & Kruleva, M. (1998). Induced androgenesis in tomatoes (*L. esculentum* Mill.) I. Influence of genotype on androgenetic potentiality. *Plant Cell Reports*, 17, 968-973.

Zayova, E., Nikova, V., Ilieva, K. & Philipov, Ph. (2008). Callusogenesis of eggplant (*Solanum melongena L.*) *Compt. Rend. ABS., 61, 11*, 1483-1488.

In: Feminism and Women in Leadership
Editor: Vicente Nardi, pp. 145-154

ISBN: 978-1-60876-270-5
© 2010 Nova Science Publishers, Inc.

Chapter 8

SO WHAT… I AM STILL A ROCK STAR: CELEBRITY AND FEMINIST MUSIC VIDEOS IN THE NEW MILLENNIUM

Panizza Allmark
School of Communications and Arts, Edith Cowan University, Australia

ABSTRACT

This chapter will look at feminist self-affirmation in mainstream popular music videos, and how the medium and its music has become the "most important cultural form for expressing third wave feminist perspectives" (Drake, 2002, p. 187). Recent work, in the late 2000s, by female popstar video musicians, Pink and Britney Spears suggest the conflation of celebrity, stardom and feminist practices of assertion to be prevalent. The concern with subjectivity is a dominant aspect of female music videos, in which the telling of a story with strong hints of autobiography abounds. The compelling nature of female music videos is attributable to the personal insights offered by the performers. As such a neo-romanticism associated with the cult of the artist and celebrity stature is conveyed. Social commentaries of success and survival address a female audience. Furthermore, there is an aggressive defiance in which the lyrics and the music video textually enact a challenge of the male domain, in which independence both financially as well as sexually and emotionally is paramount.

INTRODUCTION

In order to discuss the practice of contemporary third wave popular feminist music video artists, who provide a challenge to the narrow gender prescriptions for females, it is necessary to look at the short history of female music videos. The emergence of female address in music videos occurred in the early nine-eighties. Madonna and Cindy Lauper were pioneers in this field and achieved commercial popularity due to their visibility, style and gender performance in music videos, which was quite unlike their predecessors, and the masculine dominance of music videos of the time. Of significance, is that these musicians' highlighted white women's visibility, which celebrated a notion of girlhood that played with overt confidence, sensuality, and revelry and became a cultural dominant within music video texts. This also signaled "the commercial pre-eminence - of ironic, postmodern modes of gender performance" that can be seen in the lineage of female white music video artists (Wald, 1998 p. 588).

Lisa A. Lewis argues that it was with the 1983 release of Cindy Lauper's video 'Girls just want to have fun' which signaled a shift in the style of music videos which aimed at a distinctly female-address audience (1993, p.136). The video filled a niche in the market, which was then dominated by male pop/rock stars and masculine proclivity, which spotlighted the 'band' or 'star' on stage, and/or "male adolescent experiences and desires" (Lewis, 1993, p. 134). The 'Girls just want to have fun' video won the first ever Female Music Video award in 1984. In the video Lauper engaged in gendered female activities, such as dance, talking on the phone, fashion play and dress. 'Girls just want to have fun' became a feminist anthem and a theme for a plethora of female music videos that celebrated distinctive feminine activities and feminine empowerment.

Of crucial significance, around this time, is also the impact of Madonna's emergence as a music video artist. Madonna who has received much critical discussion (Shwichtenberg, 1993, Fiske, 1989, Lewis, 1987) was pivotal in establishing female addressed videos. Her "postmodern feminism is part of a larger postmodern phenomenon which her videos also embody in the blurring of the hitherto sacrosanct boundaries and polarities such as male/female, high art/pop art, film/TV, fiction/reality, private/public (Kaplan, 1987,p 126). Furthermore, as David Gauntlett notes

> Madonna's expressions of womanhood are close to what Angela McRobbie (1999) calls 'popular feminism' and Natasher Walter's 'New Feminism' (1998). These 'versions of feminism are also similar to the idea of empowered female living celebrated by Cosmopolitan magazine for many years: a vision that emphasizes being confident independent, pleasure-seeking and subservient to no one (Gauntlett, 2004, p. 168).

Madonna and Lauper promoted the cultural visibility of white women in popular music videos. They were the first women to attract the kind of devotion of young female fans normally associated with male rock stars (Lewis, 1990, p. 10). Madonna and Lauper set the trend for the celebration and promotion of female subjectivity within the mainstream popular music audience genre. As Sheila Whitley (2000, p. 6) suggests, "the female artists who are most prominently on Top 100 charts are primarily concerned with subjectivity, more interested in communicating and telling stories that in taking on the more masculine obsession of sonic wizardry" associated with, for example, "Radiohead, Rage against the Machine and Space Team Electra".

It should be noted that female authorship and female viewer identification is primarily associated with the female performer. The gender of the director of the video is not significant in the reception of the video. Lewis argues that a "combination of generic textual practices in music video – the female musician singing 'her' song on the video soundtrack, her on-screen performance as musician and actor…can create a context of female authorship even when videos are directed by men" (2004, p.212). Significantly, the discourses of celebrity and how it is bound up with the performer have been integral to the reception and success of the video. Furthermore, the authorial voice is paramount in sending feminist messages, and promoting the cultural visibility of women within popular music.

In a comparative nature to women's literature, personal insights and life stories provide a compelling force of female music videos. As such, the lineage of nineteenth century Romanticism prevails in rock and popular music. Whitley argues that "notions of autonomy, of seriousness, of expressive truth are important. In other words, 'the cult of the artist, of auterism, of 'poetic' elevation and 'emotional depths'"remain features of expression that are prevalent in female music (2000, p.6). Of significance is that the 'telling of the tale' is important in conveying the relationship between women and society (Whitley, 2000, p. 8). In the music videos the cult of celebrity is further amplified to highlight the relationship between the star status and the traditional notion of women as objects of the gaze, which is deeply associated with popularization and personalization.

SPEARS IN THE SPOTLIGHT

Women pop stars in particular are the objects of specularisation in which there seems to be a media fascination in finding the ordinary or 'raw' aspects to their lives. Celebrity scandals are the narrative focus of tabloid magazines. This news angle, perhaps, makes them appear more 'real'. Dyer (1979,1986) in his seminal analysis of star systems acknowledges discursive structures that produce celebrities, highlighting the intertextual approach. Su Holmes' refers to this as the 'ordinary/extraordinary' paradox, the notion that stars are constructed as being 'ordinary' (like 'us'), yet simultaneously 'distinctive' and 'special' (2005, p. 10). However, their falling star status into the realm of the ordinary or damaged females produces a cultural anxiety about the role of women. For example, "few celebrities have received more negative attention than Britney Spears. Her fall from pop stardom and descent into mental health problems and drug addiction has been well documented, not least due to her supposed status as an "unfit mother"" (Fairclough, 2008, p14). Rolling Stone magazine published a cover story titled the "The Tragedy of Britney Spears" *She was a pop princess. Now she's in and out of hospitals, rehab and court. How Britney lost it all"* (Grigoriadis, 2008). The fascination with the background life dramas of this young popstar, with her predominantly teen fan base, is quite extraordinary. Spears, notably has topped Yahoo Searches for the past four years (Jiang Yuxia, 2008, p. 1). Furthermore, *Rolling Stone* magazine has described her as "one of the most controversial and successful female vocalists of the 21st century.

The fascination with Britney Spears' life, perhaps, is due to her early representations 'as the girl next door' (Grigoriadis, 2008). Her star persona involved the clean living image of a healthy, white American girl, who the public witnessed growing into maturity. Her "whiteness signaled purity, cleanliness, and frangibility" and represented an idealised female sexuality (Railton & Watston, 2005, p.61). Her liminal teenage years revealed a more sexual persona that provided a contradictory appeal. "She had publicly vowed to remain a virgin until marriage and played the girl next door in interviews. But when performing, her outfits were tiny and tight, her dance moves sexualised and her eyes distinctly 'come-hither'" (Whyllie, 2008, p. 1). Spears' 2002 performance of 'I'm Not a Girl, Not Yet a Woman', which won a 2003 Golden Music Award and Popstar magazine award for best international video, was a testament to her changing image. From a sassy school girl in her debut hit '...Baby One More Time' (1998) to a more scantily clad temptress in her subsequent videos,

Spears presented a sexualized femininity, that bespoke of third wave feminist practices of sexual assertion. But, nevertheless, the contradictory appeal of innocence and sexuality, as well as her depicted off-screen representation as a mother, has provided debate and angst for scholars and fans in situating Spears within a feminist framework. Melissa Lowe, for example, states in her research on the reception of Britney Spears and colliding feminisms asserts that for young girls Spears is a "touch and touchy subject" (2000, p. 124). She claims that

> Unlike Madonna, we don't read Spears as using such ambiguity and self-conscious play with traditional constructs of femininity to challenge or undo dominant gender codes. And, unlike Madonna's fans of the 1980s, Spears's fans of today seem not to feel empowered by any overt expressions of her sexuality. (Lowe, 2000, p.125)

Furthermore, Su holmes argues that there is a cultural anxiety about gender roles. she contends that:

> Seeing Britney Spears 'fail' as a mother, or young women lurching in and out of 're-hab', might be seen as 'proof' of the fact that women can't 'have it all' (work, career, family, love life) and be successful. This is then seen as essentially 'reassuring' in terms of traditional gender boundaries. We might also point to the fact that women, and especially young women, are often positioned as epitomizing a decline in the cultural value of fame ('famous for being famous'). The fact that women are more likely to be conceived as 'trivial' celebrities reflects the fact that women's work (in terms of career) has always been less valued than men's. (cited in Silverstein, July, 1, 2008)

Lisa appignanesi also suggests that:

> Then as now, it seems, men can be wild and bad, transgress bounds, enter the revolving doors of what we casually call "rehab", without incurring the stigma and constraints of madness, whereas women, certainly once they have reached the maturity of motherhood, cannot. Being a bad, rebellious girl, in the style of Amy Winehouse or Lily Allen, may just about be permissible, but the socially defined limits of what is considered "sane" quickly narrow with the arrival of babies. (Appignanesi)

Holmes and Appignanesi raise very interesting points about the status of female celebrities in popular culture. Despite their rise to fame for their musical talents, women are still judged according to their adherence to traditional gender roles. Furthermore, whereas the aura of the male genius is often celebrated, in which males are revered for their talents and potential for eminence, women are judged according to their personal life stories and how they fit within limited feminine sexual stereotypes.

The cult of celebrity that encompasses Spears is phenomenal and is described "as the most public downfall of any star in history" (Grigoriadis, 2008). Nevertheless, her story is one of survival. It is a story very much attuned to a feminist consciousness that the personal is political. The music from her 2008 album 'Blackout' attributes to this feminist affirmation. In 2008, Britney Spears won top pop video of the year and Best female Video in the MTV Video Music Awards, for the song "Piece of Me" from this album. Unlike the dulcet and melodic anthem of female sisterhood in the 'Girls just want to have fun' video, which won an award 24 years earlier and embodies the values of the female collective, often associated with second-wave feminism, 'Piece of Me' is a declaration of struggle and survival which closely aligns with Spears celebrity status. It is indicative of a shift in feminism, which embraces pop culture and the cult of celebrity. 'Girls just want to have fun' signaled a celebration of female solidarity and girl culture, where 'Piece of Me' confronts the attention given to celebrity feminine behavior. It espouses third-wave feminist tendencies of 'do-it-yourself' feminism in which individual empowerment overrides a collective political identity (Bayle, 1996).

The success of this music video 'Piece of me' performed by Britney Spears is attributable to its self-reflexivity. The music video parodies Spears celebrity scandals. Key features of the video are the foray of paparazzi following Spears and the close-up images of gossip magazines. In the spotlight is Spears. She is defiant, challenging and confronting. She presents a cynical awareness of her celebrity role and how she has been depicted. The song presents her autobiography within the celebrity circus. She begins the song with "I'm miss American dream since I was 17". The lyrics highlight the emblematic status she holds, which is blonde, white and beautiful. She was the 'ideal' girl within the constructs of Hollywood/American/Globalised celebrity, before falling from grace. The chorus further emphasizes her status in the statement "I'm Mrs. Lifestyles of the rich& famous (You want a piece of me?) I'm Mrs. Oh my God, That Britney's Shameless! (You want a piece of me?)". The chart and award success of this music video seems to be deeply attributable to Spear's self-reflexive lyrics and performance in the video. It spotlights the cult of celebrity and the song's popularity is due to its tell-tailing nature. It also draws upon "third-wave tenets of confrontation and contradiction" (Shugart, Wggoner & Hallstein, 2001, p.198). Spears is confronting her scandalous media image, yet also promoting herself as a kind of *femme fatale,* through her sensual look in the video text.

Reading it as a feminist text it draws attention to female empowerment through the notion of tactics, rather than strategy. I here draw upon Michel de Certeau's notion of tactics, in which certain maneuvers, guile and inventiveness is called upon from within to subvert patriarchal constructs. Tactics make a practice available to people displaced and excluded as other by the bordering actions of strategy (Morris, 1992, p.32). Fundamentally, it is a mode of action determined by not having a place of one's own. Indeed tactics aptly relates to a feminist political subversion by cleverly playing upon 'opportunities' (de Certeau, 1985, p. 127). The tactics in the video 'Piece of Me' also refer to Tong's (1992, p. 228) evocations of Irigaray's theory of mimicry in which she asserts that "if women exist only in men's eyes, as image, women should take those images and reflect them back to men in magnified proportions." The safe viewing space of the spectator is disturbed, and the wry self-reflexive humour in the video is a tactic that confronts the viewer. Her participation in "self – deprecating parodies suggest that humor is a persuasive way of criticizing a popular genre from the inside" (Roberts, p. 174).

Since the 1960s, "front-line performers were expected to *look* feminine and in retrospect it is obvious that attitudes towards women artists had not undergone any significant change" (Whitley, p.51). Furthermore, the emergence of the "girl" in music culture is a newly privileged mode of white middle-class femininity (Ward, 1999). As previously discussed Spears had embraced the epitome of white girl femininity. However, the scandals that have surrounded her have occurred when she didn't live up to this ideal, for example by shaving her head, an alleged sex tape and breakdown which have been the staple of the tabloid press news stories that have shattered her facade. Speers 'white trash' behaviour was an affront to the privilege of white girl femininity. Spears, labeled as 'white trash', "did not display the cultural tastes appropriate to the privileges of whiteness and wealth" (Cobb, 2008, p. 6). Nevertheless, in her music video she presents and plays with the persona of white girl femininity and heteronormative beauty culture. With her long blonde flowing hair, sensual dance routines and pouts to the camera her performance in one of mimicry and defiance.

PINK COMMAND

Another female performer whose star persona plays with notions of normative femininity is Pink. By setting herself apart from her pop musical peers by dying her short spiky hair pink in her early career, she presented a parody of feminine ideals. Pink's affiliation may be aligned with previous white female musicians such as the Riot Grrrls who were influential in the 1990s with the rise of female musicians within punk and postpunk music. It was "loud, fast, and unapologetically "angry" music associated with the pre- dominantly white, middle-class women in and around the Riot Grrrl movement (Ward, 1992, p.593). The girl style revolution offered by Pink and Britney Spears for mainstream audiences, nevertheless, also follows the blond ambition and the avenues opened up by Madonna (Gauntlett, p. 161). Pink's *oeuvre* includes hits such as 'Stupid Girls' (2006), which won the 2006 MTV Video Music Award for Best Pop Video. In the video Pink parodies female celebrity star personas and the narrow stereotypes offered. She highlights contemporary cultural feminine fixations with celebrity culture. 'Blondeness', thinness, anti-intellectualism and exhibitionism are its themes. She also plays herself trying to fit in to the star system. "The problem, Pink surmises, is that if we waste our time, money and energy on trying to be someone else's idea of fabulous, we waste our potential to be something better" (Vineyard, 2006, p. 1). Pink espouses a feminist consideration of identity politics. Through the use of humour, the video "draws attention to the use of sex as a promotional device and to the commercial aspects of the star system of American corporate rock and roll" (Roberts, p.173).

Another of Pink's releases, 'So what I am still a Rockstar' (2008) is an interesting video in its use of humour and autobiography. It was also nominated for the 2009 MTV Video Music Award. The song is a reflection on the ending of her recent relationship. It is sung from the first person perspective, similar to the major 1979 hit 'I will survive' by Gloria Gaynor. 'I Will Survive' is also about independence after a failed relationship. It became an anthem for feminists and "taken up as a kind of rallying-cry of the victimized and the vainglorious, a gay anthem, a political shibboleth" (The Independent, 14 April 2003). 'So what I am still a Rockstar', on the other hand, revels in survival through occupying the position of Pink's celebrity status and reckless 'bad boy' rock behavior, which for a female artist conveys a third-wave feminist hallmark "of an 'in-your-face' confrontational attitude" (Shugart, Wggoner & Hallstein, 2001, p.195). The lyrics begin with:

> I guess i just lost my husband
> I don't know where he went
> So i'm gonna drink my money
> I'm not gonna pay his rent (Nope)
> I got a brand new attitude
> And i'm gonna wear it tonight
> I wanna get in trouble
> I wanna start a fight

Whitley asserts that in popular music "to achieve success, it seemed that women had to take men on at their own game, and within the arena of rock this involved drink, drugs and sexual promiscuity" (p.51). As I have discussed, earlier, with the example of Britney Spears there is feminist and popular culture backlash to women who have been portrayed as an ideal of white girl femininity behaving in inappropriate (white-trash) ways and, significantly, once women popstars become mothers, they need to return to traditional gendered roles of the nurturing self-sacrificing mother. Pink challenges traditional femininity. In 'So what I'm still a Rockstar' Pink enacts stereotypical masculine irreverent rebellious rock star behaviour. She gets a tattoo, smashes a guitar, chainsaws a tree and revels in the rock star attention.

Pink's behaviour also conveys the horror of the abject. In the masculine order the abject is "related to perversion" (Kristeva, 1982, p. 15). In one scene, Pink directs a couple of males to urinate in bottles. She then handles these bottles to two unsuspecting young males who consumes it, assuming it's beer. She displays contempt and amusement at the young males drinking the piss she has offered. She appears empowered by her actions. By representing the abject Pink disturbs the repressions of the patriarchal order. In her overt juvenile delinquent behavior in the video she appropriates a masculine position. Unlike the video of the hit 1979 'I will survive' which depicts Gloria Gaynor soulfully performing in the spotlight of a stage, in which she laments her broken heart and proclaims her new found strength, Pink, almost thirty years later is strong, rebellious and conveys what may be considered a masculine behavior pattern of 'acting out' at the end of a relationship. She follows the individualism and defiance of third-wave feminism. "Being empowered in the third-wave sense is about feeling good about oneself and having the power to make choices, regardless of what those choices are" (Shugart, Wggoner & Hallstein, 2001, p.195). Furthermore, it is also about self-promotion, which has been "intuitively more normative and acceptable for men than for women" (Rudman, 1998, p. 629). Pink, in her third wave feminist mode, is self-confident and confronting.

"Historically, women have been seen as less competent and competitive than are men" (Rudman, 1998, p 629). Pink's revelry and mockery of her rock star image in the video is boldly asserting her equality with her male equivalents. Lewis (2004, p. 135-136) argues that "female video musicians textually enact an entrance into a male domain of activity and signification. Symbolically they execute take-overs of male space, their erasure of sex-roles and demand parity with male privilege". Furthermore, as Lewis highlights "motifs based on street symbolism and leisure themes can become powerful social commentaries for female audiences" (2004, p. 217). It challenges the social construction of women and girls. It can be read as suggesting that we can attest social mores on how women and girls should behave and places we can be. Rather than looking inwards it is about acting outwards. It is also about speaking your mind, and not holding back. Notably, the expression of rage, discontent and taking over public space is the cornerstone of the white male rock tradition.

Pink is defiant in her video. She is behaving in many ways like a 'male' rock star, whilst still holding on to cultural notions of femininity. Again, in the video through the use of humour Pink challenges social constructs. One key scene involving her celebrity status and the role of women as objects of the gaze is when she disrobes and appears naked to a crowd of paparazzi. Rather, than a demure feminine coy pose, she parades and flaunts her body. She challenges conventional notions of how a woman should behave. She is empowered through her narcissistic display. So what, she is a rock star and in the music video this comic behaviour is given credence because she is in control and empowered by her actions. This is unlike the disempowerment of fellow popstar, Britney Spears who was caught in 'real' paparazzi photographs without wearing underwear. Her public pubic exposure was deemed inappropriate and her 'scandalous' images spread virally on the net. Of significance is that Spears' public exposure is the topic of over six hundred thousand sites on Google. However, through the music video genre this scandal may be redressed. In the realm of the music video female popstars have the opportunity, through the use of humour, to confront conventions and their scrutinisation. Spears did this in deliberately holding her dress down to cover her genital area in various scenes in the video 'Piece of Me'. Moreover, in celebrating her power and sex appeal Pink also presents an aggressively defiant girl power that can be aligned with a third wave feminist consciousness.

CONCLUSION

Third wave feminism is entrenched in popular culture. It is in the fashion and spectacle of femininity, in its myriad of forms. It is appropriated, commodified and reinscribed by the mass media. It involves confrontation and contradiction as highlighted in the previously discussed music videos. "The politics of difference that drives third-wave feminism thus are manifesting an embracing of contradiction so those apparently inconsistent political viewpoints coexist in the name of third wave feminism" (Shugart, Wggoner & Hallstein, 2001, p.195). The postmodern fragmentary nature of the music video provides a forum to display the contradictions. In the earlier years of Music Television Video (MTV), Kaplan argued that its postmodern universe, "with its celebration of the look, the surfaces, the self-as-commodity, threatens to reduce everything to the image/representation/simulacrum" (Kaplan, 1987, p. 151). She contended that there was a danger that the video format could induce the reduction of the female body to merely an image and the notion of self would be annihilated. Whilst many music videos by male performers, for example in the hip hop and rock genre, have been accused of misogyny because the portrayal of women is seen as demeaning and women are presented merely as 'eye candy', female music video performers are beginning to challenge the subservient position of women. The rise and popularity of female performers since the 1980s, when "popular music, at its worst (the image content of most music videos) usually functioned to perpetuate all the old gender stereotypes, with a few spaces for ambiguous (not feminist) alternatives" seem to have shifted (Pratt, 1990, p.39). In the new millennium, white young female performances have embraced third wave feminist practices, such as the use of irony, sarcastic discourse, wry humour and sexual confidence. For example, following the legacy of Madonna, female performers such as Gwen Stefani, Avril Lavigne and Lilly Allen, all have won various music video awards and have espoused notions of girlhood that is defiant, confrontational and celebrates female independence. Through their disparate modes of femininity they have succeeded in commercial popularity.

Nevertheless, the issue of declaring independence involving financial, sexual and emotional issues for females within popular music is not new. It has been a cornerstone of Black women's rap. Woldu (2006) argues that this self-affirmation also follows a

> long tradition in black women's music hat has its roots in the songs of the blues women of the 1920s and 1930s. Black women's ignoble social status in the early twentieth century was a double-edged sword; on the one hand (p.94) wonderfully liberating and empowering,

enabling the women to exist outside the rigid structures of the cult of true womanhood and, on the other relegating and confining them to the lowest rung in the social hierarchy.

Furthermore, Blues women, in particular, "were expected to deviate from the norms defining orthodox female behavior" (Davis 1998, p. 38). This pattern is certainly exemplified in the music videos of the white female performers that I have discussed, in which the elevation of women's life experiences and the vitality of self-empowerment are key themes. The story telling nature, and the sincerity of assertion provides an avenue for identification and exploration.

The pleasure for women and girls in viewing the videos derives from their openness to interpretation. As John Fiske (1989, p. 117) highlights, similar to watching soap operas, there is license for the viewer to insert "herself into the narrative, and to play with social conventions, rules and boundaries, in an active" way. Furthermore, the sense of power that the videos offer a female viewer in centred on fantasy and representation. It is about agency and entitlement. The videos represents a carnivalesque fantasy of rebellion for women in what they stand up, speak up and/or engage in bad boy behavior. It is a fantasy about female empowerment. The narratives that are constructed celebrate a girlhood that disrupts a patriarchal discourse of the passive feminine subject (Ward, p.588).

REFERENCES

Appignanesi, L. (2008). Out of control. *The Guardian*, March 10. http://www.guardian. co.uk/music/2008/mar/10/popandrock.women. Bail, K. (Eds.) (1996). DIY Feminism. Allen & Unwin.

Cobb, S. (2008). 'Mother of the Year: Kathy Hilton, Lynne Spears, Dina Lohan and Bad Celebrity Motherhood'. *Genders*. Issue 48 http://www.genders.org/g48/g48_cobb.html

De Certeau, M. (1985). Practices of space. In M. Blonsky (Eds.) *On Signs* (122-145). Oxford: Blackwell.

Drake, Jennifer (2002). 'The Mis/Education of Righteos Babes: Popular Culture and Third Wave Feminism' in Ronald Strickland (Eds.) *Growing Up Postmodern*. Rowman & Littlefield.

Dyer, R. (1979). *Stars* London:Educational Advisory Service, British Film Institute.

Dyer, R. (1987). *Heavenly Bodies: Films stars and society* Hampshire : Macmillan.

Fairclough, K. (2008). Fame is a Losing Game: Celebrity Gossip Blogging, Bitch Culture and Postfeminism. *Genders*, Issue 48http://www.genders.org/g48/g48_fairclough.html

Fiske, J. (1989). *Reading the Popular*. Cambridge. Unwin Hyman.

Gauntlett, D (2004). 'Madonna's daughters: girl power and the empowered girl-pop breakthrough'. In: Fouz-Hernandez, Santiago and Jarman-Ivens, Freya, (Eds.) *Madonna's drowned worlds: new approaches to her cultural transformations*, Ashgate, Aldershot, UK, 161-175.

Gaynor. G. (1979). 'I will Survive'. Writers: Freddie Perren & Dino Fekaris.

Grigoriadis, V. (2008). The Tragedy of Britney Spears. Rolling Stone, February. http://www.rollingstone.com/news/story/18310562/the_tragedy_of_britney_spears

Kaplan, E. A. (1987). *Rocking Around the Clock*. Routledge.

Kristeva, J. (1982). Powers of horror: An essay on abjection (*L. Roudiez, Trans.*). New York: Columbia University Press.

Lewis, L. A. (2004). 'Form and Female Authorship' in *Popular Music: critical concepts in media and cultural studies* Simon Frith ed. England, New York, Routledge.

Lewis, L. A. (1993). "Being Discovered: The emergence of female address on MTV" in *Sound and Vision* by Simon Frith, Andrew Goodwin, Lawrence Grossberg.

Lewis, L. A. (1990). *Gender Politics and MTV: Voicing the difference.* Philadelphia : Temple University Press.

Lowe, M. (2003). 'Colliding Feminisms: Britney Spears, & Tweens and the Politics of Reception', *Popular Music and Society*, *26, 2*, 123-140.

Morris, M. (1992). Great moments in social climbing: King Kong and the human fly. In B. Colomina (Eds.) *Sexuality and space* (1-52). New York: Princeton Architectural Press.

Pink. (2008). 'So What I am still a Rockstar'. Writers: Pink, Max Martin, Shellback. Album: Funhouse.

Pratt, R. (1990). *Rhythm and Resistance: Explorations in the Political Uses of Popular Music.* Praeger.

Railton, D & Watson, P. (2005). *Feminist Media Studies, Vol. 5, No. 1*, 51-63.

Rudman, L. A. (1998). Self-Promotion as a Risk Factor for Women: The Costs and Benefits ofCounterstereotypical Impression Management. *Journal of Personality and Social Psychology. Vol. 74, No. 3*, 629-645.

Silverstein, M. (2008). 'The Facination with Celebrity Women in Crisis' *The Huntington Post.* July 1, 2008 http://www.huffingtonpost.com/melissa-silverstein/the-facination-with-celeb_b_110201.html

Shugart, H. Waggoner, C. & Hallstein, D. (2001). 'Mediating Third-Wave Feminism: Appropriation as Postmodern Media Practice' in *Critical Studies in Media Communication. Vol. 18, No. 2*, June 2001, 194–210.

Spears, B. (2007). 'Piece of Me'. Writers: Christian Karlsson, Pontus Winnberg, Klas Åhlund Label: Jive, Producers: Bloodshy & Avant,

Tong, R. (1992). *Feminist thought: A comprehensive introduction.* London: Routledge

Whitley, S. (2000). *Women and Popular Music: Sexuality identity and Subjectivity.* London and New York, Routledge.

Woldu, G. (2006). "Gender and anomaly: women in rap'" in *The Resisting Muse ed Ian Peddie.* Aldershot, Hants, England ; Burlington, VT: Ashgate.

Wyllie, A. (2008). 'The seven ages of Britney Spears', *The Scotsman*, 27th November, 2008 http://news.scotsman.com/britneyspears/The-seven-ages-of-Britney.4741324.jp

Vineyard, J. (2008). 'Pink's 'Stupid' New Video Feautres Fakes Breasts, *Fake 50 Cent'.* MTV. January 18 2008. http://www.mtv.com/news/articles/1521044/20060118/pink.jhtml? headlines=true

In: Feminism and Women in Leadership
Editor: Vicente Nardi, pp. 155-167

ISBN: 978-1-60876-270-5
© 2010 Nova Science Publishers, Inc.

Chapter 9

QUALITY PERSPECTIVE ON WOMEN'S ROLE IN MARRIAGE: ASSESSMENT OF WOMEN'S SATISFACTION AND WORK

P.L. Rika Fatimah[*][(1)] *and A.A. Jemain*[(2)]

[(1)]Graduate Centre for Management (GCM), Faculty of Management (FOM),
Multimedia University, Malaysia
[(2)]School of Mathematical Science (PPSM), Faculty of Science & Technology (FST),
Universiti Kebangsaan Malaysia, Malaysia

ABSTRACT

Women's satisfaction related to their marriage and work bring about interesting discussion in this study. Feminism has been opening work opportunities for women to be equal to men and to allow women to be more developed and independent in society. However, conflict of the double role—women's work and women's role in marriage as a wife and mother—to women seems continuously discussed. In general, conflicts occur as consequences between the two commitments, which are demanding that women perform excellently both in their marriage and at work. The conflicts include women's time management, priority need, energy division, decision making, love and attention, etc. Therefore, it is important to assess the level of women's satisfaction with regard to her work in order to identify how strongly a woman's work influences a woman's satisfaction in married life. In this study, we assess women's satisfaction in marriage with respect to several kinds of occupations from a quality perspective. The quality perspective offers a new way of assessing women's satisfaction by using a Quality Function Deployment (QFD) method. The QFD method, which is usually applied in industry, can be adopted in assessing women's satisfaction towards their marriage and work life. QFD produces a friendly interpretation of highly complex and intangible matters around married life; thus, it makes the assessment of women's satisfaction in marriage and work easier. By using QFD, we determine the variables and dimensions with respect to marital characteristics by integrating previous studies and considering expert opinions. Many activities carried out in married life are representative of a

---

[*] Email: rika_paper@yahoo.com

woman's role in marriage. In addition, QFD also compares the level of satisfaction with respect to a woman's occupation in a clearer and simpler way. The comparison leads to the identification of which dimension is the most satisfying and which one is less than the other, with respect to a different kind of occupation. In this study, we perform the QFD method on assessing women's satisfaction by utilizing data gathered from a questionnaire survey based on 587 respondents across West Malaysia, Malaysia. The effort to enhance women's satisfaction of their success in playing the double role in the marriage and at work is our main consideration. This study may contribute a new point of view regarding the progress of feminism in the social aspect and in women's quality of life.

INTRODUCTION

Feminism allows women to play the role of taking care of the household as well as also providing financial support for the marriage. Therefore, many activities carried out by women represent the consumer aspects of their role both in the marriage and at work. Women undertake these activities to fulfill their needs which can be classified in the order of preference using Maslow's Hierarchy of Need. Generally, people first seek food and shelter before they satisfy other needs, such as leisure, career, etc. Women also give priorities to the needs, with the first priority of fulfilling family needs before considering earning money (Locke and Thomes 1976; Duvall 1976). By using the approach of Maslow's Hierarchy of Need, several important aspects contribute to the consumer aspects of women's role, which make up the entity of women's existence both in the family and the marriage (Rika Fatimah et al. 2008).

Marriage is a critical point of role transition for couples who marry for the first time. It involves moving on from their families, and from the orientation phase of their development, to the unfamiliar husband-wife relationship (Duvall, 1976). Then the marriage is developed into a family where more roles are involved such as mother-father, grandmother-grandfather, aunt-uncle, etc. A greater challenge demanded of the couples is especially to improve and maintain their marriage loyalty. The marriage loyalty indicates the capability of the couples themselves for initiating a long-term marriage by satisfying their spouse in term of fulfilling the spouse's needs (Rika Fatimah et al. 2009). In order to achieve a better quality of marriage loyalty, the couples should understand and support each other in many things. However, the condition is more complicated for women who have outside work since they must play a double role—for both outside work and household work. Therefore, the condition of the double role may influence a woman's feeling of satisfaction in the married life.

The question may occur, is it true that the women's double roles influence women's satisfaction in marriage? Is there any different level of women's satisfaction in marriage with respect to different kinds of occupations? Therefore, in this paper, we proposed a new method to determine more clearerly what activities are involved in achieving a better quality of marriage through better women's satisfaction in marriage. By using the Quality Function Deployment (QFD) approach, we deliver a systematic way to identify what is marriage loyalty and how does a women's occupation affect the level of satisfaction in married life.

QFD is a technique which is quite versatile for industrial application, we believe that it is possible to adopt this approach for marriage and women's contexts. Earlier applications included, for example, the problem of product design. The designing process related to making the customer satisfied could be achieved by applying QFD techniques to the needs put forward by the customers (see Walden, 2003). The success of QFD has attracted its implementation in other fields such as the service industry (see Bosch and Enriquez, 2005). In addition to implementation of QFD for organizational planning, Gerst (2004) has also applied QFD for social system redesign (Masui et al. 2003). Considering these applications, the QFD technique is quite flexible and can also be applied in many areas, such as social science.

In this study, we apply the QFD approach to identify the complexity of marriage and to assess women's satisfaction with respect to different kinds of occupations. The satisfaction reflects the level of executing activities of women's roles both in outside work and household work. Marriage loyalty is complex and complicated, therefore it is necessary to simplify the loyalty by deploying it in a clearer and more structured manner. In addition, women's satisfaction is obtained from questionnaires distributed to 587 respondents. The questionnaires were designed following the deployment of marriage loyalty.

We divided this study into seven main parts. First is the introduction followed by The Traditional QFD, which briefly discusses QFD. The third part will discuss the adoption of the traditional QFD in the context of marriage and women. The fourth part is the Methodology where we present our subjects and scope of research, measures and scale reliability. Result and discussion is the fifth part, presenting the implementation of QFD into the marriage and women context, blended with a brief discussion of the result. Then, in the last part, are the conclusion and references.

THE TRADITIONAL QFD

Quality Function Deployment is a product or service development process based on interfunctional teams such as marketing, manufacturing, engineering and research and development (Hauser, 1993). These interfunctional teams may apply the tools of quality in sequence to deploy customer input by identifying the design, manufacturing process, and service delivery (Day 1993). Ensuring that products enter production would fully satisfy the need of the customers by fulfilling the necessary quality levels at every stage of product development (Amaturaga et al. 2001).

The final output of QFD can be represented in the form of House of Quality (HOQ) as shown in Figure 1. The main positions of HOQ of the room, left, right, top, roof and center, represent the sequence of the process in implementing the QFD approach. The left room represents determination of Voice of The Customer. The voice can be found based on the survey of customers' needs and wants. Next, the right room indicates the process of determining the Customer Competitive Evaluation for the purpose of comparing performance of the company with its competitors. The top room represents the Technical Information Portion which contains information that relates the voice of the customer into technical requirements of the organization. Following this is the roof room, which represents the co-relationship among the Technical Portion which is shown the contradictive or supportive technical requirements inside the organization itself The last center room represents determination of the Customer Information Portion which contains information on the relationship between voice of the customer and the organization. The information is represented by symbols for easier reading and interpretation.

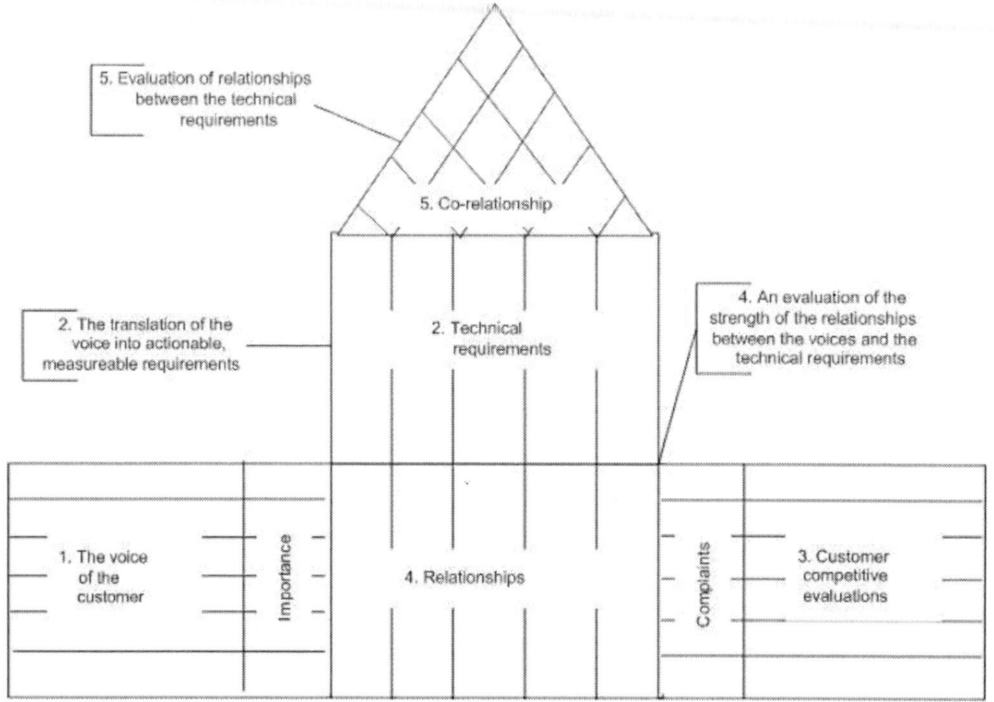

Figure 1. Traditional rooms of HOQ in organization (Rika Fatimah & Jemain 2007)

QFD FOR DETERMINING MARRIAGE LOYALTY AND WORK ASSESSMENT ON WOMEN'S SATISFACTION

As discussed earlier, the traditional QFD has five main parts represented five main rooms in HOQ. Adopting the traditional QFD, we simplified it into three main parts to deploy marriage loyalty. The three main parts represent three main rooms in HOQ for marriage loyalty which is shown in Figure 2. The first part named Voice of Marriage (VoM) which deploys dimension and variables of marriage loyalty and is located at the *center room of HOQ*. The *right room* deploys Work Assessment with respect to the dimension of marriage loyalty. The third is at the left room representing Level of Satisfaction among respondents of this study with regards to the dimension and variables of marriage loyalty.

Figure 2. Adoption of HOQ for marriage loyalty.

As represented in the center room, VoM are earlier generated by asking 50 respondents from various backgrounds about activities in marriage which are related to the development of marriage loyalty. It is important to place our respondents as the customers of the organization whose needs and wants are our main goal to fulfill (Gitlow 1990). The data of activities received were gathered by using various techniques such as conversation, complaint, confidential letter, telephone, e-mail, etc. (Bossert 1999). As a result, we have shortlisted activities mentioned by the respondents.

The list was unstructurized, unorganized, and had no specific manner which makes it hard to identify what is the specific idea of each relationship between the activities in the list. Therefore, we refer to some literature study from a previous researcher about marriage loyalty or as equal as it is. Then we involved experts on marriage and quality who are gathered in a focus group to arrange the groups, with regards to the list, into several groups that have similar characteristics (Asaka & Ozeki 1990). The characteristics are determined based on similarity in the subjects, goals and relationships that occurred. To organize the list, the focus group has done grouping into three levels of complexity. The lowest level of complexity is called an *attribute,* which is represented by the list of activities on marriage loyalty then provided into a questionnaire of the study. The higher level is a *variable,* which consists of several attributes that had similarities to each other, and are displayed in the center room. Next is the highest level of complexity, the *dimension,* which consists of several similar variables and they are also displayed in the center room along with variables of marriage loyalty. By having several levels of complexity of activities on marriage loyalty, it may give simpler and more manageable information on what marriage loyalty is (Rika Fatimah et al. 2009; Oakland 1993). The result of VoM will be discussed in the next part of this paper.

After determining VoM then we utilize the questionnaire consisting of attribute determined in VoM earlier. We asked 587 respondents for their level of satisfaction to the dimension of marriage loyalty which is represented level of satisfaction of the marriage loyalty with respect to women's occupation. We have aggregated their respond by using mod value which is to identify the most occurred value chosen by the respondent. The value being used is range from 1 for Very Dissatisfy to 4 for Very Satisfy. After processing value respond of the respondent, then we analyze the respond based on women's occupation and deploy the comparison between four major kinds of occupation in the right room of work assessment. The four major kind of occupation founded in this study are women who work with government's institution, women who work with private organization, women who run own business and women who stay at home as housewives,

Following the result in the right room, we also ask the respondent for their level of satisfaction regarding to the variable of marriage loyalty which is represent more detail activities of marriage loyalty. If in work assessment we compare the result based on respond of different kind of occupation then in this part we integrate all answer and find the mod value for each variable. The result is represented in the left room of HOQ for marriage loyalty. Completed HOQ for marriage loyalty for this study is as shown in Appendix.

METHODOLOGY

The part of methodology contains several sub-parts of subjects and scope of research, measures and scale reliability.

Subjects and Scope of Research

Duvall (1976) states that there are two cycles of family which are the cycles of growth and developed family. The first cycle represents family in phase of marriage couple then having children and raising the children into teenagers and then adults. Furthermore, in the cycle of developed family, this family landed in phase of letting go their adult children to be independent and having their own life whether both by marriage or by their own revenue. Based on the family cycle, we divided our subjects into three groups. The first group is respondent, both male and female, whose marriage length less than 12 years. The second group is for those whose marriage lasting between 12 until 17 years and the third group lasting for more than 17 years. All respondents involved must have offspring at least one since our questionnaire asking for parents relationship as well. In addition, our scope of study also limit to the respondents who are still having their marriage and live with their spouse. The rationale is that our study need to explore the activities happend in the marriage life, therefore we need respondent whose marriage life is still going on as well.

Furthermore, it is decided that 587 questionnaires returned are distributed across West Malaysia. For the survey, we have identified several regions as well as the cities of the country. The numbers of questionnaires distributed in these cities are decided based on the share of the total population contributed by the states identified in the particular regions.

In terms of length of marriage, 44.0% of our respondents are married for the period of less than 10 years, 27.8% for the period of between 12 until 17 years and 28.1% for the period of more than 17 years. According to socio-economics level, 44.6% of our respondents are in high level of economic and education, followed by 17.4% in moderate level, and 37.9% in the low level. There are many types of occupation of the respondents; however, we found that the top four occupations which also being used in our analysis are women who work as housewives (40.5%), related to government sectors (23.0%), followed by working to private sectors (19.1%), conducting their own business or as entrepreneur (11.9%) and while others for 3.40%.

Measures

The questionnaire was divided into three main parts. The first part is about background of respondents. The second part involves questions regarding relationship among the spouse, level of efforts on adjustment for marital adjustment and level of execution of roles with respect to intimacy between spouses for continuation of marital intimacy. The third part of the questionnaire consists of 3 questions on the overall opinions regarding the level of importance on issues relating to loyalty of marriage. Contents of the questionnaire are summarized in Table 1.

Table 1. Summary of Contents of the Questionnaire

No.	Parts	Sub-Parts	Likert Scale	No.of Quest.
I	Respondent Background			15 quest.
II	Details on Marriage Loyalty	Marital Relationship	1 = almost never & 4 = always	17 quest.
		Marital Adjustment	1 = almost never & 4 = always	15 quest.
		Marital Intimacy	1 = very disagree & 4 = very agree	17 quest.
III	Overall Perspectives on Marriage Loyalty	All marriage loyalty dimensions	1= very satisfy & 4= very dissatisfy	3 quest.

Scale Reliability

In this study, the most common measure of reliability which is Cronbach's alpha (α), based on Cronbach (1951), has been used. The values of 0.7–0.8 above are an acceptable value for Cronbach's alpha, and values substantially lower indicated an unreliable scale. The questionnaire in this study are found acceptable in terms of scale of reliability since we found the Cronbach's alpha (α) value range 0.899 until 0.911 for each dimension of the marriage loyalty.

RESULT AND DISCUSSION

In this section, we present the HOQ rooms for the marriage loyalty which consist of Voice of Marriage (VoM), Work Assessment, and Level of Satisfaction or also called Level of Marriage Complaint.

Voice of Marriage

After generating a shortlist of selected activities representing the marriage loyalty, we had did a literature review in order to determine VoM. Marriage implies a ceremony, a union with social life, recognition of obligations to the community assumed by those who entering this relationship (Locke and Thomes, 1976). Exploring marriage issues has been continuously done by researchers to invent and improve the quality of marriage institutions. Even though different terms are used to express the marital quality, such as marital success (Kaukinen 2004; Papp et al. 2004), marital happiness (Twenge et al. 2003), and many others, all the terms refer to the same basic need of feeling satisfied in marriage life. Successful marriage is found, mostly, if the couple feels satisfaction in running their marriage. Hawkins & Booth (2005) stated that low level of marital quality may influence some factors in married life such as happiness, life satisfaction, health and self confidence.

Many studies have explored the marriage field, especially in terms of success, by identifying what factors or variables were involved in the marital success. The successful marriages are a husband and wife who survive in marriage unions and are not broken by separation and divorce, or seriously considering divorce (Twenge et al. 2003). Other researchers have studied more on the satisfaction of marriage which has been associated with its harmony and happiness (Horowitz et al. 1997). Some of the studies also mentioned that satisfaction of marriage with job satisfaction of married women and men were increasingly likely to share both economic and domestic responsibilities throughout the life course (Larson et al. 1994; Nomaguchi and Bianchi, 2004). Another variable for successful marriage is adjustment of the husband and wife to each other in married life. A well-adjusted marriage may be defined as a union in which the husband and wife are in agreement on the important issues of marriage, such as handling finances and dealing with in-laws. In addition, a recent study was done by Rogers and May (2003) who discussed more on consensus in problems occurring in a family in which the husband and wife are together. The consensus found were status compatibility, children living arrangements, marital distress, parental symptomatology, and job satisfaction.

Based on the previous studies, we have studied the variables which can be used to explain the marriage in terms of initiating marriage loyalty. Then, we identified three dimensions being used to describe marriage loyalty. As mentioned earlier, expertise gathered in focus groups had been sought in order to provide grouping of marriage variables under the respective dimensions of Marital Relationship, Marital Adjustment and Marital Intimacy. The detail deployment of marriage loyalty is as shown in Figure 3.

The first dimension of marital relationship represents the relationship in marriage activities. The activities implied to togetherness and attachment between spouses and family included children, in-law relationship, neighbors and friends. The second dimension of marital adjustment represents the evaluations of the relationships whether they fulfill spouse's satisfaction or not. Cohesion and consensus on important matters like financial planning, social and in-law relationship were also evaluated in this dimension. Marital intimacy which represents emotional relationship between husband and wife in marriage, is our last dimension. Conflicts and affections play an important implication in this dimension. The success of the two previous dimensions may bring better intimacy which may initiate better loyalty.

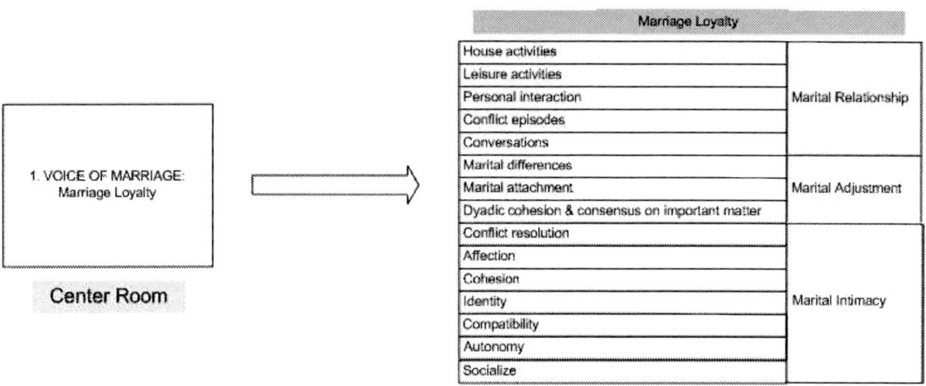

Figure 3. Center room: Voice of Marriage (Loyalty)

Work Assessment

The assessment of women on marriage loyalty involves the comparison point of view between different kinds of occupations regarding the level of satisfaction of marital relationship, marital adjustment and marital intimacy (see Figure 4).

It appears that the levels of satisfaction for two out of three dimensions are considered the lowest same by women with respect to different kind of occupation. In assessment of marital intimacy, the level of women's satisfaction is 2, dissatisfy, for occupation of government, private and entrepreneur. The result indicates that women who are working have level of satisfaction lower than those who stay at home as housewives. The responsibilities of doing outside work whatever to work with government, private or to work as entrepreneur tend to decrease women's activities to achieve better intimacy in marriage. In our study, activities in marital intimacy should be considered as conflict resolution, affection, cohesion, identity and others with reference to the center room of HOQ for marriage loyalty (Figure 3). On contrary, women who are housewives have more advantages in terms of more time and efforts to execute activities of marital intimacy rather than those who must go outside work and divide time and effort between activities of outside work and household work.

Furthermore, in assessment of marital adjustment, the result shows that level of women's satisfaction is also 2, dissatisfy, for occupation of government, private and housewives. The different from assessment of marital intimacy is that the level of satisfaction for women's occupation as entrepreneur is 3, satisfy, compare to 2, dissatisfy. The result indicate that women who are own business have more likely flexible time to manage activities for initiating adjustment in marriage life.

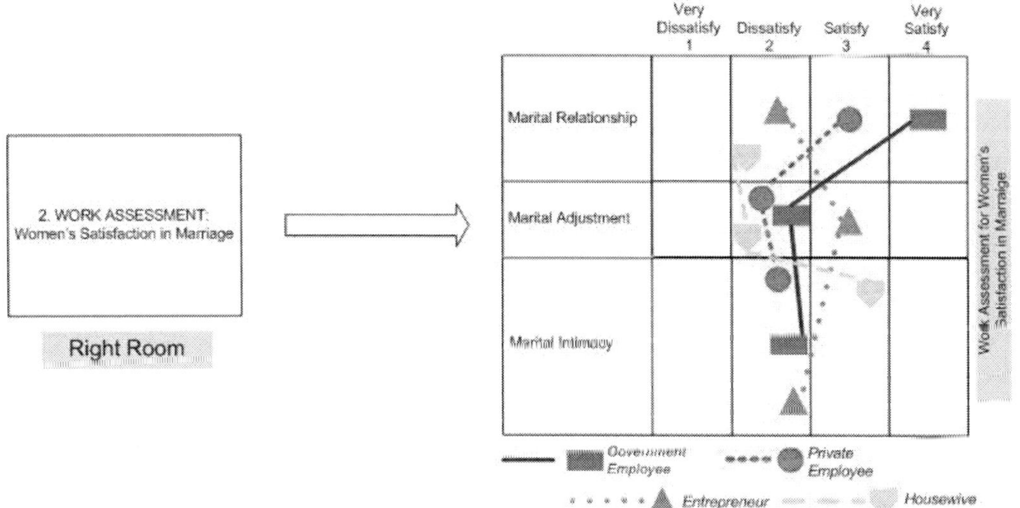

Figure 4. Right room: Work Assessment (Marriage Loyalty)

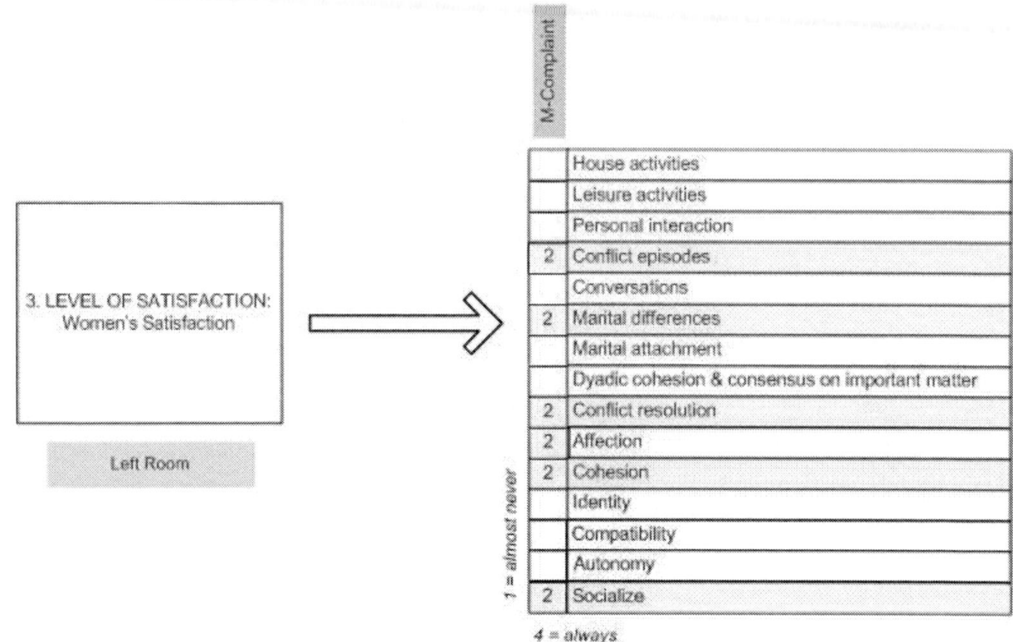

Figure 5. Left room: Level of satisfaction with the lowest value for women's satisfaction with respect to execution of activities of marriage loyalty (Marriage (M)-Complaint)

Regarding the last dimension of marital relationship, the result shows that both type of women's occupation of entrepreneur and housewives have lower level of satisfaction of 2, dissatisfy, compare to the others. Women who work with government have the highest level of satisfaction of 4, very satisfy. The result indicate that women who have flexible time tend to get used to in running activities of marital relationship. Women who own business and as housewives are more feel alike that activities of marital relationship is only routine or daily activities since women who own business and as housewives have enough time to always execute the activities of marital relationship. On contrary, women who work with private and especially women who work with government are tend to more appreciate opportunities and time that the employer given to these women.

Level of Satisfaction

Taking account the result in work assessment, we need to analyze the differences in further detail. As the result shows, there are different responses on each dimension with respect to different kinds of women's occupation. The level of satisfaction indicates women's complaint in marriage (M-Complaint) by considering the execution of activities, which are represented in variables, under the respective dimension of marriage loyalty. As shown in Figure 5, there are four variables under the marital intimacy that have the lowest level of satisfaction with 2 for dissatisfied. The variables under dimension of marital intimacy are conflict resolution, affection, cohesion, and socialize. Furthermore, two more variables with level of satisfaction 2, dissatisfy, are marital difference, which is under dimension of marital adjustment, and conflict episodes, which is under dimension of marital relationship.

CONCLUSION

The QFD method in determining the level of satisfaction based on the women's point of view with respect to different kinds of occupations in the marriage loyalty could be adopted as a new approach in marital studies. After deploying the variables and dimension of marriage loyalty, then we have carried out the comparison of women's occupation regarding their level of satisfaction of dimension. The result shows that there are the same responses to the dimension of adjustment and intimacy in marriage and slightly different regarding marital relationship. Therefore, further analysis to identify the level of satisfaction of each variable in dimension of marriage loyalty has been carried out. All of the results are presented in HOQ for marriage loyalty (see Appendix) which makes it easier for the user, policy maker, family researchers, consultant, and others to study more on marriage loyalty and gender evaluation.

As observed in the application of QFD for the marriage, QFD can be widely applied in many areas of research, apart from the manufacturing and service industry, in which QFD is commonly applied. It can be seen that QFD is quite flexible since the complexity in the marriage can be easily presented in the form of several sets of priority variables. If the complexity is not addressed wisely, then the problem inherent in the marriage cannot be tackled properly.

Furthermore, the QFD method applied in this study may be used to improve the women's quality of life. By acknowledging which variables need to be improved, it has given a more effective and efficient way of identifying which activities in married life need to be improved as well. Furthermore, QFD also provides a more informative way to compare women's satisfaction with respect to women's occupations. The information may help women and spouses to plan the proper path for their marriage so that the plan will run well and provide satisfaction for women and their spouses.

REFERENCE

Amaratunga, D, Baldry, D. & Sarshar, M. (2001). "Process improvement through performance measurement: The Balanced Scorecard methodology", *Work Study, Vol. 50, No. 3*, 179-188.

Asaka, Tetsuichi & Ozeki, Kazuo. (1990). *Handbook of Quality Tools*. Cambridge: Productivity Press.

Busch, V. G. & Enriquez, F. T. (2005). "TQM and QFD: exploiting a customer complaint management system", *International Journal of Quality and Reliability Management, Vol. 22, No. 1*, 30-37.

Bossert, J. L. *Quality Function Deployment: A Practitioners Approach.* Milwaukee: ASQC Quality Press

Cronbach, Lee J. (1951). "Coefficient alpha and the internal structure of tests", *Psychometrica Vol. 16*, 297-334.

Day, G. Ronald. (1993). *Quality Function Deployment: Linking a Company With Its Customers*. Wisconsin: ASQC Quality Press.

Duvall, E. M. (1976). *Marriage and Family Development*. New York: J.B Lippincott Company.

Gerst, R. M. (2004). "QFD in large-scale social system redesign", *International Journal of Quality and Reliability Management, Vol. 21, No. 9*, 959-972.

Gitlow, Howards S. (1990). *Planning for Quality, Productivity, and Competitive Position*. Dow Jones-Irwin. Homewood.

Hawkins, Daniel N. & Booth, Alan. (2005). Unhappily Ever After: Effects of Long-Term, Low-Quality Marriages on Well-Being. *Social Forces 84 (1)*, 451-464.

Hauser, J. R. (1993). "How Puritan_Bennet used the house of quality". *Sloan Management Review* (Spring).

Horowitz, Allan V. McLaughlin, Julie & White, Helene Raskin. (1997). How the negative and positive aspects of partner relationships affect the mental health of young married people. *Journal of Health and Social Behavior 39*, 124-136.

Kaukinen, C. (2004). Status compatibility, physical violence, and emotional abuse in intimate relationships. *Journal of Marriage and Family 66*, 452-471.

Larson, R. W. Richards, M. H. & Perry-Jenkins, M. (1994). Divergent worlds: the daily emotional experience of mothers and fathers in the domestic and public spheres. *Journal of Personality and Social Psychology 67*, 1034-1046.

Locke, H. J. & Thomes, M. M. (1976). *The Family: From Traditional to Companionship*. New York: Prentince-Hall.

Masui, K. Sakao, T. Kobayashi, M. & Inaba, A. (2003). "Applying Quality Function Deployment to environmentally conscious design", *International Journal of Quality and Reliability Management, Vol. 20, No. 1*, 90-106.

Nomaguchi, K. M. & Bianchi, S. M. (2004). "Exercise time: gender differences in the effects of marriage, parenthood, and employment", *Journal of Marriage and Family, Vol. 66* (May), 413-430.

Oakland, J. (1993). *Total Quality Management*. 2nd ed. Oxford: Butterworth-Heinmann.

Papp, L. M. Cummings, E. M. & Schermerhorn, A. C. (2004). "Pathways among marital distress, parental symptomatology and child adjustment", *Journal of Marriage and Family, Vol. 66*, (May), 368-384.

Rika Fatimah, P. L. & Jemain, A. A. (2007). QFD approach in determining importance of family performance: gender evaluation in Malaysia. *International Journal of Population, Vol.13, No.2*, 2007, 179-198. Universitas Indonesia (UI): Indonesia. [Indexed]

Rika Fatimah, P. L. Jemain, A. A. & Ibrahim, K. (2008). Women-Family in quality perspective. Social Indicators Research: *An International and Interdisciplinary Journal for Quality-of-Life Measurement, Vol.88, No.2*, September, 355-364 with DOI: 10.1007/s11205-007-9196-1. Springer.

Rika Fatimah, P. L. Jemain, A. A. Khairul Anuar, M. A. & Mohamad Nasir, S. (2009). Quality_Marriage Deployment in determining priority needs for initiating marriage loyalty. *Quality & Quantity International Journal, Vol.43, No.3*, May, 401-416 with DOI:10.1007/s11135-007-9115-1. Springer.

Rogers, S. J. & May, D. C. (2003). "Spillover between marital quality and job satisfaction: long-term patterns and gender differences", *Journal of Marriage and Family , Vol. 65*, (May), 482-495.

Twenge, J. M. Campbell, W. K. & Foster, C. A. (2003). "Parenthood and marital satisfaction: a meta-analytic review", *Journal of Marriage and Family, Vol. 65*, (August), 574-583.

Walden, Jim. (2003). "Performance excellence: a QFD approach, *International Journal of Quality and Reliability Management, Vol. 20, No. 1*, 123-133.

APPENDIX: HOQ FOR MARRIAGE LOYALTY FOR ASSESSMENT OF WOMEN'S SATISFACTION IN MARRIAGE WITH RESPECT TO WOMEN'S OCCUPATION

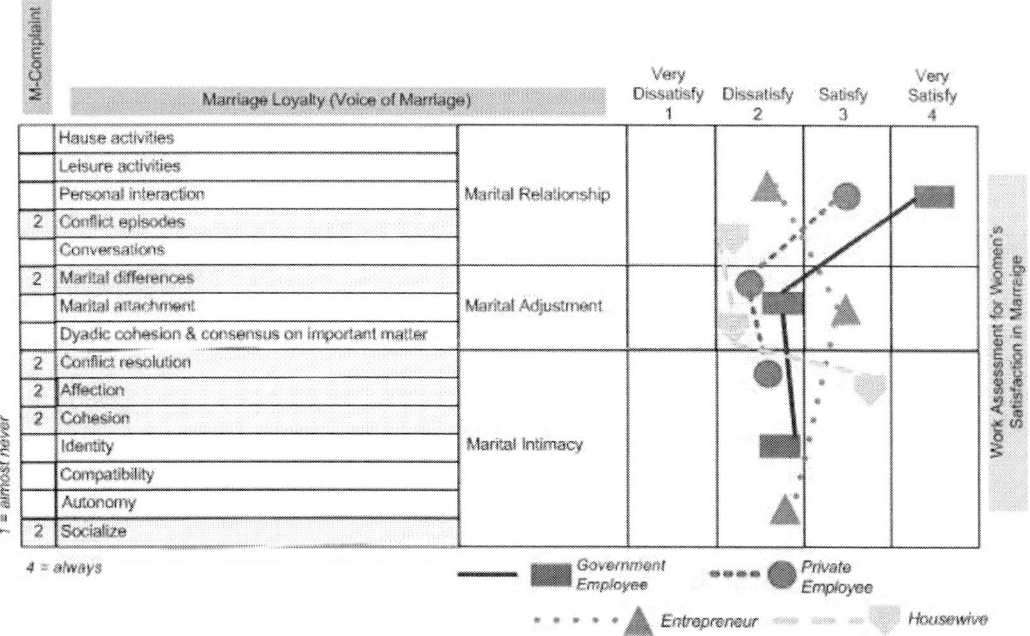

In: Feminism and Women in Leadership
Editor: Vicente Nardi, pp. 169-178

ISBN: 978-1-60876-270-5
© 2010 Nova Science Publishers, Inc.

Chapter 10

CRITICAL MASS AND THE GLASS CEILING : A STUDY OF FEMALE POLITICAL LEADERS

Sol Encel, Dorothy Campbell and Scott Campbell

University of New South Wales, Australia

Vickers, in a detailed critique of the concept of "women's interests", observes that "formal politics, which involves decision-making by governments and international organizations, has been marked, historically, by women's virtual absence; despite a few women presidents and prime ministers, governing is an activity dominated by men" (Vickers, 2006: 5).

Male domination also entails the exclusion of women from positions of political power and authority. The role of exclusion as an aspect of power was stressed, years ago, by Wright Mills in an essay on the structure of power in American society. Like Vickers, he saw decision-making as the essential substance of politics. "Power has to do with whatever decisions men make about the arrangements under which they live, and about the events which make up the history of their times". Correspondingly, power entails the ability to set the agenda and exclude the powerless (Mills, 1963: 23).

The history of women's participation in politics is a notable example of the use of power as a form of exclusion. In 1929, Virginia Woolf remarked in her essay, *A Room of One's Own*, that "the history of men's opposition to women's emancipation is more interesting perhaps than the story of that emancipation itself".

Resistance by a male-dominated society has meant, among other things, that the progress of women's political participation has taken place in fits and starts, a point stressed by Maurice Duverger in the well-known report on the political role of women published by the United Nations in 1955. Duverger observed that the low level of female political participation reflected the secondary role of women in society at large, and especially the widespread belief among men that political activity is a masculine prerogative (Duverger, 1955: 127).

This low level of participation is clearly exemplified by the slow progress of entry to legislative and executive positions on the part of women. The effort involved in obtaining the vote in Britain, the United States and some Continental European countries during the two decades before 1914 generated a high level of activity, which then dropped away. A notable case is that of New Zealand, where women obtained the vote in 1893. The first woman was not elected to parliament until 1935, and she had few successors until the 1960s. Similarly in Australia, where women were given equal political rights in national affairs with the adoption of the federal constitution in 1901, the first woman was not elected to the national legislature until 1943 (although women did better in the state legislatures). From 1901 until 1972, only 42 women had been elected to state or national legislatures. In 1972, the number was 16 out of a total of 728 seats, i.e. 2.2 per cent. In Canada, only 20 women had been elected to the House of Commons by 1972 (Encel, MacKenzie and Tebbutt, 1974: 245).

In the United States, the number of women in Congress rarely rose above 2 per cent until the 1970s. Even then, remarked one commentator, they were "permanently excluded from the informal network of power relationships which is the key to the workings of that complex legislative machine:" (Gehlen, 1969: 36.). Pat Schroeder, who was elected to Congress in 1972 as one of 14 women, felt that she had "broken into and entered a private club", and describes the various indignities to which she and her female colleagues were exposed.(Schroeder, 1999: 19). A journalist who interviewed female congressmen found that women were totally excluded from a select circle run by the (male) Speaker of the House of Representatives, called the 'Board of Education' Some of her respondents had not even heard of it (Lynn, 1979: 413). Jeane Kirkpatrick, who served as a diplomat during the Nixon presidency and was a serious possibility for the Republican vice-presidential nomination in 1988. observed that men "do not bar women from taking part in politics, but only hamper their efforts to participate in power " (Kirkpatrick, 1974 : 20). During the Nixon presidency. women occupied no more than 13 of the 300 senior administrative positions.

THE GLASS CEILING

Reporting on a 1978 survey of women in legislative and executive positions around the world, Reynolds maintained that the glass ceiling for women in politics had risen slowly over a period of 50 years, especially during the preceding decade, when women had attained a significant number of ministerial cabinet posts. The next glass ceiling to be broken through would see women filling the top jobs in areas such as defence, finance, and foreign affairs. "Then will come the highest glass ceiling---women competing on a gender-neutral playing field for the very top job as president or prime minister " (Reynolds, 1999: 572).

Reynolds' conclusion echoes the words of Geraldine Ferraro, US vice-presidential candidate in 1984. In her speech conceding defeat, Ferraro declared that "a door had been opened that can never be closed again". Her speech, reported in the *Washington Post,* was accompanied by an editorial which claimed that "from now on women will be considered for high public office not as tokens or obligatory fixtures...but by the same standards that are applied to men" (*Washington Post,* 19-11-1984). Although these claims were evidently premature, it is notable that since Pat Schroeder retired from Congress in 1996, Nancy Pelosi has become Speaker of the House of Representatives, Condoleezza Rice and Hillary Clinton have succeeded one another as Secretary of State, and Sarah Palin ran for vice-president in 2008. In the 111th Congress, elected in 2008, there are 92 women, 75 in the House of Representatives and 17 in the Senate.

Reynolds noted that, in spite of increasing numbers of women in national legislatures and executive governments, very few had attained leadership positions. When his survey was conducted in 1998, there were only five women at the level of heads of government or heads of state, and only 22 had attained these offices since 1959, starting with Sirimavo Bandaranaike in Sri Lanka.. Increased numbers were not, in themselves, a sufficient reason for the growth of female participation at the governmental level, given a range of ideological and religious obstacles. Wilma Rule has listed these obstacles as "narrow gender roles, restrictive religious doctrines, unequal laws and education, male-biased party leaders or other political elites, and some voters" (Rule , 1994: 15)

There has, in fact, been a considerable growth in the number of women in top leadership roles since Reynolds' survey. As of February 2009, we identified 69 women who had attained these positions since 1959, of whom 16 were in office at the time. In the latter part of this paper, we examine the careers of these women to identify factors which have been important in shaping their careers and are likely to be relevant to female participation in politics at various levels.

Critical Mass

The concept of 'critical mass', borrowed from nuclear physics, has become an important sub-plot in the literature dealing with women in politics. Its early use is commonly attributed to Kanter's study of male-female relations in a corporate setting (Kanter, 1977). The idea was extended a decade later by Dahlerup, who linked the increased political role of women with the massive increase in female labour force participation (Dahlerup, 1997). In a later paper, she refined that argument to stress that critical mass was an inadequate concept and that 'critical acts' were more important (Dahlerup, 1988).

The concept received an official imprimatur through the international convention on ending discrimination against women, which declared in 1997 that "if women's participation reaches 30 to 35 per cent (generally termed a 'critical mass') there is real impact on political style and the content of decisions". Quoting this declaration, Sawer remarks drily that, although the concept has swept the world, an increasing number of studies have demonstrated that there is no simple relationship between an increase in the numbers of women and the passage of legislation beneficial to women (Sawer, 2008:) A similar point is made by Mackay, who deplores the 'intellectual laziness' exhibited by the uncritical use of the concept, and adds for good measure that reality is 'too messy' to be explained by simplistic notions of critical mass (Mackay, 2004: 115).

At all events, the figure of 30-35 per cent is well above current levels. Reynolds' survey found a worldwide average of 12,5 per cent, with the highest ratios being just over 18 per cent in Western Europe and North America. This has now risen, according to the Inter-Parliamentary Union, to a world average of 18.4 per cent in 2008. Between 1999 and 2007, the proportion of women holding ministerial portfolios rose from 8.7 per cent to 15.2 per cent. Higher scores are to be found in Australia and New Zealand (Curtin, 2006: 106-7). In Australia, figures available in January 2009 produced an overall result of 30 per cent (i.e. including federal and state legislatures). In the federal parliament, the figure for the lower house (House of Representatives) was 27 per cent, and for the upper house (Senate), which is elected by proportional representation, 36 per cent.

An interesting symptom of the increased prominence of women as top leaders was the formation of the Council of Women World Leaders, under the auspices of the Aspen Institute, in 1997. In January 2008, the Council included 37 living women who were former presidents or prime ministers. All of them are included in the present study.

WOMEN ON TOP

The ascension of women to top political posts represents the latest stage in the fluctuating history of female political participation. Whereas Reynolds, in 1999, could identify no more than 22 women who had become heads of government or heads of state, the research reported in this paper found a total of 69 (as of February 2009). One important symptom of change is that disabilities traditionally associated with the female gender have become much less salient. A striking example was the appointment of a woman, Carme Chacon, as Spanish defence minister in 2008, while she was pregnant. In addition, the new cabinet had a majority of women. This was described at the time as a 'tectonic shift' (Day, 2008). Another female first was the appointment of Johanna Sigurdardottir as Iceland's first woman prime minister in 2009. Sigurdardottir is also the world's first openly gay political leader, having married the author Jonine Leosdottir in a civil ceremony in 2002, at age 60. Welcoming her appointment, an Icelandic writer observed sardonically that the country's dire financial situation called for an emergency government, preferably made up of women. "They couldn't be worse than the men" (Gunnarson, 2009).

Vital Statistics

Among our 69 subjects, drawn from 55 countries, nine were heads of state and 54 heads of government (which, in 12 cases, also meant heads of state). Sixteen were incumbents. We included two marginal cases---Aung San Suu Kyi in Burma (Myanmar) and Julia Gillard (Australia). Although Aung San Suu Kyi has never exercised political power, she was elected by a clear majority in Burma's last free election in 1990. (Aung San Suu Kyi is listed as an honorary member of the Council of Women World Leaders). Julia Gillard, appointed deputy prime minister following the Australian general election in November 2007, had acted as prime minister for a total of approximately four months at the time of writing, generally because of prime minister Kevin Rudd's frequent trips overseas.

Since a number of the countries represented could not be regarded as significant in international terms, we constructed a rating scale which included strategic importance, population, and economic wealth. We invited ten raters to make the assessment, which gave the following results:

High	18 (e.g. France, Germany, UK)
Medium	23 (e.g. Australia, Poland, Portugal)
Low	22 (e.g. Dominica, Guyana, Malta)

There was a remarkably wide range of ages. The modal age of our subjects when they attained the top job was in the range 40 to 50 (24 out of 63), but the dispersion was much wider, from 32 ro 77. The youngest—age 32—was Radmila Sekerinska, who became prime minister of the small landlocked republic of Macedonia, formerly part of Yugoslavia, in 2004. Her tenure was brief, from May to December of that year. Previously, at age 30, she had been elected leader of the Social-Democratic Union of Macedonia (SDSM). She also served as deputy prime minister in 2006, and was again elected president of SDSM.

At the other end of the scale, Janet Jagan became president of Guyana in 1997 at age 77, following the death of her husband, Cheddi Jagan. She had previously been deputy Speaker of the legislature, following the election of her husband as president in 1953, when Guyana was still a British colony. The British government, fearing Communist influence, suspended the constitution. At the first free election in 1992, supervised by former US president Jimmy Carter, Cheddi Jagan was returned as president. Janet replaced him following his death from a heart attack in 1997, but resigned in 1999, observing that she was "a little more battered and a little wiser" (*Economist,* 1999) She died in 2008..

In terms of tenure, there was again a wide divergence. The modal range was between one and five years, but nine had lasted less than one year, while 12 had held office for more than five years. Aung San Suu Kyi's tenure—zero—is clearly a world record. Close behind was Rosalia Arteaga of Ecuador, who served for two days in 1997. Leaders who served more than 10 years included Sirimavo Bandaranaike (Sri Lanka), Eugenia Charles (Dominica), Indira Gandhi (India), Mary McAleese (Irish Republic), and Margaret Thatcher (UK).

Dynastic/Family Connections

Family connections have always played an important role in politics This is true for both sexes, but evidently more in the case of women. Patterns of family connection also differ, especially when the widows of male political leaders inherit their husbands' roles. Assassination has also been a significant factor in the case of women, especially in Asia. Our earliest subject, Sirimavo Bandaranaike, succeeded her husband, S.W.R.D. Bandaranaike, following his assassination in 1959. In due course, she was succeeded by her daughter, Chandrika Kumaratunga.

In summary, we identified the following patterns of relationship :

Daughters	7
Widows	7
Other connections	3

In addition, six of the fathers or husbands of our subjects had been assassinated. Z.A. Bhutto, one-time prime minister of Pakistan, was executed by the regime of the military dictator Zia ul-Haq. In turn, his daughter Benazir, also an ex-premier, was assassinated during her election campaign in 2007. Agathe Uwilingiyimana (Rwanda) was also assassinated in 1993.

Occupational/Educational Background

Political leaders and legislators enter the political arena by diverse routes. This remains true despite the increasing professionalization of politics. In the case of our 63 subjects, diversity is clearly reflected in their wide range of occupational and educational backgrounds, as shown below :

Lawyers	18
Economists	11
Trained teachers	6
Physicians	3
Natural scientists	5
Other university qualifications	19
Other/N.A.	7

Not surprisingly, lawyers are well represented (22 per cent). The proportion is markedly less than the case in the United States, where 34 per cent of members of the 111th Congress gave their previous occupation as 'attorney'. The figure of 22 per cent is, however, markedly higher than is the case in Australia, where the proportion of lawyers in the federal parliament in 2009 is 13 per cent.

Out of the remarkable diversity shown by our subjects, a few examples may be chosen for special mention. Gro Harlem Brundtland, Norwegian prime minister on three occasions between 1981 and 1996, was a medical specialist before entering politics. She achieved international notoriety by appointing seven other women to her cabinet of 18. (Subsequent Norwegian governments have maintained similar ratios). Before becoming prime minister, she was minister for the environment, and had remained at the forefront of the environmental movement ever since. In 2007, the UN secretary-general appointed her as special envoy for climate change. After leaving politics in 1996, she became director-general of the World Health Organization from 1998 to 2003.

Another physician on our list, Michelle Bachelet, was elected president of Chile in 2006, after a career in public health, including the public health portfolio. She was also minister for defence (2002-2004). She entered politics as a student, involved in underground resistance activity during the Pinochet dictatorship. Her cabinet includes equal numbers of men and women.

Radmila Sekerinska, prime minister of Macedonia in 2004, qualified as an electrical engineer and worked for several years as an assistant in the Faculty of Electrical Engineering at the University of Skopje, the Macedonian capital. After leaving office, she obtained a master's degree from the Fletcher School of Law and Diplomacy at Tufts University in Boston. She also won a prize as a 'Global Leader of Tomorrow', awarded under the auspices of the World Economic Forum.

Another woman with an engineering background was Maria de Lourdes Pintasilgo, prime minister of Portugal in 1979. She graduated as a chemical engineer at age 23, and after post-graduate work at the national Nuclear Energy Board, worked for a six years with a large industrial conglomerate. She left the company to enter politics, and became minister for social affairs. In 1979, the Portuguese president asked her to become prime minister in a caretaker government. During her three months in office, she was able to make social security universal. In 1986, she ran unsuccessfully for the presidency, but was elected to the European parliament in 1987. She died of a heart attack in 2004, aged 54.

Political Affiliation

There has been much argument about the links between feminism, Left-wing politics, and state action. State action has been a necessary, though not sufficient, condition for rectifying imbalances between the sexes. This requires political involvement by women's groups. The majority of feminist activists take a Left-wing stance because Left-wing parties are, on the face of it, more disposed to take up women's problems (although this disposition cannot be taken for granted), and women as a whole do not vote in the majority for Left-wing parties (Encel and Campbell, 1991: 3-14).

The careers of female political leaders provide some support for a connection between feminism and Left-wing politics, although the link is not overwhelmingly strong. Thirteen of the women in our study were clearly associated with Left-wing parties, and a further 13 were associated with parties generally regarded as Centre-Left. Eleven were associated with Right-wing/conservative parties. The remainder did not lend themselves to a partisan classification.

The difficulties of making such an analysis have been noted by some feminist writers. Childs and Krook have stressed the limitations of quantitative methods, such as critical mass, arguing for a case-by-case approach (Childs and Krook, 2006: 21-25). .

Against the Grain

A particular aspect of women's political careers is the extent to which they have attained leadership while going against the grain of their own society or political system, not always successfully. We identified at least 15 such cases among our subjects, including countries as diverse as Sri Lanka, Pakistan, India, Bangla Desh, the Irish Republic, Germany, Malta, Peru, Ecuador, Bolivia and the United Kingdom. Sirimavo. Bandaranaike, the first woman to become prime minister of a sovereign state, was written off as a political cipher when she succeeded her murdered husband. "What does she know of politics?" asked one of her relatives (Rettie, 2000). In the event, she made a major impact, including the renaming of the country, previously Ceylon. Mireya Moscoso Rodriguez, who succeeded her husband as president of Panama in 1999, was similarly written off as a political ignoramus. She told a press correspondent that she "wanted to prove to Panama and the world that women can use power to accomplish anything they want, even in a country as full of machismo as ours". Responding to some male friends who warned her that she would have to demonstrate that a woman could lead, she declared that "I will show you that I am not only as good as a man, I will be as good as three men" (Riley, 1999). In the event , she served her full term of five years, and was responsible for an extensive social program, including rural electrification, the modernization of the health and education systems, and the building of a major bridge.

A rather different case was that of Beatriz Merino Lucero, the next woman to become leader of a Latin American country, in this instance Peru, in 2003. She was also the first Peruvian woman to graduate from the Harvard Law School. However, rumours surfaced that she was a lesbian, and she was dismissed by President Alejandro Toledo.

In Europe, a notable instance was the election of Angela Merkel as German chancellor in 2005. Apart from the handicap of being a woman in a country where women have traditionally not been expected to play a role in public life, she is also a Protestant leading a predominantly Catholic party, the CDU/CSU.

In some respects, the most striking case of a woman achieving political leadership against the grain is that of Margaret Thatcher, British prime minister from 1979 to 1990. Lovenduski observes that Thatcher became leader of the British Conservative Party despite the fact that the system was weighted against women. She owed nothing to the women's movement, nor to a quota system for women in party selection procedures (Lovenduski, 1999: 196). Gloria Steinem, former editor of MS magazine, commented that Thatcher 's success was actually a setback for the women's movement. "The disillusionment of having someone who looks like us and behaves like them brings a dangerous loss of energy and mutual trust" (Steinem, 1984: 147). Germaine Greer, as is her wont, was even more blunt. "Thatcher's unparalleled success", she asserted, "underlined the fact that British men find women alien and threatening. Having Thatcher at 10 Downing St has done nothing to dispel their unease...when the reaction comes to Thatcherism it will give vent to misogyny that has been bottled up for years"(Greer, 1988: 89-90).

Steinem also drew a parallel between Thatcher and women such as Indira Gandhi and Benazir Bhutto. "When existing interests don't have a suitable man to serve them, class or caste may mitigate the disaster of sex and allow a woman to rise. Thus, the conservative and party interests represented by Thatcher, and the ruling family tradition represented by Indira Gandhi, have allowed them to become exceptional women in national power"(Steinem, 1984: 147). .

In the British case, at least, these pessimistic prognoses have not been borne out. The electoral victory of the Labour Party in 1997 saw a sharp increase in the number of women in parliament (mainly on the Labour side). The proportion of women in the House of Commons rose to 18 per cent, close to the European average (Mackay, 2006: 102). Women have also occupied a wide range of portfolios in the cabinets of Tony Blair and Gordon Brown.

It is probable that female political leaders are still cutting against the grain, and that the demand for affirmative action of some kind (such as quotas) will continue. The present study suggests that, apart from greater numbers, women leaders are drawn from an increasingly diverse range of backgrounds. Family connections, for instance, which were once considered to be of particular importance, account for only a small minority of cases. We may expect that women's political careers will no longer go against the grain, but increasingly resemble those of men---at least in countries with democratic/parliamentary institutions.

CONCLUSION

The glass ceiling has clearly risen since the 1990s. Although female political leaders are still in a minority, it is now a significant minority. The spectacle of a woman holding a major office of state, including president or prime minister, is no longer to be marvelled at. Samuel Johnson likened a woman preaching to a dog's walking on its hind legs (Boswell, 1791). Complete acceptance of women in top jobs may well have to wait until they constitute a critical mass, but the numbers are evidently moving in that direction. In this short paper, we have used qualitative methods to make a modest contribution towards the exploration of these changes.

REFERENCES

Boswell, J. (1791). *The Life of Samuel Johnson,* 31 July 1763.

Childs, L. & Krook, M. L. (2006). 'Gender and politics: the state of the art', *Politics, 26(1).* 18-28.

Curtin, J. (2006). 'Advancing women's interests in formal politics: the politics of presence and proportional representation in the Antipodes', in Chappell, L. & Hill. L. (Eds.) *The Politics of Women's Interests,* Oxford: Routledge, 93-110.

Dahlerup, D. (1987). 'Confusing concepts', in Sassoon, A. S. (Eds). *Women and the State,* London: Hutchinson, 120-29.

Dahlerup, D. (1988). From a small to a large minority: women in Scandinavian politics,' *Scandinavian Political Studies, 11,* 275-98.

Day, E. (2008). 'Women signal changing of the guard', *Observer* (London), 25 June, 7.

Duverger, M. (1955). *The Political Role of Women,* Paris: UNESCO, 137. *Economist (*1999), 14 October, 22.

Encel, S. MacKenzie, N. & Tebbutt, M. (1974). *Women and Society : an Australian Study,* London: Malaby Press, 245-6.

Encel, S. & Campbell, D. (1991). *Out of the Doll's House,* Melbourne: Longman Cheshire, 3-14.

Gehlen, F. (1969). 'Women in Congress', *Trans—Action, 6(11),* 36-40.

Greer, G. (1988). 'Thatcher', *Lear's Magazine,* May/June, 89-90

Gunnarson, V. (2009). 'Iceland gets world's first openly gay prime minister', *Guardian Weekly* (London), 6 February, 6.

Kanter, R. M. (1977). *Men and Women of the Corporation,* New York: Basic Books.

Kirkpatrick, J. (1974). *Political Woman,* New York: Basic Books.

.Lovenduski, J. (1999). 'Sexing political behaviour in Britain', in Walby, S., (Eds.) *New Agendas for Women,* Basingstoke: Macmillan, 190-209.

Lynn, N. (1979). 'American women and the political process', in Freeman, J. (Eds.) 2nd edn, *Women: A Feminist Perspective,* Palo Alto: Mayfield Press, 413-22.

Mackay, F. (2004). 'Gender and political representation in the UK', *British Journal of Political and International Research, 6,* 99-120.

Mills, C. W. (1963). 'The structure of power in American society', in Horowitz, I. L. (Eds.) in *Power, Politics and People : The Collected Essays of C .Wright Mills,* London : Oxford University Press, *23.*

Rettie, J. (2000). 'Sirima Bandaranaike', *Guardian* (London), 11 October, 22.

Reynolds, A. (1999). 'Women in the legislatures and executives of the world', *World Politics, 51(4),* 549-72.

Riley, M. (1999). 'Leader navigates treacherous waters', *Sydney Morning Herald,* 1 September, 17.

Rule. W. (1994). 'Parliaments of, by and for the people: except for women', in Rule, W. & Zimmerman, J. (Eds.) *Electoral Systems in Comparative Perspective: Their Impact on Women and Minorities,* Westport: Greenwood Press, 1-36.

Sawer, M. (2009). *"Women and elections"* in Le Duc, L. Niemi,G. & Norris, P. (Eds.) *Comparing Democracies: Elections and Voting in the 21st Century* (forthcoming).

Schroeder, P. (1999). *Twenty-Four Years of House Work—and the Place is Still a Mess',* Kansas City: Anderson McMeel Publishing.

Steinem, G. (1984). 'The Ferraro factor', MS, October, 144-50.

Vickers, J. (2006). 'The problem with interests: making political claims for "women", in Chappell, L. & Hill, L. (Eds.) *The Politics of Women's Interests,* Oxford: Routledge, 5-38. *Washington Post* (1984), editorial, 19 November.

In: Feminism and Women in Leadership
Editor: Vicente Nardi, pp. 179-186

ISBN: 978-1-60876-270-5
© 2010 Nova Science Publishers, Inc.

Chapter 11

ASSAULT: FROM THE TOP DOWN

Marilyn Lanza,[*] Frederick McMillan, Jennifer DeMaio, and Trudy Lefebvre

Edith Nourse Rogers Memorial Veterans Hospital 200 Springs Road
Bedford, MA 01730

ABSTRACT

In most bureaucracies, support for the assault victim comes at mid-level in the hierarchy. When, for example, a nurse is assaulted, she/he is most likely to seek assistance from another staff nurse or from the nurse manager. If a committee is formed about the high number of assaults, it usually begins at mid-range and is elevated as it becomes more formalized. In our case, violence concern started at the top of the hierarchal pyramid and led to the training of a team of counselors who intervene when an employee has been assaulted.

ASSAULT: FROM THE TOP DOWN

Patients assaulting nursing staff is hardly a new concept but has been documented in the literature since the early 1980's.[1,2] Such assaults are a common occurrence; so common that Fagan-Pryor, Femea, & Haber[3] found that 50% of their respondents (N=220) had experienced assault. Although most assaults do not result in life-threatening injuries, serious injuries do occur, such as severe sprains, lacerations, fractures, and head trauma.[4,5,6,7,8]

Though the number of nurses who have been assaulted is estimated to be high, it is difficult to determine the exact number. The reasons for this are multiple: there is no standard reporting mechanism, the definition of assault varies, and many incidents are not reported for a multiplicity of reasons. A study by Coombs,[9] for example, found that 85% of nurses had experienced verbal abuse or had been threatened with violence. Data from multinational

[*] Corresponding author: E-mail: marilyn.lanza@va.gov Tel: (781) 687-2388 Fax: (781) 687-3337
This work is supported by the Edith Nourse Rogers Memorial Veterans Hospital

studies have shown that 75% of all nurses have been assaulted at least once in their careers [10,11] and a study across Veterans Health Administration (VHA) facilities of patients who had assaulted two times or more in a 2-year period found that in 83% (N = 5,959) of the incidents, nursing staff was the target of the assault.[12]

Underreporting of assault is common. Reasons for not reporting physical events (both specific and recurring) and nonphysical events include (a) considering assault part of the job, (b) considering the assault a minor or an isolated incident, (c) perceiving it as unnecessary to report, (d) considering the work environment non-supportive, and (e) being too busy.[8] Underreporting, thus skewing the actual number of assaults, plays a major role in violence against nursing staff not being taken seriously.

Reaction to Assault

The most common consequences of both physical and nonphysical violence reported by nursing staff are frustration, anger, fear, anxiety, stress, and irritability, with the frequency of reporting being much greater for nonphysical violence for each of the consequences.[13]

Lanza[7] conducted a descriptive exploratory study in which nurses reported various short-term (1 week or less) and long-term (more than 1 week) reactions to patient assault, including family pressures to change jobs and/or leave nursing. Nursing staff who had experienced assault reported a variety of emotional, physical, social, and cognitive responses. There are indications that some staff members felt that they would be overwhelmed if they allowed themselves to recognize their feelings. Some stated that if they permitted themselves to recognize the likelihood of being assaulted, they would not be able to function. Others indicated they considered assault part of the job or even that they themselves somehow were to blame for the assault. Some of the staff members who received the most severe injuries indicated less fear of the assailant than did staff members who were more mildly injured.[7] Numerous studies have reported similar findings about the intensity and variety of victim reactions.[4,14,9,10,15,16,2,17] Poster and Ryan[17] and Whittington and Wykes[18] documented that these reactions continue up to one year after the assault, suggesting that nurse victims suffer post-traumatic stress syndrome or disorder (PTSD).

Victims' reaction to being assaulted does, however, not depend on the degree of the assault.[7] Someone who suffers a "mild" verbal assault may be severely traumatized. If counseling of assault victims is to be effective, the counselor's view of the assault is of minor importance. It is the victim's perception of the assault, which is key. The victim and the counselor must explore possible solutions to the particular problems that the assault has caused for the victim. For example, how does a female nurse who is a single parent of two teenagers cope with their demand that she quit her job after an assault? The children challenge her, telling her that she is crazy to work in a place where she can get hurt. She, however, is their sole support and is likely to make the most money in nursing so she feels compelled to take the side of the institution against her children. Thus, rather than unifying the family, the assault causes additional stress for all family members.

Assault is now much more publicly recognized by such influential bodies as the American Nurses Association but assault continues to be an everyday event for too many nurses. Various short term solutions have been suggested, e.g. education to prevent and intervene with assault. Such measures decrease the assault risk but do not eliminate assault.

Some administrators anticipate discussion of assault prevention but they do not appreciate the prevalence of violence against staff. Though nurses would prefer to work in a non-violent environment, they realize that they will continue to be exposed to violence as the economic downturn forces hospitals to have fewer beds. As a consequence, less seriously-ill patients will receive their treatment as out-patients, leaving the proportion of seriously-ill patients on in-patient wards to continue increasing.

The Hospital CEO Advocates a Top-down Approach

The CEO at our particular VHA facility was concerned about the number of staff who had been assaulted. She believes that when employees suffer burnout from verbal or physical assault, they need special concern and an outlet to vent their feelings and help to achieve a new focus.

Per mandate from the CEO, a task force consisting of the author (as chair), the director of the employee assistant program (EAP), the director of staff education, and a nurse from quality management was commissioned to design, develop, and implement a program for counselors who would be available to assaulted employees in need of exploring their reactions to verbal and/or physical assault or battering by patients, patients' families, or other employees. The CEO believes that peer support can play a major role in the success of any wellness program and recovery of an assaulted employee. To help overcome the fear, guilt, shame, and low self-esteem that often accompany assault, employees are strongly encouraged to access their peer counselor for guidance and assistance. In addition to providing assaulted staff with the opportunity to receive emotional and tangible peer support through times of crises and to help anticipate and address potential obstacles, the program can fortify or reinforce current programs, e.g. employee assistance programs and employee health programs, but cannot replace them. The current model, the Victim Assessment Support Team (VAST) conducts all peer support activities in conjunction with the Employee Assistance Program and Employee Health Services and also fits well into our program the Vertically Integrated Violence Intervention Network (VIVIN), which addresses or focuses on all aspects of aggression.

For reference, we defined:

the assaulted employee as any employee who is put in fear of being struck by another person. This fear may be caused by verbal threat or abuse, by menacing gestures, or by a sudden move, by itself or accompanied by a verbal threat.[19]

the battered employee as any employee who experiences actual physical contact from another person, whether or not a physical injury occurs.[19]

The goals of the task force were to:

(a) design the components and processes of a program that will provide staff with support in an "on demand" basis
(b) define the role and responsibilities of the VAST counselors
(c) solicit volunteers among the employees to be trained as counselors

(d) develop the program to train the counselors
(e) train the counselors
(f) assign the counselors to the nursing units
(g) introduce the counselors and the program to the staff on each unit

Introductory meetings

Meetings were held with Program and Nurse Managers to introduce the concept and attain support for the program. The number of counselors required per ward varied depending on the nature of the ward. In order to recruit counselor referrals, we attended various hospital meetings and we were then in a position to ask administrators to begin considering possible candidates to serve as counselors. The human resource director met with the task force to discuss possible incentives for prospective counselors to consider, e.g. potential for performance incentive or incentive awards and the sense of fulfillment in being able to help a co-worker. Posters describing the VAST program were posted throughout the hospital.

The recruited counselors had to fill their primary job responsibilities first and serve collaterally as a VAST counselor, i.e. they could not abdicate their job responsibilities by participating in the program. Counselors would be trained and have on-going supervision with a mental health professional. The peer support would consist of meeting with an assaulted employee for no more than two visits prior to referral to a mental health professional, if necessary. Typically, the counselor would ask how the victim was feeling and coping with the assault and any problems would be addressed specifically.

Application process

Staff interested in serving as a VAST counselor, were to obtain permission from their supervisor and then complete an application. As part of the application, applicants completed a questionnaire, which included their experience and the skills they could offer. Among the characteristics required of an applicant were:

- Strong interpersonal skills
- High motivation
- Ability to maintain confidentiality
- Ability to maintain objectivity
- Understanding of boundaries
- Flexible and adaptive
- Responding well to crisis
- Kind, compassionate, empathetic
- Ability not to personalize things

In addition, applicants were to have

- No time and leave issues
- No disciplinary actions against them

Training

Once referrals were screened and accepted, education of the applicants was necessary. The training consisted of a half-day session during which literature on Peer Counseling and Violence in the Workplace was presented and discussed. Relevant tapes and literature were made available to the applicants and Continuing Education Units were awarded for attendance.

The applicants reviewed the expectations of the VAST counselors:

- Counselors offer "peer support", which is not to be considered a substitute for therapy or help from EAP.
- Support consists of no more than two sessions – if more sessions are needed, the individual is referred to either EAP or Employee Health.
- Employees seen by the VAST counselor have been identified either by themselves, by a supervisor, or EAP as having been assaulted on the job, either physically or emotionally.
- Counselors will adhere to the protocol set forth in the Violence in the Workplace hospital memo.[20]
- VAST counselors must fulfill their primary job responsibilities first and serve collaterally in their position as counselor.
- Any conflict in roles will be addressed at the supervisory level.
- Counselors must attend a monthly meeting with EAP/Dr. Lanza for support and on-going education.

The specific aspects of intervention by VAST counselor were discussed:

On-scene response: Peer counselors are contacted by the ward and arrive soon after the assault. They work to calm the victim, notify family members, and direct the victim to other helping resources, if necessary.

Initial contact with affected staff ("outreach"): Many staff, even if aware of available services, do not make use of them. Outreach to victims is, therefore, an important part of the counselors' job, as outreach increases victims' awareness and provides additional opportunities to obtain support.

Individual assessment of the assaulted employee: Victims exposed to severe trauma may benefit from an initial assessment from a peer rather than a professional. During this assessment, the counselor may be able to establish a relationship with the victim, provide education about trauma and its impact, and set the scene for continuing support and monitoring. The assessment will also provide an opportunity to determine the risk of the victim experiencing long term problems, to assist with triage decisions, and to possibly refer the victim to more intensive individual help. An interview schedule was developed for the assessment. Included as part of the interview is a questionnaire entitled "Victim's Reactions to Assault" which asks victims specific information about their reaction such as what feelings were evoked by the assault and whether the victim experiences any difficulty returning to work. The questionnaire clarifies issues to be further explored by the counselor and help determine whether the victim should be referred to EAP.

Active individual follow-up: Perhaps the most important modification to many current approaches is the inclusion of systematic individual follow-up with particular victims (e.g., those identified as "at risk" on the basis of level of exposure or those who are absent from the workplace for longer than expected periods). Follow-up telephone or face-to-face contact by the counselor and EAP provides the victim with multiple opportunities to self-refer or to make use of other available helping resources. Many of those who suffer intense acute stress responses may have only a few symptoms after several weeks or months. However, if PTSD symptoms persists and are frequent at 3-4 months post-trauma, follow-up at this time period enables more effective determination of whether referral to more specialized care is needed.

Mental health training

The task force and the future counselors discussed crisis management, traumatic intervention, depression, burn out, and domestic violence. Problem assessment, stress management, communication facilitation, and listening skills were shared, as were cross-cultural issues. The future counselors were concerned with suicide assessment, when to seek mental health consultation and referral information, ethical issues, confidentiality issues, limits of their service, and liability.

The counselors covered a variety of situations by role-playing, e.g. a white, female nursing assistant who was hit in the chest, a black male nurse who was pushed, a Hispanic woman who was yelled at because of her accent. Each person played both victim and counselor. Feedback was given by the other group members.

Counselors as consultants to supervisors/managers

As needed, the counselors – now VAST team members - should train, advise, and support supervisors/managers, who are core elements in the comprehensive workplace response. The nursing supervisor will determine whether an assaulted employee is capable of remaining on duty and if not, the supervisor follows local policy for management of workplace injuries and places employee off duty. If the employee is capable of remaining on duty, the supervisor will offer the assistance of a peer counselor at this time. If no peer counselor is on duty, the supervisor provides the employee with a list of VAST counselors and offers to help set up a first appointment. This service is available to all shifts.

Referral to VAST

The VAST program will accept referrals of victims by:

Self-Referral. This is the preferred mode of entry. Self-referrals to the VAST program often indicate a high degree of motivation and commitment on the part of the victim.

Supervisor/Employee Assistance Program Referral. This mode of entry involves a third party who has either observed or been advised of possible work-related impairment.

Confidentiality

For employees entering treatment, confidentiality is critical. VAST counselors must, therefore, inform victims of the limits of their confidentiality and consider potential role conflicts (e.g., supervisor providing peer support). These will be consistent with the law as well as with departmental policy and may include the following:

> The confidentiality of victims, referral sources, and program records are protected by strict adherences to Federal Confidentiality Law (42 C.F.R. and HIPAA)

VAST counselors must not volunteer information to supervisors and should advise supervisors of the established confidentiality guidelines.

Launch of the program

After the employee training, we sent representatives to meet with the CEO as well as with all employee and assistance bodies to explain about the function of the team and the counselors.

The team of counselors was now ready for referrals. They were trained in terms of goals, the process of counseling, and how to avoid potential conflict.

Continuation of program

Because of the concern of the hospital's CEO, the VAST program was created and with her support, it has been implemented at all levels of the hierarchal pyramid. The program has become highly appreciated by both assaulted staff and their supervisors, and continues to develop as new issues are brought up by counselors at the monthly meetings with EAP and Dr. Lanza.

REFERENCES

[1] Lanza, ML. The reactions of nursing staff to physical assault by a patient. *Hospital and Community Psychiatry,* 1983, 34, 44-47.

[2] Lion, JR; Snyder, W; Merrill, G. Underreporting of assaults on staff in a state hospital. *Hospital & Community Psychiatry.* 1981, 32, 497-498.

[3] Fagan-Pryor, EC; Femea, P; Haber, LC. Congruence between aggressive behavior and type of intervention as rated by nursing personnel. *Issues in Mental Health Nursing.* 1994, 15, 187-199.

[4] Anderson, C. Workplace violence: Are some nurses more vulnerable? *Issues in Mental Health Nursing.* 2002, 23, 351-366.

[5] Lanza, ML. Nurses as patient assault victims: An update, synthesis, and recommendations. *Archives in Psychiatric Nursing,* 1992, 6, (3)163-171.

[6] Lanza, ML. Psychotherapeutic treatment of violence. In Tardiff K ed.. *Medical Management of the Violent Patient.* New York: Marcel Dekker, Inc.;. 1999, 311-334.

[7] Lanza, ML. Workplace violence in health care settings. In Kelloway K, Barling J, Hurrell, JJ Jr. eds. *Handbook of Workplace Violence.* Thousand Oaks, CA: Sage Publications; 2006, 147-167.

[8]   Gerbrich, S; Church, T; McGovern, P; Hansen, H; Nachreiner, N; Geisser, MS; et al An epidemiological study of the magnitude and consequences of work related violence: The Minnesota Nurse's Study. *Occupational Environmental Medicine.* 2004, 61, 495-503.

[9]   Coombs, R. Violence against nurses: the facts. *Nursing Times.* 1998, 94, 43-45.

[10]   Dehn, DS. Violence against nurses in outpatient mental health settings. *Journal of Psychosocial Nursing Mental Health Services.* 1999, 37, (6)28-33.

[11]   Quintal, AS. (2002). Violence against psychiatric nurses: An untreated epidemic? *Journal of Psychosocial Nursing.* 2002, 40, (1)46-53.

[12]   Blow, FC; Barry, KL; Copeland LA; McCormick, RA; Lehmann, LS. Ulmann ES Repeated assaults by patients in VA Hospital and clinic setting, *Psychiatric Services.* 1999, 50, (3) 390-394.

[13]   Lanza, ML; Zeiss, RA; Rierdan, J. Non-Physical violence: A risk factor for physical violence in health care settings. *AAOHN Journal.* 2006, 54, (9)397-402.

[14]   Chambers, N. We have to put up with it don't we? The experience of being the registered nurse on duty, managing a violent incident involving an elderly patient: a phenomenological study. *Journal of Advanced Nursing.* 1998, 27, 429-436.

[15]   Janoff-Bulman, R. *Shattered assumptions: Towards a new psychology of trauma.* New York: The Free Press; 1992.

[16]   Lanza, ML; Kayne, H; Hicks, C; Milner, J. Nursing staff characteristics related to patient assault. *Issues in Mental Health Nursing,* 1991, 12, (3)253-266.

[17]   Poster, EC; Ryan, JA. A multiregional study of nurses' beliefs and attitudes about work safety and patient assault. *Hospital and Community Psychiatry.* 1994, 45, (11),1104-1108.

[18]   Whittington, R; Wykes, T. Staff strain and social support in a psychiatric hospital following assault by a patient. *Journal of Advanced Nursing,* 1992, 17, 480-486.

[19]   Occupational Safety and Health Administration. (1996). Report on violence in the workplace: Guidelines for preventing workplace violence. Retrieved August 24, 2005, from http://72.14.207.104/search?q=chche:i5UmYdwIvMJ:www.osha.gov/Publication/osha3148.pdf+National+Institue+of+Occupational+Safety+and+Health+(1996).+NIOSH+Report+on+Violence+in+the+Workplace&hl=en&ie=UTF-8.

[20]   Waghorn, K. (May 8, 2007). Violence in the workplace. *Hospital Memorandum #132.14.* Available from the Public Affairs Officer, Edith Nourse Rogers Memorial Veterans Hospital, 200 Springs Road, Bedford, MA 01730).

In: Feminism and Women in Leadership
Editor: Vicente Nardi, pp. 187-190

ISBN: 978-1-60876-270-5
© 2010 Nova Science Publishers, Inc.

Chapter 12

WOMEN LEADERSHIP IN ORGANIZED CRIME

Petter Gottschalk
Norwegian School of Management, Norway

INTRODUCTION

Often, women are considered victims of organized crime. A typical example is trafficking in women, where women are exploited in prostitution by criminal organizations. However, there are examples of women playing a quite different role in organized crime.

The Story of Alete

For example, Frossard (2007) tells the story of *Alete*, who was the daughter of Jose Baptista da Costa in Brazil. He was killed in 1981. This crime remains unsolved – like most other homicides involving the cupola - despite the fact that suspicion fell on a former policeman and aspiring competitor. Arlete took over her father' business to protect the territory. Arlete was dissatisfied, claiming that she should receive half the monthly proceeds from her territory. Se decided to use violence to resolve the question. She contacted three policemen - all of them later killed in crimes that have also remained unsolved - known for the violent dealings in the criminal underworld. Arlete and her three bodyguards also invaded competitors.

The Story of Suely

Another example of daughter takeover in Brazil is *Suely Correia de Mello*. Her father was murdered in Rio de Janeiro over a territory dispute for the 'jogo dos bichos'. According to an interview given to a major national newspaper, Suely, a lawyer, had the ambition of becoming a public prosecutor, but was tried and found guilty of murder. She was one of the richest bankers and owned a real estate company created solely to manage the innumerable properties she had acquired during her lifetime (Frossard, 2007).

Mafia Women

According to Allum (2007), Sicilian mafia women are perceived as loyal and subordinate wives who do not interfere with their husband's criminal projects and decisions. In contrast, Camorra women have always been much more involved and aware of their men's activities. They are not passive onlookers, but are the active backbone of this criminal organization, and have become increasingly involved, sometimes out of necessity, and sometimes because of a specific criminal intent.

Women in the Neapolitan criminal underworld of the Camorra mafia take on active, formal roles as directors of legal companies, which represent the front-end of the organization. They also take on leadership positions internally, making strategic decisions regarding the clan's activities, taking matters into their own hands, and even killing. For example, in May 2002, in Lauro, a town in the province of Avellino, a shoot-out between women from the Graziano clan and women from the Cavas clan left three women dead and six injured. According to Allum (2007), this suggests that Camorra women are now definitely taking centre stage as major players.

As directors of front-end companies, Camorra women received public contracts, as was the case of *Maria Orlando*, mother of Lorenzo Nuvoletta of the Nuvoletta clan, or Antonietta Di Costanzo, wife of Antonio Orlando, the uncle of Lorenzo Nuvoletta. (Allum, 2007).

Anna Mazza in Napoli became involved in Camorra activities when rival gangs murdered her husband, Gennaro Moccia, capo and boss of Afragola. She became known as 'the Black Widow'. She supported her sons in avenging their father's murder and became the leader of the gang, directing its activities and influencing its ideology. She became a capo in her own right - one of the most dangerous and most bloody. She led the group while her sons were in prison. When her eldest, Angelo, became a leader of the Alfieri confederation, her leadership role grew less important, although she still managed local criminal activities, as well as relationships with politicians, while her sons were involved in regional Camorra warfare. Today, it appears to Allum (2007) that she still runs the clan, directs its activities, and visits her sons in prison.

Women Entrepreneurs

Successful women entrepreneurs in organized crime are hard to find. It is somewhat easier to find successful women entrepreneurs in legal businesses. For example, Reavley and Lituchy (2008) conducted a six-country analysis of self-reported determinants of success. They studied female entrepreneurs in Canada, Ireland, Czech Republic, Poland and Japan. The women became entrepreneurs because they felt rejected - e phenomenon sometimes labeled the 'push factor'. While some women defined success in terms of profits, many used non-financial factors such as number of clients, number of employees, years in business, or because 'my peers say so'. The most important factor identified in the study was networking. Business education and training was second.

The contribution of female entrepreneurs is seldom acknowledged in neither legal nor criminal business. For example, in a study of female immigrant entrepreneurs, Low (2008) found that female immigrant entrepreneurs made a significant contribution to the Australian economy. The study examined the economic contributions of a group of Asian-born women entrepreneurs in Sydney. The empirical study showed that they make significant economic contributions to the creation of new businesses and jobs in addition to other non-quantifiable economic benefits to Australia.

The Story of Georgia

In the United States, *Georgia Durante* saw the local mafia as her ticket out of boredom and poverty. In Rochester, New York, Durante started running errands for local Mafioso Sammy Gingello. These errands involved taking packages into New York City, and she claims that she once delivered a letter directly to the powerful New York boss Carlo Gambino. She was also instructed to keep an eye on local comings and goings and to keep Gingello informed - a traditional female role in organized crime according to Longrigg (2007): when men's movements are restricted or attract more attention, it is often easier for women to pick up information.

Georgia Durante's principle role was as a driver: she started driving for mafia associates who collected extortion money from premises including building sites. Sometimes these shakedowns involved violence, and she became an expert at getting away fast from the scene of the crime. According to Longrigg (2007), Durante's mafia career was in some way similar to a man's: she was attracted to local mafia figures by their money and the strange fascination that violence exerts; she saw her way out of a dreary existence by associating with them. As they got to know her, they began to give her more-demanding tasks She always accepted these commissions, feeling they gave her status and enjoying the trust that was invested in her. It gave her a sort of fascination to be trusted at this level. She felt connected to fear, but the thought never crossed her mind that she might be in any kind of danger. She was too engrossed in the intrigue.

The Role of Women

The research by Allum (2007), Frossard (2007) and Longrigg (2007) can be found in a book entitled 'Women and the Mafia - Female Roles in Organized Crime Structures'. There are many more research chapters in the book, all trying to shed new light on the role of women in organized crime. For example, the emancipation of women in society at large might have an impact on female roles within such organizations. The very interesting, while still incomplete, analyses in the book demonstrate a wealth of ideas even if they cannot yet lead to definite conclusions. One of the many interesting insights in the book is the underestimation of female criminality, the main reason being judges considering women's roles in criminal episodes as victims or at the most accomplices.

In a study of legal entrepreneurs, Seet et al. (2008) was interested in differences between female and male entrepreneurs in Singapore in terms of personality traits. Personality traits studied included sociable, decisive, authoritative, goal-oriented, self-confidence, anxious, risk-taking, intuitive, internal locus of control, optimism, self-confident, and leader. Their results showed that a majority of the female entrepreneurs regarded themselves as more anxious as compared to their male counterparts. Females rated themselves lower in the aspects of self-confidence and optimism. The study findings also showed that Singaporean male entrepreneurs have significantly higher internal locus of control than their female counterparts.

REFERENCES

Allum, F. (2007). Doing It for Themselves or Standing in for Their Men? Women in the Neapolitan Camorra (1950-2003), In: Fiandaca, G. (red.), *Women and the Mafia - Female Roles in Organised Crime Structures*, Studies of Organised Crime, Springer, NY: New York, 9-18.

Frossard, D. (2007). Women in Organised Crime in Brazil, In: Fiandaca, G. (red.), *Women and the Mafia - Female Roles in Organised Crime Structures*, Studies of Organised Crime, Springer, NY: New York, 181-204.

Longrigg, C. (2007). Women in Organised Crime in the United States, In: Fiandaca, G. (red.), *Women and the Mafia - Female Roles in Organised Crime Structures*, Studies of Organised Crime, Springer, NY: New York, 235-284.

Low, A. (2008). Economic outcomes of female immigrant entrepreneurship, *International Journal of Entrepreneurship and Small Business, 5 (3/4)*, 224-240.

Reavley, M. A. & Lituchy, T. R. (2008). Successful women entrepreneurs: a six-country analysis of self-reported determinants of success - more than just dollars and cents, *International Journal of Entrepreneurship and Small Business, 5 (3/4)*, 272-296.

Seet, P. S. Ahmad, N. H. & Seet, L. C. (2008). Singapore's female entrepreneurs - are they different? *International Journal of Entrepreneurship and Small Business, 5 (3/4)*, 257-271.

INDEX

A

Index

D

danger, 40, 152, 189
data collection, 22
database, 117
dating, 9, 17
death, 173
debates, 37
decision making, x, 76, 78, 155
decision-making process, 107
decisions, 4, 78, 112, 129, 169, 171, 183, 188
defence, 170, 172, 174
deficiency, 141
definition, 39, 52, 179
delinquent behavior, 151
delivery, 157
democracy, 91, 110
demographic characteristics, viii, 76, 77
demographic factors, 2
demographics, 113
denial, 38
Department of Justice, 48
dependent variable, 25, 63, 83
depression, vii, 1, 18, 32, 184
depressive symptoms, 6, 10
developing countries, 109
deviation, 8
dichotomy, 36
dictatorship, 174
dietary, 14
dieting, 21
differential rates, 32
directives, 76
disabilities, 172
disabled, 122
disappointment, 103
disaster, 176
discipline, 35, 57, 62, 63, 65, 66, 116, 117, 119
disclosure, 32, 72, 98, 106
discomfort, ix, 97, 99
discounting, 118
discourse, 33, 35, 36, 103, 152, 153
discrimination, 76, 77, 92, 118, 122, 132, 171
diseases, 135
disorder, 15, 47, 180
dispersion, 173
disposition, 175
dissatisfaction, 6, 7, 9, 14, 15, 16, 21, 23, 24, 25
disseminate, 105
distress, vii, 1, 10, 11, 13, 15, 162, 166

distribution, 22, 80, 91, 100, 114, 138, 140
divergence, 173
diversity, 15, 33, 120, 122, 140, 174
division, x, 77, 89, 155
division of labor, 77, 89
divorce, 110, 162
DNA, 135, 142
doctors, 99, 106, 109
do-it-yourself, 149
domestic violence, 184
dominance, 34, 38, 76, 89, 145
dream, 149
drinking, 151
drought, 135, 141, 142
drug addict, 147
drugs, ix, 97, 99, 104, 105, 128, 151
duties, 132
dysplasia, 106

E

ears, 188
earth, 114, 117
eating, 6, 7, 8, 9, 10, 15, 17, 18, 21
eating behavior, 6, 8, 15
eating disorders, 15
ecology, 127, 132, 135
economics, 160
education, xi, 100, 107, 124, 153, 170, 183
educational background, 174
educational institutions, 122
educators, 71
egalitarianism, 78, 90
ego, 11
elderly, 186
election, 172, 173, 176
electromagnetic, 143
e-mail, 102, 159
emancipation, 169, 189
embryonic stem, 99, 128
embryos, 100, 104, 108, 110, 128, 140, 141
emotion, 53, 70, 72, 106, 108
emotional, vii, viii, ix, 51, 52, 53, 54, 55, 56, 57, 58, 59, 61, 62, 63, 64, 65, 66, 67, 68, 69, 70, 71, 72, 73, 97, 98, 99, 101, 102, 147, 152, 162, 166, 180, 181
emotional abuse, 166
emotional experience, 166

F

G

H

N

O

Q

R

S

W

Y